Now, When I Was A Kid…

Nostalgic Ramblings By

Dan McGuire

ISBN: 1-4033-8374-X (e-book)
ISBN: 1-4033-8375-8 (Paperback)

This book is printed on acid free paper.

Published by Back When Books, P.O. Box 232, Wood Dale, IL 60191
in cooperation with
1stBooks Library, 2595 Vernal Pike, Bloomington, IN 47404

1stBooks – rev. 09/14/04

To the Joy of my life, who still brings out the kid in me.

"The stories you are about to read are true. Only the names have been changed to protect the innocent."
—variation on the introduction to the popular radio and television drama *Dragnet*

Actually, most of the names in this book are unchanged, except where my memory proved faulty.

When these pieces were first published, I used aliases for almost everyone except my family. (They might have preferred to remain anonymous, but it would have been difficult to pull off.) Even though there were no scandalous revelations being made, it seemed appropriate somehow to extend that courtesy to the folk who appeared here and there in these recollections.

As I was putting this book together, however, I had second thoughts. The folks, young and old, who appear herein comprised the world as I knew it in my youth. They are largely responsible for the fact that my memories of those years are overwhelmingly positive. I think it's the least I can do to let them have their moment in the spotlight, such as it is.

My lifelong pal, Chuck Schaden, deserves recognition (if that is the word) for causing this book to happen. When he launched *Nostalgia Digest* magazine, Chuck encouraged me to put down a few memories of the good times we enjoyed together in the neighborhood of our youth. What began as an occasional contribution evolved into a regular column that ran for over eleven years.

John V. Leigh, our principal at James Giles Elementary School, served the local school district for 39 years. As the town grew and added more schools, he became District Superintendent. Were he still with us, I should like to present a copy of this book to him as a token of a former student's esteem. Mr. Leigh would be embarrassed to be singled out, but he was a truly wonderful man and a dedicated educator. He was loved and revered by several generations of parents and pupils alike.

In the years that I was growing up, our little community was all but overrun with kids. That fact, plus my fading memory, may have caused me to attribute some comments or activities to the wrong individual. Also, to simplify things, I have borrowed a trick from

Mark Twain, and some of the kids mentioned are actually composites. So, in the unlikely event that any of my former cohorts reads this book and can not recognize himself or herself, I apologize for depriving them of their fifteen minutes of fame.

But in the stories you are about to read, there really is no need of name changes to protect the innocent. Because there are no bad guys in any of these reminiscences. My cast of characters had its share of the minor human frailties common to working class folk anywhere. Yet, as a whole, they represented the qualities that have long made the U.S.A. stand out as a land of promise. Generous, neighborly, honest, patriotic, hard working – in short, good people.

My path from short pants to a high school diploma and that first full-time job stretched from the late 1930s to the mid 1950s. For the record, let me acknowledge that adult participants of that era would not describe it as "just a bowl of cherries." Among other things, we went from the tail end of the Great Depression to World War II, followed by the so-called "Cold War."

I do not mean to gloss over the hard times, tragedies and sacrifices experienced by many Americans in those years while I was growing up. This book is largely a tribute to the grown-ups who supported one another, endured together and managed in the process to shelter us kids from most of the bad stuff. Thanks to them, my playmates and I were able to revel in the carefree adventure of just being kids. The memories collected herein are a celebration of the overriding good stuff that enables an old geezer to look back at those years and say, "Ah, yes, those were the days!"

Dan McGuire

FOREWORD

Growing up in Chicago in the good old days:

Danny McGuire and his family had moved into their house on Ottawa Avenue not long before my family moved into ours, just two doors north, in the summer of 1939.

It really wasn't Chicago, but an unincorporated area of Norwood Park Township in Cook County. A decade went by before the area was incorporated into the Village of Norridge and became a Far Northwest Side suburb of Chicago.

My birthday that year, the first in our new home, made me eligible to enter grammar school in the fall. Danny would have to wait until the following year, because he was almost exactly one year young than I.

I don't remember exactly how we met, but I was the new kid on the block and we hit it off immediately. We've been close friends ever since.

As pals through the years, we shared a great many life experiences.

We hung out together on the block, welcomed other new kids to the street and attended James Giles Elementary School, less than a block from our houses. I had the teachers a year before Danny did and so could clue him in on how to deal with their idiosyncrasies. Sometimes we were asked by those teachers to remain after school as punishment for separately committed offenses.

But usually, after school, we played "Cops and Robbers," "Kick the Can," "Statue Maker" and other kids' games, and then ran home to listen to *Jack Armstrong* and *Captain Midnight* on the radio.

We collected and traded comic books. (He liked *Batman and Robin* and I thought *Captain Marvel* was tops.)

In our early years, we raced our tricycles up and down the sidewalk. Later, we raced each other on roller skates and scooters and, still later, we mounted our trusty two-wheelers for daring bike races. Once Danny's bike hit an obstacle on the street and he took a header over his handlebars and landed in the bushes. I helped him limp home.

We loved to go "Trick or Treating" on Halloween, and as we moved into the upper grades at James Giles School, we started begging for candy and other goodies on streets beyond Ottawa Avenue.

We went to nearby grocery stores on errands for our mothers, mowed the lawn for our fathers, and acted silly for all the neighbors when, on a summer evening, they were all sitting out on their front porches getting some fresh air.

The Irving Park Road shuttle buses and streetcars took us to the Patio Theatre ("Pay-Show") at Austin Avenue, or to the Portage Theatre at "Six Corners" (Irving Park, Cicero, Milwaukee), or to the Irving Theatre at Pulaski Road, where we saw, on most Saturday afternoons, a double feature, a color cartoon, a chapter of an exciting cliff-hanging adventure serial and plenty of Coming Attractions.

By the time we reached high school—we were still a year apart at Steinmetz High—we were taking the Addison Street bus ("The Boulevard Route") downtown to see a movie and a stage show at the Chicago or Oriental Theatre, or even going to see a live radio show at the Merchandise Mart.

We were starting to notice girls, and we were obliged to seek out friendships with older guys who had driver's licenses and access to their family automobile, so we could hitch a ride with them and not be obliged to take a date on the streetcar.

Gosh, it seems like just yesterday that we did all those things together.

Those were good times, and you can be sure that Dan and I have reminisced *ad nauseam* about them often over the years. Too many times, if you ask our wives.

In 1976, Dan started writing his recollections of those thrilling days of yesteryear for the *Nostalgia Digest*. This led to a regular column that became a welcome feature in the magazine and continued for eleven years.

Now he has gathered many of those recollections for this book and, while I didn't participate in *every single* activity described by Dan, I was there for a lot of them.

And I think you will find that you were there, too.

Chuck Schaden
Those Were The Days radio show host
Nostalgia Digest publisher

Since 1970, Chuck Schaden has been producer and host of "Those Were The Days," a weekly panorama of the great classic shows (and some all but forgotten ones) from The Golden Age of Radio. Aired every Saturday from 1 to 5p.m., Central Time, the program originates from Public Radio station WDCB-FM in Glen Ellyn, Illinois. It can be heard worldwide on the streaming website of the College of DuPage: www.wdcb.org

CONTENTS

At Home And Around The Block

The Neighborhood

The Big, Wide World

Families from 4300 block of Ottawa Avenue gather at a picnic in nearby Schiller Woods. At left, parents Jessie and Ray McGuire hold the author's brothers Alan and Dickie. In center group of kids, the author stands at left in second row, next to his pals Chuck, Peter, and Jimmy. Chuck's brother, Kenny (in striped shirt), stands in front of him. Their parents, Toby and Mary Schaden, are at the far right. (photo courtesy C. Schaden)

At Home And Around The Block

Let The Games Begin. You're It!

In the golden years of my childhood, long before noise pollution was recognized as a social ill, our neighborhood often was subjected to a deafening din. The cause was not any of our modern culprits: auto traffic, boom box radios, construction, jet aircraft overhead, etc. It was us kids.

If we weren't in school, sick, eating meals, doing chores or listening to a favorite radio program, we usually were outside playing. We played in the streets, in alleys, back yards, the school yard—and we didn't play quietly. The degree of noise we made was a measure of what a good time we were having.

On my block alone, the gang (in that relatively innocent era the word *gang* carried no connotation of delinquency) included nineteen kids who were within a couple of years of my own age. Another dozen were only a tad younger or older, and because our block was so populated with kids, there was an added spill-over of friends from the next block and across the alley. Depending upon the game being played and who was around, anywhere from half a dozen to perhaps thirty kids might be engaged in our boisterous activity.

Sometimes two or three games were played in overlapping territory. It then became necessary to yell over and around other players, and things got even more raucous.

Amazingly, mothers could single out the voices of their own offending offspring from amidst this robust ruckus. Often a mother would lean out a window and put our lusty lungs to shame with her own sonic–boom soprano shout: "Billy! Stop all that SCREAMING!" By implication, we were all chastised, and for a little while we lowered our voices in the vicinity of Billy's house.

About a dozen games stand out in my memory as those we played most frequently. Several of the most popular games were in the search or chase category.

The simplest of these was "Tag," more commonly referred to as just "It." The game almost always began spontaneously. Half a dozen kids are standing around, digging holes in the lawn with the heels of their shoes, and someone says, "Let's play Tag." The rest look around, nodding heads at one another, and someone says, "Okay.

2

You're 'It'!" Everyone takes off at a run. *It* singles out someone to chase and tag, thus passing on the unwanted title.

The taggee cannot retag the taggor, so the title of *It* keeps getting passed around. This rule, plus the challenge of catching the faster runners, saves slow pokes from always being *It*. There are no prearranged boundaries. The radius of play is instinctively governed by the number of players. If the group spreads out too far, *It* will get tired and discouraged and shout, "I quit!" Also, you must not get too far out of range and lose sight of who is *It*— or suddenly *It* will be you.

The more daring players make wild dashes past *It*. Sometimes several such risk takers converge and a chain reaction results. *It* tags one, who immediately passes it on to another, and yet a third receives the tag (en passant, as the chess players say). As the cluster breaks up and fans out, all still running, everyone else hollers, "Who's *It*?"

"Hide and Seek" also required an "It" person. Whoever was *It* faced a wall, or covered his or hers eyes, and counted to one hundred. The rest of us ran to hide. The boundaries usually were anywhere from alley to alley on the south half (the most densely populated) of our block. Garages, gangways, partially enclosed porches, bushes, parked cars and a dozen or more other places made good spots for hiding. Even a thick tree trunk would do, if you stood sideways and resisted peeking around.

In the traditional "Hide and Seek" game, *It* went looking for hidden players. After spotting one, he returned to the home base, or "gool," and announced to the neighborhood at large: "One, two, three on Jimmy, behind Swensons' lilac bush! Not free, not free!"

If the kid he spotted actually was Tommy, Tommy would pop out and cry: "Oley, oley, ocean,[1] free! It's Tommy, not Jimmy!" He then was entitled to a count of 50 in which to hide elsewhere.

As each player was located and correctly identified, he came back to gool and waited for the others to be caught. After the last person was found, that game was over and the person caught first became *It* for the next game.

---

[1] The terms *oley, oley, ocean* and *gool* were passed down by generations of kids who played these street games. There are several variant forms, but my inquiries in later years indicate that nobody knew their origin, what they meant, or even the correct spellings.

"Fifty More" and "Kick the Can" were variations of the game that were a bit more involved. In "Fifty More," players could try to sneak back to gool when *It's* back was turned or he stepped away looking for other hidden players. If they could get there before *It* spotted them and did the "One, two, three on Margie" routine, they could touch gool and shout: "Fifty More!" This freed all previously captured players to run and hide while *It* returned and counted to 50.

"Kick the Can" literally used an old tin can, which *It* banged on the sidewalk while he covered his eyes and counted as the players ran to hide. Again, players could sneak back to gool, where the can remained while *It* searched. A running kick sent the can clattering down the street, to be retrieved by *It* while his captives fled.

Obviously, these variations had the potential of being very frustrating for whoever was *It*. The game often broke up after he had been obliged to count to 50 several times and became disgusted. Or he grew so cautious that he wouldn't stray ten yards from gool, was unable to spot any of the hiders, and they all got bored. Once, when Peter was *It*, he got fed up and just went into his house without saying anything. We all stood or crouched restlessly in our hiding places for about twenty minutes. When we figured it out, boy, were we ever mad at - - -

Aw, shucks. I think my mother's calling. I gotta go. I wanted to tell you about "Statue Maker," "Mother, May I?" and a whole bunch more. Tell you what. Meet me here when the next issue comes out, okay? Good. See you then. Meantime:

Oley, oley ocean, free! New quitter!

Let The Games Continue. You're Still It!

Hi! Glad you could come back. Remember last time, I was telling you about favorite games the kids on my block played? "Kick the Can," "Fifty More," etc.

Hide-and-seek type games required an "It" person to do the seeking. Nobody especially wanted to be "It," so we often resorted to the "guilty finger" process to select an unfortunate designee. Whoever suggested the game turned around and closed his eyes. Someone traced an imaginary circle on his back as the gang recited in sing-song voice:

"Make a round circle,

Color it purple,

Some-bod-ie poke!"

One of the group then poked the center of the circle. As the poked player turned, everyone wagged a finger in his face and chanted:

"Who's got the guilty finger?

Who's got the guilty finger?"

If you were lucky enough to actually pick the kid with the guilty finger, he became "It" instead of you. Trouble was, with 6, 8, 10 or more kids playing, the odds always were against you.

A more democratic method was counting potatoes. Everyone, including the Counter, held out two fists. The Counter went down the line, tapping each fist with his own and counting off: "One potato, two potato, three potato, four. Five potato, six potato, seven potato – more!" The fist that was tapped on the word "more" was eliminated by its owner placing it behind his or her back. By repetition, other hands were removed from the count until only one remained. The body attached to that hand was "It."

Some games required leaders rather than "It" persons. Everyone was happy to volunteer because being leader gave you a sense of power over the other players. The "one potato, two potato" process of elimination became a necessity to insure that no one felt slighted because they never got to be the leader.

In "Mother, May I?" players lined up across the street, about three houses down from the goal line at the corner. The leader called out instructions to each one in turn: "Jimmy, take eight baby steps forward." Or: "Judy, take five giant steps forward."

5

Before moving, the player must ask, "Mother, may I?" If the leader replied, "Yes, you may," the player made his move. "Baby steps" were toe-to-heel, which didn't get you far. "Giant steps" were the longest stride you could manage without a running start. You might also be told to take "scissor steps." This required leaping forward and alternately landing with legs spread wide apart and then with feet together.

When asked, "Mother, may I?" the leader could say, "No, you may not," and give a different order. This could be repeated several times. Sometimes a player would lose the rhythm and forget to ask "Mother, may I?" before moving forward. Then the leader would triumphantly hold up a hand and demand: "Stop! Go back. You didn't say 'Mother, may I?'" The player then had to return to his or her spot and lost a turn.

Some sadistic leaders would tell a player to take twenty giant steps forward, and the player would quickly calculate that this would put him over the goal line, making him the winner and the new leader. But when he asked, "Mother, may I?" the leader would say, "No. You may take one scissor step forward."

Occasionally a leader might originate a little trickery such as telling Eddie to take seven "regular steps" forward. After asking "Mother, may I" Eddie would start forward, but the leader would hold up a hand and say, "Stop! Those are giant steps. Go back and lose a turn." Many a game was interrupted for loud arguments about such smart-alecky tricks.

A few players were prone to forget and move too quickly without asking the crucial question. Thus they were forever lagging behind. By common consent, leaders would compensate by occasionally permitting them to make great moves forward.

Our gang most often played a version of the game that required each player to first ask, "May I?" To which the leader usually would reply, "Yes, you may." But then the player had to confirm his permission by asking, "*Mother,* may I?" Invariably, as the game speeded up, everyone fell victim to a short attention span and missed a turn. So, even the better players were sometimes reduced to stomping their feet in frustration at their own dumbness.

The leader also could order you backward, theoretically prolonging the game (and his rule) forever. But a lot of cheating went on. Players on the edges sneaked up a few feet when the leader was dealing with someone on the opposite side of the street. Or an occasional car passed by, everyone moved aside and when the line reformed, everyone was five or six feet closer to the goal. Besides, leaders eventually started to tire of that role. Itching to be part of the action, they would let someone make it across the goal line.

"Red Light, Green Light" was a simpler, swifter version of the same idea. The leader turned her back and called out, "One, two, three, Green Light!" Everyone started walking forward as fast as they could (no running allowed, though). The leader called, "Red Light!" (without the "One, two, three" preface) and turned quickly. If she saw you still moving, you were sent back.

A favorite trick, when the players were stopped, was for the leader to call out, "One, two, three, Yellow Light!" Anticipating the green light command, half the players would start forward. The leader would turn swiftly, point and say triumphantly: "Jimmy, Bobby, Margie and Barbara – all back to 'Go'!"

"Statue Maker" involved being swung around by the arm and sent spinning across the yard to land in the goofiest possible position. After a gallery of statues had been created in this fashion by the Maker, a "buyer" came along. He picked a statue he liked and asked the Maker, "How does it work?" The Maker turned an imaginary key in the statue's back, and: *"Viola!"* The statue came to life and gave a show of crazy antics until the Maker turned it off. It would then "freeze" in something akin to its original form. This was repeated with each statue until the buyer made a purchase. Then the roles changed and another array of statues was created.

Perhaps because it did not lead to a conclusive finale, "Statue Maker" tended to be a short-term cure for boredom in between more organized games. At some point, when the buyer had selected a statue and was paying the Maker, the statue would come to life and try to run off, with the buyer giving chase and the other statues breaking their poses to call out encouragement to one party or the other. When that happened, the game sort of fizzled out and someone would ask the inevitable question, "What'll we do now?"

Some games were favored more by one sex than by the other. Girls were good at jumping ropes. Most boys weren't. We sometimes joined in when two people turned one long rope.

(Remember: "Teddy bear, teddy bear, turn around"? Or: "Fire, fire, false alarm. Georgie fell in Margie's arms. How many kisses did he get?") But when two ropes started twirling in tandem, that was it for us boys.

Why couldn't boys jump rope? (They were agile enough at climbing trees and walking fences.) Partly, I think, because the girls had better rhythm. But boys really did jump; whereas girls actually skipped, one foot lifting a second behind the other to let the rope slide under as it skimmed the sidewalk.

Games like "London Bridge" and "Kitty in the Corner" were genderless, while "Hop Scotch" offered challenges to both sexes. You had to lag a stone into squares chalked on the sidewalk, each progressively farther away. Then you hopped on one foot down the column, landing only once in each box. Still standing on one foot, you stooped to retrieve your stone, then hopped back.

Halfway up the column was a set of two side-by-side squares. Here you could pause with one foot in each square, but to turn back you must leap and twist around so as to land facing the opposite direction, again with one foot in each box. At the far end, designated "Sky Blue," was a half moon space in which you could put both feet down, turn around and rest before starting to hop back home.

Soldiers, cowboys and Indians, cops and robbers—all variations on a theme—attracted mostly boys. Girls occasionally joined in (or had their own games) playing an Army nurse, a gun moll or Dale Evans (the movies' "Queen of the Cowgirls").

When we played soldiers, everyone wanted to be a G.I.; nobody wanted to be "the enemy." So we had to make do with battles in which we routed imaginary Jap machine gun nests or blew up Nazi ammunition dumps. Otherwise, the bank robber, rustler and desperado roles were popular – until they were captured. Then the bad guys, bored with being stuck in jail, inevitably said, "I know what. Let's play we have a jailbreak!"

When the groups were large and enthusiasm high, some games went on all afternoon. They recessed at supper hour, then resumed and went on until dark. They usually ended in a familiar pattern.

A couple of mothers would call their wandering offspring. If we were out of sight down the block, these players conveniently would not hear at first. The calls were soon repeated, now more emphatically. Continued deafness brought further calls in a few minutes – this time from male voices.

At this point, the players' hearing improved miraculously. Callees began to disperse and shout toward home: "Com-ming!" To their pals, they yelled back: "My ol' man's callin'. I gotta go. See yuz tomorrow."

Thus did the games go on....

Afterthought: Almost every male who experienced such calls from home in that era will tell you of a similar scenario upon arriving home.

First you would be confronted by Mother, hands on hips, demanding rhetorically: "Where have you *been*, young man? I've been calling you (sometimes it was "I've been yelling my head off...) for half an hour."

It really was more like ten minutes, but to protest would be to admit that you heard her call – and failed to respond. So you gave the humble apology: "I'm sorry, Mom. We were playing (and the guilt-laden lie:) and I didn't hear ya."

At which point Father, in a nearby armchair, lowered the evening paper to interpose: "You know you're supposed to come in when it gets dark. When your mother calls, you get yourself home here!"

End of discussion. Note the implication that Father, having once been a boy himself, *knows* that you heard your mother and ignored her call. The proper response was to utter a simple "Yes, sir" before diplomatically removing yourself to another part of the house.

Many of my male contemporaries speak of their father's dreaded razor strop, which usually hung as a forbidding reminder in the bathroom. But most acknowledge that their fathers seldom, if ever, resorted to using it on their young behinds.

Our love and respect for our parents made knowing that you had displeased them punishment enough. For the next week or so, at least, you would come home when called.

During his daily perambulation, the author pauses in front of the McGuire homestead. Note the early version of whole-house air conditioning. A canvas awning can be lowered to keep afternoon sun from the front windows. An open window in the attic allows rising hot air to escape during the day and welcomes any cool breezes at night.

A rare photo of the McGuire boys; together and standing still. Alan stands beside the author, who holds brother Dickie.

Ya Wanna Trade Comics?

Summer days held endless possibilities for us kids in the 1940s. But rain that didn't let up could pose a problem. What can you do when you're about played out with card games, checkers, Monopoly and Sorry? We pondered this together, Jimmy, Pete, Judy, Bobby, Wayne, Tommy, Shirley, Chuck and me. We'd been nearly three hours on Wayne and Shirley's front porch – the only one on our block big enough to hold all of us without two or three having to sit on the steps and get soaked.

The answer to our youthful quandary came from next door, as twins Wilbert and Willard dashed across the gangway and up the steps, hugging bunches of comic books under each of their four arms. Wilbert reached the porch two strides ahead of his brother, shook off raindrops dog fashion and asked, "Anybody wanna trade comics?" Primed to partake of any new diversion, we answered more or less in unison with a chorus of affirmatives.

With a leap from the steps to get a good running start, we raced home through the rain and returned shortly with armloads of our own comics. Staking out small sections of the porch to display our collections, we began an excited round robin of negotiations.

Trading was a one-on-one operation. Each trader wanted to see and evaluate what everyone else had to offer. During the next half hour, only a few trades took place as we browsed through each pile to see what was available. Once we'd zeroed in on our personal selections, the serious negotiating began. After about an hour, the trading tapered off and we all began skimming through our new acquisitions. Some comics had changed hands several times, unread by traders who possessed them briefly but then "traded up" for something more appealing.

Eventually, parents called us home for supper. We dispersed, happily anticipating days of comic book read-a-thons.

That group trade was a novelty. Like the tango, it took only two to trade comic books, although threesomes were not unusual. Most trading was done spur-of-the-moment, when other activities temporarily fizzled.

The rules were unwritten, but universally agreed upon – and simple. You traded a "like new" comic only for one in comparable condition. Torn or badly worn issues of a highly regarded comic might be worth one issue of a less valued series that was in almost A-1 condition. We would have been at a loss to explain why, but

coverless comics had little appeal and were infrequently traded, even for other no-cover issues. Occasionally, two denuded editions of very popular comics might purchase one copy of a less desirable series that still retained its cover.

Girls were at a slight disadvantage in trading. They usually bought fewer comics than us boys, and their tastes ran to series such as Wonder Woman, Little Lulu, Archie and Sheena of the Jungle. These had limited trading value to those of us who preferred male hero types; although as puberty began to kick in we came to appreciate Sheena and the wonder lady somewhat. (A youthful chauvinist, I found Sheena quite exciting when some jungle tribe tied her to a stake as a sacrifice for their gorilla mascot.)

We all had our favorites. Batman and Robin, Tarzan and the Lone Ranger were mine in the adventure category. Their heroic exploits were the more thrilling to me because they all were mortal. With no super powers, they fearlessly faced the danger that their daring adventures could prove fatal. (Unlikely, of course, since none of their various publishers would be so foolish as to kill their respective golden goose.)

Not so that tooth pretty boy, Captain Marvel, that Chuck idolized. With his shouts of "Shazam!"

13

and those great bolts of lightning, Billy Batson was forever changing into the flashy superhero at the first sign of trouble – except that often he was too dumb to spot the danger or too slow to react. That enabled the bad guys to slug or gag him when all he'd gotten out of his mouth was "Shaz—!" (Decades later, I read that Captain Marvel actually had been intended to poke a little fun at Superman—only to surprise his creators by becoming a smash hit himself. How revolting!)

Anyway, having favorites complicated the trading system a bit. Your favorites were not my favorites (see above), and each of us placed an otherwise excessive value on his. As a result, many favorites were traded only rarely, usually after they became badly shopworn.

Varying proportions of all our youthful incomes were spent on comic books. Only the most severely tattered were ever discarded, and most of us probably accumulated 200, 300 or more before outgrowing the addiction. (I know, I know. Some never did outgrow it.) But no prestige was attached to either the quantity or quality of our collections. Saving comics was just something kids did.

Floyd didn't understand this. He tried to impress us with tales of 5-foot-high stacks of comics in his attic. Yet he always brought out a familiar pile of about 50 or 60 to trade. He explained that his mother would permit him only one quick trip to the attic because it was so dusty up there and he suffered from asthma. A strict churchgoer, Floyd's mother may also have restricted his comic purchases. However many comics his collection comprised, it included an inordinate number of Bible Story and Classics Illustrated comics, which tended to go begging.

I do not mean to scoff. Today, my own "collection" consists of a few dozen unread and carefully preserved Classics Illustrated reprints that I purchased during the publisher's last days.

Those who collected comics half a century ago (when it was *just* a collection, not an investment) undoubtedly have at some time mused: "If I had all the comics that passed through my hands as a kid, I could sell them for a small fortune today." But if you had them, could you part with them now? Think of the wealth of memories they hold of buying, reading, trading, reading and trading again!

During a period when I was flush with paper route income, I actually subscribed to the Walt Disney and Bugs Bunny/Porky Pig (Looney Tunes) comics and received every issue in the mail. These were supplemented by "special edition" comic book versions of *Snow White* and other Disney films. Along with 100-plus others in like-new condition, they constituted a collection that I treasured long after I'd outgrown actually reading them.

When I married, I left this precious remnant stored in the family basement. During an over-enthusiastic cleaning binge, my mother mistook them for junk—*junk?!*— and gave them to a Boy Scout paper drive.

Over time, I eventually forgave her. But neither of my daughters was named after her.

At his Comic Kingdom shop in Chicago, Joe Sarno displays some classic early editions from the thousands in his collection.

Dan McGuire

Icicles, Igloos And Angels In The Snow

What you did was, you stood with feet together, hands at your sides and fell straight backward into the snow. You moved your arms up in an arc until they met over your head, then brought them back to your sides. Next came the tricky part.

Without using your hands, you thrust yourself to a sitting position and used the forward momentum to spring to your feet. If you completed the process without falling back or stumbling into the area just vacated, your efforts were rewarded with an impression in the snow that looked roughly like the silhouette of a Christmas angel.

In the pre-television years of my youth, sculpting snow angels was one way that kids entertained themselves when outside alone on a winter day.

Knocking down icicles also could occupy an hour or more of idle time. Once winter had a good start, there was likely to be a bumper crop of frozen drippings all around the gutters and overhangs of your house.

Smallfry couldn't reach up and pull icicles down as some tall fathers might. The job required a broom or mop handle. Even so, many icicles were too short for a good shot at them. Or thick ones would break off at midpoint. It didn't count unless you got the entire icy stalactite at or near its base.

To accomplish that required a lot of jumping—sometimes with a running start—and wild flailing of your stick until a lucky blow found its mark. If the snow was good packing, you could try lobbing snowballs at the out-of-reach stubs. This method, however, required both a strong arm and excellent marksmanship.

To my knowledge, no one ever succeeded in eliminating the icicles from all four sides of his or her house. Usually, both interest and energy were exhausted about halfway around. Or a friend showed up to dispel our boredom and we departed, sucking on two of the thickest icicles.

Early in the season, when street puddles were crusted over but not yet frozen solid, cracking the ice was great fun. A thin layer of ice could be stomped flatfooted, but you had to take care lest your shoe submerge above the sole and heel. This called for both precision and good balance.

16

As temperatures fell and puddles froze thicker, it became necessary to use the heel of your shoe like a hammer. It took more work to punch smaller holes in the surface. This was not recommended activity once galoshes weather began. Heels were apt to tear, resulting in leaky galoshes, wet feet, colds and distressed mothers. ("What have you been *doing* to those galoshes? They were new last winter.")

Once you got started stomping frozen puddles, there was a tendency to become more determined in your efforts to leave no icy surface uncracked. This often led to carelessness and/or misjudgment.

I once stepped easily through a layer of ice that was thinner than it looked. Beneath it was a deeper puddle than I expected. My shoe, sock and pants cuff were soaked. As my foot turned numb with cold, I fervently longed to warm it on a register at home. Instead, I had to occupy myself outside until I was dry enough that Mom wouldn't notice.

Two kids and only one sled? No problem. Alan McGuire pushes brother Dickie on the snow-covered sidewalk along Ottawa Avenue. When he gets tired, they can take turns belly flopping.

Auto traffic in our neighborhood was negligible. When our streets became slick with ice or packed snow, we could belly-flop to our hearts' content without worrying our parents.

Belly-flopping involved holding a sled chest high and getting a running start. On the run, and without letting go, you bent, let the

17

sled drop to the ground beneath you and literally fell on top of it. Properly done, your belly (well padded by your winter garb) absorbed the impact. Thus the term "belly flop."

Immediately upon touchdown, you elevated your legs so that your feet wouldn't drag. Simultaneously, you had to shift your hands to the two front handles that gave you a measure of control over the sled's direction.

You could burn off plenty of energy just belly-flopping on a straightaway course. Or you might try zig-zagging around obstacles. In a spirit of daredevilism, we sometimes crashed head-on into piled snow. Or we'd get up a head of steam and run up a slope that would send us flying off sideways into a snowbank.

Once I belly-flopped eight blocks over to my friend Harvey's house. Half a block away, I hit the ground on a high-speed run. Ten feet later, I slid over a parking space that someone had salted. The sled ground to an abrupt halt, but I kept going. I arrived at Harvey's house with skinned palms, a cut lip and a loose front tooth.

When you were with a buddy, you could take turns pushing each other or compete for speed and/or distance in belly-flops. In groups, we sometimes had races, taking turns as rider and pusher.

"Hey, let's race to the end of the block."

"Naw. Too far. The pushers'll drop dead."

"Okay. How's this? From the end of the block to the Schadens' big tree."

"Good. Pick partners and line up. Odd man out can be starter."

A few round-robins of that race course would leave everyone fairly pooped. Rather than admit it, we'd find some excuse to dispute the outcome of one or more races. That would precipitate an impromptu snowball fight.

What with all the switching off of partners during the races, no one was specifically on anyone else's side. So it became pretty much an every-man-for-himself free-for-all, last one standing wins.

Sometimes we had more organized combat, with snowballs made and stockpiled for several days. Then the two sides would face off over the back yard fences, with one yard separating us.

We threw our best fast balls from behind trees, bushes and walls of packed snow. We aimed chest high and usually were lucky to hit an outflung arm or leg. We all wore winter caps, so at that distance, if

18

a missile chanced to hit someone's head, it did no real damage, although the victim might be stunned for a moment. Often as not, the thrower stood up and peered in surprised concern at his hitee, making him the prime target for a barrage of the enemy's next eight or ten lobs.

In more cooperative efforts, we built perhaps a thousand snowmen over the years. (Occasionally the girls exerted their influence and we created a snowwoman.) In twos and threes, we would work together on one figure. In larger groups, we could produce a whole snowperson family of assorted sizes and genders.

One year at least a dozen kids on our block decided to construct an igloo in Wayne's back yard. The outer walls, with about a ten-foot diameter, went up easily enough. We rolled and stacked dozens of huge balls such as you'd use to make a snowman. The snow was good packing and we tamped handfuls between sections to make them solid.

Getting a roof to stay on was a challenge. To give it support, we put four partial walls inside with an opening in the center. It looked like a wheel with the hub missing. The result was that we had four small rooms that all faced into one another.

The roof still had to be patched very gingerly. Someone sat inside and held each small segment from below as it was padded and tamped into a snug fit. There were dozens of partial collapses before we got a complete roof in place that was packed solidly enough to last for awhile.

We put the finishing touch to our frozen architecture by adding an Eskimo-style crawl-through entrance. Then we celebrated our success by dragging most of our parents (singly or in pairs) out into the cold to inspect our handiwork and heap lavish praise upon us.

For a few days, the igloo was our prime gathering place. But we couldn't actually do much inside. Crawling in, you had to take care not to raise your head lest you poke a hole in the entryway ceiling. Maximum capacity was two kids per room and one seated Indian-style in the center. But this meant removing our heavy winter coats because of the cramped space. It also required sitting almost motionless because any movement might damage a wall.

With occupancy limited to one kid per room, we could play cards or board games in the center. Except that very little light came through the tunnel entrance.

Several of us asked parents for candles but were told that these would likely cause our roof to melt. (It made sense to us and didn't prompt the whining arguments we would have raised for what probably was their real concern: that we would set ourselves afire.) We had to make do with flashlights that were continually going dim.

Except for telling spooky stories, escaping from the chilly wind for brief periods, resting between other activities or just hiding out, the igloo soon fell out of favor. One day, with no prior discussion, but apparently by mutual inspiration and consent, we had a sort of demolition party.

We began with a mock attack on the igloo, bombarding it with snow cannonballs. We crawled inside, stood up and poked our heads through the roof, prompting laughter and a few poorly aimed snowballs from our cohorts. We ran and threw ourselves into the walls. In about fifteen minutes, we undid a week's hard labor. We lay laughing in the jumble of bodies, buried in mounds of snow that had been our magnificent edifice.

During subsequent winters, someone occasionally would suggest building another igloo. The idea invariably got a chilly response. Everyone remembered how much work had been involved in the building and what the ultimate outcome had been. Once was enough.

Ice skating was not part of our winter regimen. No one owned shoe skates. A few kids had skates that strapped onto their street shoes. These got little use because there were no ponds nearby and no park with a flooded skating area.

Instead of skating, we engaged in what you might call ice skimming. This could be done on any prairie (kid slang for vacant lot) where water had accumulated and then frozen. Usually there were plenty of rough spots, protruding rocks, bushes and other plant life. This gave an added challenge to the sport.

In ice skimming, you made a running start from outside the frozen area. At the ice's edge, you hurtled forward, assuming a stance of legs slightly apart, semi-rigid, and arms outstretched for balance. The object, of course, was an exhilarating slide across the ice. If you had

Skating ponds were where and as you found them in the author's boyhood town. One of his future classmates tries out her new 2-blade skates on a semi-frozen stretch of Ottawa Avenue. (photo courtesy Nancy Gisselbrecht Simandl)

to raise a foot—or leap into the air—to avoid one of the obstacles, that added to the excitement.

Often the surface wasn't uniformly frozen and we got our shoes soaked. Spills were not infrequent in ice skimming. These resulted in plenty of sore rumps, skinned palms and torn knees in pants or snowsuits. A pratfall in a bad spot could send us home with the seat of our pants soaked and our bottoms chapped. Or, worse luck, the pants might be ripped.

We endured the injuries stoically. The damage to clothing, however, was one more trial for long-suffering mothers trying to stretch thin household budgets. These were certain to elicit stern maternal chastisement, the more painful because we knew it to be justly deserved.

One year Jimmy's dad emptied a barrel of junk from their garage and let Jimmy have the battered barrel. We dismantled it and used the staves for skies. We waxed the undersides and tied them onto our shoes with cords and strips of cloth. For propulsion, we resorted again to broom and mop handles.

Our makeshift skies were primitive. Forward motion was not easy or smooth. But it was as close to that rich person's sport as any of us got before we reached adulthood.

Dan McGuire

I'm glad that my youngsters grew up in an area with easy access to sled hills, skating ponds and toboggan slides. It's reassuring, too, to observe that the art of making snowmen is not forgotten – and occasionally I even spot a snow angel on someone's lawn.

I've yet to see a group of today's smallfry get together and pool their talents to construct an igloo. If they ever do, it probably will be furnished with a Coleman lantern, Nintendo games, a cell phone and a CD boombox.

Mother's Little Helper

My mother was always a very neat housekeeper. It couldn't have been easy in the days when she had three rambunctious boys running through the house, tracking in mud and snow, spilling various liquids, touching walls with unwashed hands, cluttering every room with discarded clothing, toys, games and trinkets of unknown origin.

Mom probably would have liked to have at least one daughter. Fortunately for her, though, I was the type of son who enjoyed being Mother's Little Helper. (Well, at least until one of my pals hollered for me from our gangway.)

Typical of her era, my mother spent a lot of time in our kitchen. Since I often was there eating a cookie or a slice of jelly bread, I observed many of her chores. At an early age, I began helping her wash dishes.

I know it was early because I had to stand on a chair at the cast iron sink. It was a single basin design, with individual hot and cold faucets. The porcelain coated drain portion was ribbed and inclined so that water ran back into the basin.

My first efforts involved sturdy items such as silverware and heavy glass coffee cups. Later, I was entrusted to do everyday tumblers, dishes, plates and such. I learned to rinse under a small trickle of hot water, which also kept the dishwater warm. I became adept at stacking dishes and plates at an angle atop overturned cups so that they would drain almost dry before being wiped.

Mom always did the sharp knives and items such as pots and pans that required real scrubbing. At first she also did the tall glasses, because my short fingers couldn't reach milk rings at the bottom. Soon, though, I learned to scrunch up the dishrag and twist it down inside the glass to accomplish this.

Wiping was sort of boring compared to plunging your arms deep into the soap-sudsy water. But I enjoyed taking three or four plates at once, wiping the upper and under sides, then repeatedly flipping one from the top of the stack to the bottom.

It was also in the kitchen that Mom set up her ironing board. This was in the pre-wash-and-wear years, remember. Almost everything except towels got ironed after washing.

Nor did we have spray irons or readymade plastic sprinkler bottles. Mom used a returnable soda bottle, with a metal shaker head on a cork base inserted into its neck.

My first attempts at ironing involved handkerchiefs. Simple, you say? Perhaps; but after a few washing, "hankies" began to lose their square shape. Then it became a bit of a challenge to fold them over several times and still have all the corners come out nice and even. (In this apprentice period, Mom could do all the rest of the ironing in about the time it took me to flatten ten hankies.)

Later, I graduated to pillow cases and wash pants. Mom let me try shirts occasionally, but she always had to finish them. I never could master the sleeves or areas around pockets and collars.

To some extent, I suppose my willingness to be so helpful could be explained by the fact that I was easily entertained. It was fascinating to me to watch the fabrics become perfectly smooth as the iron floated over them. I liked the hot touch of the material and its steamy dampness. Sometimes too damp. Watchful, even as she performed some other task, Mom sometimes would raise a hand policeman fashion and say, "Whoa, Dobbin! That's a sprinkler you're using, boy. Don't pour on the whole bottle."

A fun part of helping with this chore was my frequent "testing" of the hot iron. I loved to wet my fingers with my tongue and let the iron "kiss" them. It never ceased to amaze me when this resulted in an instant of sizzling on my fingertips yet I was able to pull them away unburned.

Another laundry item that did not get ironed was socks. These were folded – or rolled, actually. Mom would match two, then roll them together from the toe upward. At the top, she turned one partially inside out and over both rolled socks, snugging them into a neat ball ready for their respective dresser drawers.

This was an easy job. I could do it on the living room couch while listening to Captain Midnight or Tom Mix and His Ralston Straight Shooters. Matching 25 or 30 pairs could be approached as a game. Dad's weren't hard to identify. But my brothers' socks and mine were all alike except for minor variations of size.

In seven or eight years of helping Mom roll socks, I never equaled her talent for producing a nice round ball. Even years later, during my tour of duty in the Army, I sometimes was "gigged" for the sloppy socks in my foot locker display.

On the other hand, my bunk-making skills always passed inspection. At home, Mom changed our sheets and pillow covers weekly. But I fluffed my pillow, tucked in and remade my bed each morning. This practice at home made it easier for me to meet Uncle Sam's (and the platoon sergeant's) tight-corner standards in boot camp.

Saturday mornings often found me lounging on the living room couch listening to "The Adventures of Frank Merriwell" or Smilin' Ed McConnell and his Buster Brown kids' show. When Mom came to vacuum the rug, I had to strain to hear. But I didn't mind because I sort of liked that distinct smell of warm rubber as the brushes revolved, and I found the hum of the vacuum somewhat hypnotic.

As Mom maneuvered the vacuum cleaner around the couch, and especially as she poked its snout underneath, there was something about the whine of its motor that sent shivers like electricity through me. As the Electrolux approached, I would lie there anticipating the weirdly pleasant tingling sensation. (Was I the only kid thus attuned to those electric vibrations? Fearful of the answer, I never had the nerve to inquire among my friends.)

My occasional assertions that "I can do that!" eventually won me the opportunity to operate the vacuum cleaner. What a thrill to watch the rug come magically clean as it sucked up threads, scraps of paper, pebbles, specks of dirt or dust.

When a string resisted being picked up, I would go back over it six or seven times. (Sometimes Mom observed this persistence and teasingly chided, "If you get that spot much cleaner, it's going to make the rest of the rug look dirty.") If the uncooperative string still clung to the rug, I would stop to loosen it by hand, then run the machine over it one more time and experience a feeling of victory as it disappeared.

Vacuum cleaners were of all metal construction in those days before plastic. When they picked up a pin or a button you could hear it rattle past the brushes, into the funnel section, on up the tube and into the bag. Occasionally, I'd snag a wayward marble from behind a chair. I hated to lose them, but there are few sounds so resonantly satisfying: *Ka-choonk, ka-choock-a...clickety, clackety...*CLUNK!

Dusting was almost fun. All you had to do was run the silky cloth over tabletops and other wooden furniture and watch the surfaces renew their Johnson's Wax shine as if by magic.

On wash day, I got to hang some of the easy items (again handkerchiefs, towels, etc.). To reach the clothes line, I had to move the clothes pole that propped it up. Even then, I could work only at the middle, where the line sagged lowest. Mom showed me how to overlap corners of two items so as not to run out of clothes pins. But I broke a few of the wooden pins in the process by pressing them on too hard.

Probably because I was deadly on buttons, Mom taught me how to sew them back on. This proved to be another useful talent during my Army career. (Having read *The Adventures of Huckleberry Finn*, I already knew the correct way to thread a needle.)

In previous columns, I've recounted how I helped Mom wash windows in those years before triple-tracks and thermal panes. And how my first bike, with its oversized basket, enabled Mom to save the cost of tipping a delivery boy when she needed a few items from Elmer's Grocery. Where these more routine household tasks were concerned, I suppose my availability and enthusiasm were due at least partly to the fact that, unlike a female offspring, I was not expected to perform them on a regular basis.

Even so, since she was not blessed with any daughters, my mother probably felt pretty lucky to have a helper like me around. Of course, I didn't scrub or wax floors. Or scour tubs and toilets. Or wash walls. On mend clothes. Or do laundry. Or cook. Or –

Well, heck, I was just a kid, after all. Besides, even the greatest Little Helper doesn't want to put his mother out of a job. She has a right to feel needed, too, you know.

The Children's Menu
A Kid's Checklist Of Memorable House Specialties

The days between Thanksgiving and New Years are rich with activities, sights, sounds and smells that stir up fond memories for the child who remains in each of us. Having possessed a hearty appetite and a sweet tooth since before I could hold a spoon, I find the aromas of holiday cooking especially evocative.

Christmas cookies. The words are almost an incantation. They conjure visions of decorated serving dishes and bowls piled high with seemingly infinite varieties of marvelous munchables. Besides the half dozen types that Mom baked, we savored samples with relatives, neighbors and at school parties.

Can you single out one cookie and say, "This is my absolute favorite"? Me neither. Still, the cut-outs always will be most representative of Christmas for me.

Shaped like Santas, angels, reindeer, bells, stars and other holiday figures, our cut-outs were covered with red and green sugar sprinkles. Between the cooking tray and the serving dish, a few of the delicate reindeer legs always broke off. Mom didn't want to serve any broken cookies to guests, so she dispensed them among her three willing volunteer cookie tasters.

When Walt Disney's classic movie *Snow White and the Seven Dwarfs* was re-released in the 1940s, Mom bought a set of Snow White cookie cutters. As I recall, it included the heroine and seven dwarfs, but no prince, henchman or wicked queen/witch. Dopey was my favorite character, but I confess I usually reached for a Snow White cookie when these were passed around. They were larger.

High on everyone's personal preference list, I expect, would be chocolate chip cookies. Are these as popular elsewhere in the world as they are in America? Perhaps because mothers tend to bake them year-round, special occasion or no, they are a perennial favorite of most red-blooded American youth.

Made from scratch (natch!), Mom's chocolate chip cookies had just the right amount of genuine Hershey's chips in every mouthful. Served hot, they boasted a soft chewy texture. After setting and cooling for awhile, they acquired a pleasurable crunchiness. Call them Almost Home or anything else, no commercially produced chocolate chips—not even those from your local bakery—will ever quite measure up to the ones that came fresh from your mother's oven.

Besides being a champion cookie baker, Mom baked most of the standard pies – apple, peach, mince (a *must* whenever Grandpa Farr was a guest), pumpkin, etc. Because pies and cakes were frequent fare for dessert, we didn't think of them as special treats. Cherry pie is an exception, though.

In the back yard of our old homestead there grew a large and productive cherry tree. During its season, Mom gathered enough cherries to prepare eight or ten pies – if she could get to them "before those greedy robins and wrens eat every last one of them!" Many of these were donated to neighbors because, silly kids that we were, my brothers and I didn't care for them.

Grandpa Farr cured us of this folly by coaxing us to eat small slices covered with huge gobs of vanilla ice cream (an idea we then assumed to be Grandpa's own invention). After a few such samplings, we began taking larger slices and soon discovered that the pie tasted pretty good even by itself. Now that the old cherry tree is long gone, I own to a special fondness for cherry pie a la mode.

More vividly than the pies themselves, though, I recall a byproduct we called cinnamon rolls. If one of her offspring was kibitzing while she prepared a pie, it always happened that Mom ended up with more dough than she required for the pie's bottom and covering. As she finished trimming the edges, she would wonder aloud, "My, what will I do with all this left-over dough?"

The answer was instantaneous: "Make cinnamon rolls!"

Part of the joy of cinnamon rolls was that Mom's "helper" got to roll the dough out flat and thin. Mom sprinkled cinnamon and sugar liberally over the entire surface. Then she curled the dough into a long ropelike coil. Her assistant cut this into one-inch sections that went into the oven on a cookie tray. The result was a super delicious dividend.

When Mom removed the tray from the oven with her handmade pot holders, the helper was allowed to carefully select one to sample and be sure they were baked just right. I always enjoyed that first one most, while it was so hot that it burned the roof of my mouth.

Cakes were a more frequent dessert than pies. They came in a greater variety of flavors and shapes. They were round, square, oblong, layered. Some were plain, most were iced, a few had fillings. Without exception, they were delicious, in the mouth-watering way that only a mother's homemade cakes can be. Yet, my brothers and I were unanimous in our choice of the outstanding favorite – chocolate cake with chocolate frosting.

Mom learned, to her perpetual frustration, that it was useless to take a poll when she was contemplating what type of cake to offer her brood. The answer was always the same: "Chocolate! With chocolate icing!"

Speaking of chocolate, at our house, homemade fudge didn't qualify as a dessert, so mom made it only occasionally. (She probably figured that our teeth were rotting fast enough already from all the penny candy we consumed.) Since she liked fudge a lot herself, I suspect Mom sometimes whipped up a batch because she felt that *she* had earned a treat.

Helpers sometimes got to stir the mix in the bowl while Mom went about other kitchen chores. Achieving the proper smooth, thin texture could tire young arms, so Mom usually finished up. A batch would fill an eight-inch square pan. The slices were an inch square and almost as thick. They were super rich and would melt on your tongue like butter.

Mom and Dad liked nuts on their fudge. Alan, Dickie and I (the "finicky eaters," as Grandma Farr dubbed us) preferred it plain. Mom usually compromised by scattering some chopped nuts in one corner.

Another byproduct of Mom's baking was the bowl that would need cleaning afterward. Whoever was fortunate enough to come in for a drink of water and find Mom mixing fudge or cake frosting would ask excitedly, "Can I lick the bowl?"

Cleaning the bowl is an art for which kids have a natural instinct. First you scrape up as much of the leftover substance as possible with Mom's wooden mixing spoon, As you warm to your task, Mom is likely to caution you: "Don't scrape a hole in my bowl."

Soon this method becomes ineffective as you retrieve only small dabs. Now you begin running your pointer around the rim and inside. Then you lick your finger with the satisfaction and concentration of an infant sucking its thumb.

One rather unusual treat at our house was Mom's version of fried potatoes. Mom had an early vintage deep fryer that she didn't use much. It was a mess to clean and it spattered a lot of grease around her stove. But if we were having pork chops or steak, she sometimes elected to serve fried potatoes.

Mom didn't use a slicer to produce the traditional long cubed stick of potato. Instead, she cut the peeled potato into coin-shaped slices. These came out of the fryer looking like American fries but tasting like French fries, only better because they tended to cook more evenly. We called them American French fries.

In the summertime, we enjoyed a number of especially delicious ice cream treats. Sometimes it was simply a safety cone scooped full of ice cream from a pre-packaged half gallon Dad bought on his way home from work. Late in the evening, we'd all sit on the front porch and watch dusk settle over our block as we contentedly licked the "flavor of the day."

Some nights we all walked ten blocks to Thomson's Grocery. Thomson's dairy section included a small soda fountain. In addition to the usual fountain treats, they sold their own house label brand of ice cream, hand-packed in pint containers. In those years before we all became calorie- and fat-conscious, there were many excellent brands of "natural" ice cream, but none were more flavorful than Thomson's.

Most times we bought two pints of vanilla and two half gallons of Dad's Old Fashioned Root Beer. We went just before dark and returned home at a faster pace so the ice cream wouldn't melt in the summer heat. When we got home, it would be just soft enough to mix into *Black Cows* that were definite contenders for World's Greatest.

Mom produced her tallest tumblers and stuffed them with the ice cream. Dad poured in the root beer, ever so sl-ow-ly, so the glass filled without foaming over. We drank without straws, spooning out bites of ice cream as we went. As the levels went down, Dad would add a little more root beer until the bottles were empty. (Once uncapped, the root beer would quickly go flat, even in the fridge.)

My technique was to save a little ice cream and let it soften at the bottom of the glass. Then I stirred until it was completely dissolved into the last inch or so of the root beer. The final couple of gulps of this mixture was just scrumptious.

When we had all drained our glasses, my brothers and I would point and laugh at each other's foam mustaches.

Sometimes Dad would vary this routine by purchasing cream soda (the clear type) and chocolate ice cream. It was an equally thirst quenching change of pace from our Black Cows. I took the same satisfaction in mixing up the last of the ice cream and soda.

I don't know if this was a McGuire family invention, but none of my friends ever mentioned enjoying similar concoctions. In years since, I've encountered a few folk who remember mixing vanilla ice cream in cream soda, but none who ever used chocolate. (Wonder if I could have marketed something in bottles and made my fortune. Hmmm.)

When my father felt ambitious, he prepared his own private recipe malted milk shakes. It required two more pints of vanilla ice cream and Mom's largest mixing bowl.

Dad started by beating two eggs into a cupful of milk. He added more milk and a few chunks of ice cream and began mixing with Mom's hand-cranked beater. As the ice cream dissolved, he added more. More milk, more beating and along the way the addition of some Hershey's chocolate syrup and Carnation malt powder.

The process continued until all the ice cream was used up and the bowl was about to overflow. The deliciously thick malted milk had to be scooped out with a measuring cup and poured into our glasses. Mom added a soda fountain touch[1] by serving them with Salerno butter cookies.

A few other memories of edible treats involve things not homemade but home grown. For instance, the crab apple tree in Shirley's yard across the alley from our back yard. We'd been told the apples could make us sick. Apparently no one told the apples. The kids on our block munched about a barrelful each summer. They were a bit tart, but on an afternoon when we'd been playing hard they provided a refreshing pick-me-up.

---

[1] There still are a few soda fountains in America where old fashioned mixers are used to produce "malts" as scrumptious and loaded with real ice cream as those we made in our kitchen. I know of one in Saugatuck, Michigan, and another in Minong, Wisconsin. I've not discovered any others recently, but I'm always on the lookout.

During the war years, Wayne's folks and mine had victory gardens side by side in a vacant lot. Wayne and I sometimes did our patriotic bit by pulling weeds until we got bored. Then, to reward ourselves, we yanked up a couple of carrots that were growing tall. To be sure they were sanitary, we gave them a few good wipes on our pant legs. We ate them walking home, our pleasure increased by the satisfying crunching sound of each bite. If it's true that we consume several bushels of dirt in an average lifetime, I don't know of a more congenial way to eat my quota than by chewing on a carrot plucked fresh from the good earth.

From Christmas cookies to raw carrots may seem like a real giant step. But a child's imagination wears seven-league boots when deciding what constitutes a treat to eat. Thus does the spirit of Christmas repast engulf me with diverse mouth-watering memories.

No doubt you could contribute a few favorites of your own. However, you must excuse me now. I detect the irresistible aroma of freshly baked brownies wafting in from my wife's kitchen. Perchance she may require the services of an experienced taste tester.

Editor's Note: Many readers who grew up in small towns or rural areas probably have eaten crab apples or carrots plucked raw from a garden. But some of Dan McGuire's boyhood pals remember him eating Oreo cookies *without separating the two halves and licking off the cream filling!*

Train Up Your Child

A white spear from atop Engine 498 stabbed a shaft of light into the blackness ahead as the 8-wheeler highballed through a starless night. The rhythmic rumbling of the big engine's wheels echoed across the sleeping countryside. Rounding a bend, the iron horse accelerated on the straight-away. Suddenly the black Cyclops' eye spotlighted an engineer's nightmare ahead. The switch track had been left open!

Braking was futile. Momentum propelled the engine forward at breakneck speed. Its wheels lost contact with their rails, sought them desperately at the end of the gap, missed by inches. Followed by its tender and the string of cars stretched out behind, the engine briefly took wing over the embankment, then succumbed to gravity and plunged downward.

The nighttime quiet was shattered by the bone-crunching, ear-splitting impact of metal upon metal. Vulgarly, it repeated itself from engine to caboose. Then stillness returned…and darkness enveloped the wreckage.

I flipped on the basement light and surveyed the carnage caused by my carelessness. "What a hellova mess!" I muttered – then gave a nervous glance toward the stairway, mindful that a passing parent might have overheard my outburst.

Moments later, with the offending switch reset, Ol' 498 proceeded on its way again. Part of the magic of electric train sets was that even the most disastrous derailment or collision was so easily set aright.

Ol' 498, a late 1940s vintage Lionel, was my last and favorite train set. Its cars boasted self-locking couplers, which also unhooked themselves when backed over a special section of "tripper" track. I had added extra tripper sections and four remote-controlled switching tracks. By maneuvering over twin sidings, I could add, drop off and reposition cars without ever touching the train.

My track was laid on a ping pong table that had been retired because of a crack in the middle. I had extended it to half again its original length by attaching a plywood board with makeshift 2x4 legs. Extra track, switches and cross tracks enabled 498 to change direction and travel a variety of routes. I gradually enhanced the layout with a

33

mini-town and station, tunnels, crossing gates and other accessories. A lot of paper route earnings went into improving 498's environment.

Some kids got their first electric train set at a very early age. This enabled Daddy to have it well broken in by the time they were able to set up and operate it themselves. (Photofest/ICON)

To the best of my recollection, all of my buddies possessed at least one electric train during those youthful years. Many of us started out with one of the wind-up models when our folks felt we were not yet ready to care for the more expensive electric version. Such fears were not unfounded. Some of us (those with more doting parents) went through several sets before we learned to be less reckless – or more wreckless.

Sharp curves taken at high speed sent many a train crashing into a cabinet or table leg. (Thus did many a Marx leave its mark.) Placing coins on the track to short circuit the current was a favorite trick. (Good for laughs, but not so good for the transformer.) And, oh, how we loved to string Christmas tree tinsel across the track to see it sparkle as it disintegrated.

Several of my pals visited our basement frequently to take a turn at Ol' 498's controls. They all had trains of their own, but no permanent set-up. That meant operating on a living room or bedroom floor and having to pack everything away when mothers needed to vacuum or just grew tired of having to step over the tracks.

Among my friends' sets, streamliners seemed to predominate. Modeled on the forerunners of modern diesels, they had a sleek, shiny attractiveness. Jimmy's set even featured miniatures of real extended-length Pullman cars. Still, I preferred the old coal-eating black workhorse locomotives.

If there was any junior engineer I envied, it would have to be Peter, whose 12-wheeler American Flyer traveled on realistic 2-rail track. Pellets dropped into the engine made it puff smoke like a real steam locomotive. American Flyer always ballyhooed this realism in its advertisements; but it was expensive, and they were the first of the big three manufacturers to go out of business.

Bobby's oversize train set (whose maker I can not recall) was a memorable oddity. The engine weighed a ton, and it ran on track at least twice the width of the major brands. Bob claimed that his dog, Ranger, had once dozed with a paw next to the track and the passing train clipped all its nails.

At the peak of my model train enthusiasm, I subscribed to *Model Railroader* magazine. I marveled at the photographs of incredibly realistic layouts and an amazing variety of engines and cars, all perfectly scaled and flawlessly detailed. These were the work of true model train hobbyists. Nothing came readymade from a box. Everything was patiently hand-crafted by the model railroaders themselves.

These dream outfits were done in HO scale – one-half the size of the factory-produced O gauge sets. Today, most commercially made sets are HO, but they are heavily plasticized. They pale by comparison to the sturdy metal sets like Ol' 498.

Because he knows no better, my son was thrilled with his plastic made-in Taiwan set (with its delicate track that was forever coming apart). Like a first kiss, your first electric train set is an indelible memory.

The great tycoon Samuel Insull said it about a century ago: "Every boy should own at least one electric train." That was the year that he gave his son the South Shore Line.

The steam locomotive engine on this 1940s Lionel catalog cover is similar to the black beauty that headed up the author's last and favorite electric train set. The manufacturer celebrated its 100th year in 2000 and highballed into the new century still producing what many consider to be the Cadillac of electric trains. (Lionel, L.L.C.)

My Stars! How They Shined!

How often at night, when the heavens are bright
With the light from the glittering stars,
Have I stood there amazed, and asked as I gazed
If their glory exceeds that of ours.
—verse from *Home On The Range*

This reverie was inspired by a shooting star.

Late on a fall evening, the moon was a mere sliver of white in a cloudless sky. I stood admiring an unusually plentiful array of stars.

The shooting star burst into view near the Big Dipper's handle. It sped south over our back yard, its bright tail streaming far behind, and burned out high above the trees on the next block. A short trip from my perspective; but in reality probably a hundred miles or so – in about three or four seconds.

The other stars, momentarily dimmed by its brilliance, resumed winking at me. Their performance was a fact undeniably worthy of recognition. But now I was distracted, remembering a time when shooting stars were not so rare.

When I was a young tree climber in our almost rural suburb of Chicago, summer nights often provided a shower of stars. Year-round, the sky glittered with a multitude of stars that now are enjoyed only by our country cousins. On summer nights that were too hot for sleeping, my brothers and I were allowed to sit late on the front porch. Our parents would try to help us identify the various constellations.

I never really "saw" much more than the two dippers and the three stars which formed a belt for the mighty Orion (the Hunter). I could not make out hide nor hair of his dog, perhaps because I could not imagine anyone naming a pet Sirius. (Is he kidding?)

Meanwhile, though, I was on the lookout for shooting stars. On any night, there was a chance that one or two would flash across the sky. "Wow!" I'd cry to my family. "Did you see that?"

Usually these were random sightings, but from time to time there were nights when shooting stars would appear in clusters, minutes apart. One year, the newspapers forecast that an especially spectacular meteor shower would pass overhead for at least three nights. Wayne's family joined mine on the front lawn. We spread blankets on the grass and lay on our backs gazing skyward.

One of the neat things about watching meteor showers was that you did not need any special equipment. Telescopes or binoculars would only limit the amount of sky you could observe. Using the naked eye while flat on your back assured you the best seat in the house.

The heavenly fireworks streaked by faster than we could point a finger and exclaim: "There goes one!" Every few minutes a chorus of "Ooooh!" or "Aaaah!" gave approval to an especially bright streamer of light or one with an unusually long tail. Between nine people, we counted 169 before the two mothers made that non-negotiable declaration that "It's time these kids got to bed."

These stargazing evenings aroused my curiosity and enabled my parents to steer me to our newly acquired set of Encyclopedia Brittanica Junior. There I learned that what we call shooting (or falling) stars really aren't stars at all.

They begin as meteoroids, metallic masses ranging from pebble size to asteroids weighting tons. Unlike stars, which have stationary orbits, the meteoroids zoom wildly through space. When one chances to enter Earth's atmosphere, friction heats it white hot. The luminous streak we observe from below is called a meteor (from the Greek word *meteoron,* meaning "thing in the air"). Usually, they are burned to dust long before they can reach Earth. The rare chunks that survive and strike Earth are called meteorites.

That celestial show enjoyed by our little group on the front lawn was most likely the Perseid Meteor Shower, an annual display that lasts several days during the month of August. Named for the constellation Perseus, from which astronomers believe it originates, the shower was first reported by the Chinese in A.D. 36. It typically sends about 50 meteors an hour hurtling toward Earth at 35 miles per second. (Faster than a speeding bullet, I reckon.)

Last year, 157 astronomers joined in a worldwide observation to define the size and timing of the Perseid shower. They counted a total of 32,041 meteors.

I confess, dear reader, that sharing the foregoing educational data with you obliged me to revisit the encyclopedia. The trip actually was prompted by the current interest in Halley's Comet. This year (1986) that famed comet is making its first appearance to Earthlings since

1910. In some areas it has been visible to folks with strong eyes or telescopes since late November.

The comet is named in honor of astronomer Edmund Halley, who deduced that supposedly separate sightings in 1531, 1607 and 1682 actually were the same celestial body. He correctly predicted that it would return in 1758 on its elongated orbit around the sun.

Last summer, my father was keenly anticipating his second look at Halley's Comet. He was concerned by reports that it would be less brilliant because it won't come as close to Earth as it did in 1910. Knowing that he was only one year old at that time, I asked how he could have much recollection of the event.

"I'm like the auto maker whose entire production run turned out to be lemons," he explained. "I have total recall."[1]

Actually, his memory of the 1910 sighting probably was reinforced by many parental retellings. But he insists that he remembers his father holding him aloft on several evenings and saying, "Take a good look, sonny. You won't see this again until you're twice Papa's age."

In mid-February, after passing behind the sun, Halley's Comet will reappear. We will get our best view in March and April as it starts back into space and makes its closest approach to Earth (39 million miles!) on April 11. Then it will be a memory until 2062.

For city dwellers, the sighting of Halley's Comet is hampered by a modern problem: light pollution. Progress has enabled us to make our streets safer by keeping them well lighted at night. Regrettably, it also has made possible the proliferation of all sorts of commercial lighting.

As urban areas grow, skies nearby are filled with the overflow of light from shopping centers, all-night gas stations and convenience stores, lighted roadside advertising, etc. Observatories (including Palomar, with its 200-inch telescope) built in originally dark countrysides, are experiencing difficulty with background glow.

At a favorite North Woods getaway spot, I'm still able to marvel at the sight of a star-filled sky. At home, light pollution prevents me

---

[1] Look, my father said it. I'm just reporting it. So, please don't send me any poison pun letters.

from seeing any but the brightest stars (a mere handful, usually) – and I haven't seen a meteor shower in years.

Back on Ottawa Avenue in the old neighborhood, we did without the luxury of streetlights until my late teens. Even the main drag had only three per block. You would travel a long way to find an all-night business or a lighted billboard. Very little artificial light interfered with the observation of what folks take for granted deep in the heart of Texas.

Now when I observe the lonely Big Dipper, I empathize with a friend's nostalgia for the great radio programs that vanished when we became infatuated with television. My attention wandered for a few years, and when I looked again the view of our nighttime sky's glory was greatly diminished. On occasions when I'm able to stargaze from some remote lake or woodland, it's clear how much I'm missing.

My father retired to a small town down south, where his second look at Halley's Comet will be better than my first. I'm pleased for him, but I'd sure like to witness another of those nightlong gala shows put on by Mother Nature and her incredible shooting stars. Maybe the next time the Perseid Meteor Shower passes overhead we could get lucky and have a power outage that brings on one of those New York-style blackouts.

Front Porch Sitting: A Lost Art

In the carefree days of my boyhood, sitting on the front porch was a national pastime. Moms, pops and old folk relaxed there in the evening. Couples in love courted there, sometimes in the luxury of a 2- or 3-seater swing hung from the ceiling. Kids spent more time on porches than anyone else, simply because they had more time to idle away.

My Webster's dictionary describes *porch* as "a covered entrance to a house, usually projecting from the wall." That definition doesn't precisely jibe with the front porches I remember.

For one thing, it makes no mention of the porch being elevated. As I mentally stroll down my street in the old neighborhood, the front porch of every bungalow is at a level requiring five to seven stairs. A short patch of sidewalk leads directly to the stairs, a squarish front porch and the front door. A few homes have L-shaped porches.

Every house has a front entrance facing the street and some form of porch. Some frame houses have porches that project across the entire width of their front, completely covered by an extended roof. Most others have porches formed by a recess at one corner of the house, covered by an overhang of the second story flooring.

Whatever their construction, front porches collected kids singly and in "bunches" from early Spring until late Fall. Full width porches like Wayne's could—and often did—hold a dozen or more rowdy boys. (Wayne's mother seemed to have an infinite patience with all the stomping and hollering.)

On rainy days, boys and girls from the length of our block often congregated on Wayne's front porch. We formed groups and played card games, Monopoly, checkers, Chinese checkers, Sorry, etc. Porches were a great place to wait out thunder storms. You could watch the rain pour down, marvel at the crackling lightning bolts and wait to have your teeth rattled by the thunder clap that followed. All from the dry, comfortable safety of the porch.

The chest-high enclosures on porches were great for ducking behind. Many a shoot-out occurred there with injuns, "dirty rotten coppers," Nazis and cattle rustlers. Sometimes the porch was a jail cell when we were captured. Then we would wait until our guards were distracted, hang over the edge and drop to the ground to escape.

41

As we grew more daring, we sat on the edge, pushed ourselves off and were rewarded by a satisfying stinging sensation on the bottom of our feet as we hit the ground.

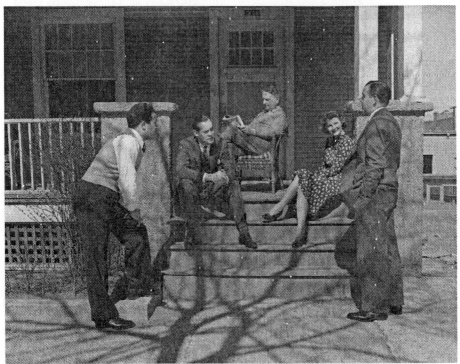

Folks gather on and around the front porch to chat and share neighborhood news. Their visit is no doubt more relaxed and enjoyable while the kids are off playing elsewhere. (Retrofile.com)

If there were no adults watching, we often stood up on or walked along the top "rail" of the porch enclosure. A rafter at roof level provided a hand-hold for the less sure-footed.

What we called the porch's railing, really wasn't— again according to Webster's. Rather than a series of posts with a sloped top rail, as on an inside staircase, there were three boxed panels, about ten inches wide, each with a flat section atop it. (Brick houses had brick sections topped with concrete slabs.) Positioned on either side, at heights just above the stairs, they were perfect for sitting on with your legs drawn up and your back propped against the next higher section or the post at the porch level.

On Sunday afternoons and warm-weather evenings, the front porch afforded an ideal gathering place for young, old and in-between. While the grown–ups relaxed and reviewed their days with each other, younger members were up, down and asking, "Wanna see me jump from *this* stair, Dad?" Sometimes the adults sat on chairs or the steps, affording their offspring access to the porch swing. Youthful exuberance often had to be restrained with a reminder that this was not a park swing and was meant for gentle rocking.

A radio placed at a nearby window might provide background music or the play-by-play of a baseball game. Neighbors passing by would exchange howdies or pause at the bottom of the steps for a few moments of joshing and sharing tidbits of neighborhood news.

Often two or more neighbor families would meet on one porch. Kids gravitated to the lawn for some acrobatics, to chase fireflies in the gathering dusk or to engage in subdued games that would not disturb the adults. Such meetings provided our parents with a social forum that differed from the man-talk and woman-talk which took place over back yard fences. In these brief times of respite from their homemaking and breadwinning efforts, the grown-ups learned what was going on in their neighbors' lives and the community at large.

These front porch visits also helped shape a wide-reaching neighborhood bond – the community spirit, if you will, that today is most often triggered only by some specific crisis. Because they knew their neighbors, folks were alert to strangers and crime was minimal. Misbehaving children would be scolded by someone from a nearby porch. Whether or not the offenders knew the adult, they paid heed.

These same mischievous youngsters, as they grew, would begin to take part in the front porch conversations. Thus did they begin to develop community ties, an enduring respect for tradition and a sense of personal involvement in the well-being of their neighborhood and their neighbors. When they became adults, their time spent on the front porch would help strengthen their patriotism and a commitment to their role as citizens of the larger community.

On our block, porch-sitting often included free musical entertainment. In the middle of the block, Mr. Trieb would practice at the only electric organ I had ever seen outside of a church or movie theatre. In those pre-noise pollution times, the mellifluous sound carried soothingly to both ends of the block.

Next to the corner, almost directly across from our house, the teen-aged Sell boy played drums and his older sister played the accordion. From up the street, Paul Schoenfeld, the fire chief's son, would join them on their wide front porch with his trombone. Several friends from farther away often came over to fill out the combo with trumpet, clarinet, sax and/or banjo.

For a pick-up group, the young musicians gave a passable performance. They ranged from straight pop tunes, old and new, to swing and Dixieland jazz. The neighborhood kids would congregate on the lawn and sidewalk in front of "Sell's Band Shell." With a readymade audience, my pal Chuck and I would launch into slapstick dance routines. These got laughs from our friends but caused our folks to roll their eyes in embarrassment on the porch across the street.

With the coming of winter, only kids spent time on the front porch, and that infrequently. Usually, it was too wet, cold or snow-covered for sitting. What sitting we did was more likely to occur when we slipped on the icy top step and bounced down to the sidewalk in our padded snowpants.

What's become of front porch sitting? In older (pronounced "low income") neighborhoods and rural communities, it's not entirely a lost art. Regrettably, though, the tensions of city life and our lifestyles in general have taken their toll.

In the 1950s, television began to replace radio as the dominant home entertainment medium. Besides requiring visual attention, early television sets did not lend themselves to being moved onto the front porch. Many folk resisted the lure of TV to a degree, but soon home air conditioning became more available and affordable. Even without TV, a cool living room became more inviting than sitting outside when no breeze offered relief from the heat and the mosquitoes were out in force.

Developers spotted the trend and quickly modified the styles of houses they were building. In the suburbs, many "front" doors face a side driveway. There simply are no porches. Back yard patios serve as more private substitutes. What some of my neighbors refer to as their porch is really a five-by-five concrete slab, with metal foot scrapers, outside the door.

Our house has a single step at the front entrance. Somehow, our children found it adequate for many hours of reading, coloring and sitting with friends, parents and grandparents. I can't tell you how many bottles of bubble-blowing liquid have been spilled there.

Obviously, that one stair does not offer the hiding, climbing and jumping opportunities of my old front porch. But given the imaginative free spirits of the young, perhaps it, too, will one day be remembered as a special place,

Meanwhile, urban dwellers are increasingly less likely to know who their neighbors are. The passing parade continues to pass by, fireflies set the evening aglow in front yards, bats swoop up bugs overhead and the stars twinkle competitively in the heavens. But, due to a shortage of front porch sitters, they mostly do so unseen and unappreciated.

A Tale Of Two Fathers

Each June we have an opportunity to honor the male parent whom we may have neglected or failed to appreciate most of the year. I shall gratefully pay tribute to my father, still healthy and independent at age 76. In this column, though, I would do homage to two other fathers, now gone, who were key figures in my "formative years."

Their names were Toby and Lafe. I knew that only from hearing their wives and other adults address them thus. To me they were Mr. Schaden and Mr. Cleghorn. All grown-ups were either Mr. or Mrs. to kids of that era.

Mr. Schaden was a banker (in Chicago's famed Wrigley Building, no less) and wore suits and ties. He and Mrs. Schaden attended the mysterious Catholic church. Mr. Cleghorn worked for the Glider Trailer Company, finishing the interior of house trailers (the kind that owners actually towed around behind their cars). He wore overalls on his job and, as often as not, around the house as well. He occasionally donned a suit and accompanied Mrs. Cleghorn to our Presbyterian church. At Christmas, as he passed along the line after service, Pastor Thurston would shake his hand enthusiastically, smile and say, "Happy holidays, Lafe. I'll look forward to seeing you again come Easter."

From my youthful perspective, these two gentlemen appeared as different as Mutt and Jeff.[1] Yet they shared one important trait. They were the fathers of my two best friends.

We all lived on the same block of Ottawa Avenue. (Our favorite bus driver, calling out street names as we approached, would announce it as: "Otto-wawa, best street in town!" We always assumed that his home must be somewhere on Ottawa, but perhaps he just liked the sound of it.) I spent almost as much time in Wayne's and Chuck's homes as in my own, and was looked on, I suspect, as a sort of pseudo-stepson.

It was Mr. Cleghorn who introduced me to the noble pastime of fishing. One summer afternoon, he handed cane poles to Wayne and me and drove us to a nearby forest preserve area. Seated on the banks

---

[1] Readers born after 1950 may not know that Mutt and Jeff were popular comic strip characters. They were similar to such comic movie duos as Abbott and Costello, or Olson and Johnson, or... Oh, never mind.

of the Des Plaines River, we spent several hours pulling in bullhead catfish, which he freed from the hooks. As he tossed each one back into the murky water, he would observe, "Nice fish, but not a keeper." By day's end, two 8-year-olds were permanently hooked on fishing. It became a frequent summertime sport for Wayne and me when we were old enough to ride our bikes to the river.

When I was 12, I dipped into my savings for the neatest bicycle accessory ever – a speedometer. Made by Stewart Warner Corporation (once a giant manufacturing company in Chicago), the shiny circular speedometer was about five inches in diameter and clamped onto the center post of your handlebars. It had a red needle and a dial marked off with speeds up to 50 miles per hour. A cylinder and gear arrangement on the front wheel connected to a cable that ran up to the speedometer's internal works.

After amazing myself by actually getting this device installed on my bike without help, I took it out for a test run. Barreling down one of our usually deserted back roads, I was approached by Mr. Cleghorn in his black Ford sedan. He flagged me down and, in a man-to-man fashion typical of his Kentucky upbringing, he asked, "Where y'all headed so hell bent fer leather?"

I proudly pointed out the new prized possession centered on my handlebars. He grinned and said, "Wanta check 'er out for accuracy? Grab ahold of the door handle and hang on tight."

Without hesitation, I took hold of the door handle with my right hand and firmly gripped the handlebar with my left.

Mr. Cleghorn put the car in gear, started up and eased us forward slowly. As he accelerated, I called out our speed at 10, 20, 30 and 40 miles per hour. When I shouted that we had hit the top speed of 50, he slowed to a halt and informed me that the Ford speedometer had registered about 42 m.p.h. at that point. But it was still pretty close, he said, when I called out 40.

That was a bit disillusioning, but still okay with me. The speedometer had proved to be fairly accurate until we got up over 30 m.p.h. Under my own power, I would seldom exceed 30 m.p.h. anyway, except maybe heading down a long, steep hill.

Without being told, I sensed that this test run was something not to be widely discussed. Had my mother or Mrs. Cleghorn heard about it, Mr. Cleghorn undoubtedly would have caught an earful.

Wayne's house had a front porch that was seven or eight steps high and extended the width of the house. It was completely closed in below, but Chuck and I had discovered a loose board on the side away from the steps. This enabled us to squeeze into the area beneath the porch. It was almost high enough for us to stand upright, and it made for a really neat "hideout."

The dank, gloomy space there was littered with rusty nails, broken glass and other debris left by the builders. We sneaked in only when we thought no one was watching, because we knew we really shouldn't be there. Mrs. Cleghorn had spotted us crawling in on a couple of occasions and shooed us out. She undoubtedly worried that we'd get hurt, but the spot was so inviting that her scoldings deterred us only for short periods.

One day, Mr. Cleghorn (who'd probably been informed of our trespassing) must have seen us crawling in again. Feigning ignorance, he came and wiggled the loose board. In a stage shout, he called to his wife: "Melville, honey, bring me my hammer and some nails, wouldja? I'm gonna fix this here dang loose slat."

Chuck and I stood trapped and trembling as he paced slowly outside until Mrs. Cleghorn dutifully arrived with a metal toolbox. There followed a terrible pounding that made me think of a wooden casket being sealed. Chuck and I huddled in frozen silence. To reveal our presence was to invite the wrath of two sets of parents. For the moment, entombment seemed the lesser evil.

We waited several anxious minutes to be sure the coast was clear after Mr. Cleghorn finished his "repair." Surprisingly, for a professional carpenter, he had not succeeded in making a very permanent fix. A few kicks from the inside loosened the board again. Like thieves in the night, we crept out. The next day, we began searching for a new hideout.

One of my earliest recollections of Chuck's father is from the World War II period when he and my father (both classified 4F) were volunteer air raid wardens. Slightly paunchy and wearing metal rimmed glasses, Mr. Schaden looked somewhat miscast in a tin pot helmet, lugging a large fire extinguisher to training sessions.

He was always a civic minded man. He served as water commissioner for several years and was active in promoting the growth and improvement of our then unincorporated little village.

Though more reserved than Mr. Cleghorn, he had a mischievous sense of humor.

Chuck was off playing elsewhere one day when I came calling, "Yo-oh, Chuck!" His father stood atop a ladder, painting the gutters of their house. With nothing much else to do, I lingered, watching and occasionally distracting him with questions. (No doubt he was also worried about dripping paint on this inquisitive young rubberneck.)

Pausing in his work, he looked down at me thoughtfully. "You know," he observed, "I could paint faster if I used both hands. Do you suppose your father might have a left handed brush that I could borrow?"

"I'll go see," I replied, and dashed home to inquire. My father raised his eyebrows and nodded thoughtfully when I presented him with Mr. Schaden's request. He took me down to the basement and rummaged around a bit in the paint cabinet, but finally concluded that he had worn out his only such tool.

Mr. Schaden didn't seem unduly disappointed when I informed him. After awhile, as I continued to gawk, he paused again and mused, "I'll bet this trim would look great with a two-tone paint job, like a barber pole. Think you dad has any striped paint?"

"I'll bet he does," I answered enthusiastically. Again I ran to check, but was obliged to report: "No striped paint, but he's got a can of black and white checkered paint you can have."

Mr. Schaden considered this possibility for a moment, then shook his head. "Nope. That probably wouldn't look good with this trim."

More painting. More gawking. Then: "Gee, this brush is going to need a steam cleaning when I get done. Do you s'pose your dad could lend me a bucket of steam?"

I ran home and back again, a little less swiftly this time. "Sorry," I reported. "My dad's bucket has a hole in it."

He nodded understandingly. After a bit more brushing, he appeared about to say something else when Chuck came running up the block and called, "C'mon, Danny. We're all going to the school yard for a game of peggie-move-up."

I fell into step with my buddy and waved goodbye to his father. Mr. Schaden sighed–probably regretful at losing his messenger–and waved his brush in reply. A giant glob of paint arced downward and splattered on the sidewalk. I'm not certain, but I thought I overheard an uncharacteristic expletive from atop the ladder.

One afternoon my mother sent me on an errand to Elmer's Grocery. Walking home with my bagful of groceries, I spotted Mr. Schaden's car at the curb, slightly tilted. He was just getting out to check the problem. I stopped to help him gaze at a completely deflated rear tire.

"Pretty flat, isn't it?" he asked me.

I nodded my agreement. "Want me to help you change it?"

He did a swell Groucho Marx imitation with his eyebrows. But as he tossed his suit coat and tie onto the back seat, he smiled and said, "Sure. Stick around. I may need some help."

I stood just out of the way and watched admiringly as he jacked up the car's rear and removed the hub cap. Our streets were unpaved then, just dirt and gravel. When he had the first lug nut off, Mr. Schaden stopped and held it in his hand thoughtfully.

"Uh oh," he said, turning to me with a concerned expression. "Now we have a problem. If I take off these nuts and put them all down in the stones, we'll likely lose half of them."

I was about to offer to hold them when I noticed the dish-shaped hub cap lying between us. "How about puttin' 'em in there?" I suggested.

His expression brightened. "Good idea," he agreed. "By golly, I'm glad you hung around!"

When the spare tire was in place, he rewarded me with a ride the remaining three blocks to home. He even tuned the car radio to one of my favorite adventure series. That night, at supper, I was able to impress my family with the story of Mr. Schaden's flat tire and how I saved the day for him.

Years from now, will any of my son's pals remember me as fondly as I recall Mr. Cleghorn and Mr. Schaden? I hope so. On Father's Day this year, let's remember all the fathers, our own and others people's, who influenced and enriched those glorious years of our childhood.

Special Delivery Memories

"Leen-Co!"

The hearty voice in our gangway announced another weekly visit of our Linco Bleach delivery man. His two-syllable cry, half shout and half sing-song, posed the unspoken question to housewives: "How's your bleach supply today?"

Linco Bleach came in an opaque blue glass gallon jug with the company's name and some product information embossed on the side. A ring handle on the jug's neck made for easy carrying and pouring.

The Linco man usually arrived with one jug hanging from each of his crooked index fingers. My mother bought only one gallon at a time. But if he happened to catch our neighbor in her back yard and sold her a gallon over the fence, he would save himself some walking.

At the stairwell to our basement, he paused. If my mother did not respond momentarily, he would repeat his cry. Or, if he spotted me playing in the yard, he would enlist me as a messenger to locate her.

Mom usually anticipated his visits and would appear shortly at the basement door. They would exchange a few pleasantries along with a gallon of bleach and some coins. Sometimes Mom turned over an empty jug. Like almost all bottles in that era, Linco jugs were returnable.

With a polite "Thank you, ma'am," the Linco man would be on about his business. His vocal identification could be heard five or six times more as he progressed up our block.

Linco's cheery representative was one of a small parade of delivery people who plied their trades in our neighborhood. In my pre-teen years, their regular arrivals were among those things that could be counted upon like the changing seasons.

The milkman's visits were daily except Sunday. He'd been making these rounds, we knew, at least since the days when our parents were children. In nostalgic recollections, adults sometimes described milkmen making deliveries from a horse-drawn wagon. They often would be awakened early in the morning, alerted to the approach of the wagon by the slow "clop, clop, clop" of the horse's hoofs on a cobblestone or red brick street.

In the neighborhood of my youth, the milkman had progressed to driving a square-shaped utilitarian truck about the size of today's recreational vans. But its cargo section was insulated and tall enough for him to stand erect inside. Like its horse-drawn predecessor, it was painted an appropriate milky white with the dairy's name emblazoned on each side.

The milkman was out doing his job while many people were still abed. The rattle of bottles in his metal carrying tray inspired the WWII hit song "Milkman, Keep Those Bottles Quiet." (photo courtesy of Elmhurst Historical Museum, Elmhurst, IL)

Milk was available in quart and half-gallon bottles or in one-gallon jugs with a metal carrying handle secured around the large neck (all returnable). The milkman also sold butter, eggs and real cream in pint and quart bottles.

For regular customers, the dairy provided an insulated metal box with a hinged lid. Large enough to store a gallon of milk and some smaller items, the box would be set in a shaded corner on the front porch. Many folk weren't awake yet when the milkman arrived. The box was a convenient and safe place for him to leave your merchandise. It held in some of the products' chill on summer mornings and hid them from prowling animals.

Gallon jugs were stacked four apiece for transportation in square metal mesh racks. (These are now considered treasures by collectors.) Between curbside and porches, the milkman carried up to eight quart bottles in a rectangular metal mesh basket. This often produced a clanking, clanging noise which was the inspiration for a World War II hit song. Popularized by the Andrew Sisters and others, and supposedly being sung by Rosie the Riveter, who had worked all night on a swing shift, it was called "Milkman, Keep Those Bottles Quiet!"

Regular customers usually had a standing order with the milkman. They could vary it by leaving a note in the milk box. This also was a perfect place for the milkman's weekly bill and the customer's payment.

We bought most of our dairy goods at Elmer's Grocery. But once or twice a week, to tide us over some shortage, Mom would order from the milkman. To signify our needs, she would leave a note tucked into the neck of an empty quart bottle on the porch. The milkman was alert to such notes from a lot of non-regular customers. In my memory, he never missed one of ours.

The unhomogenized milk we enjoyed then had a little extra bonus. All the cream rose to the top. By pouring carefully from a gallon jug, you could capture about half a cupful.

Oh, and every child of the 1940s and before remembers the phenomenon of milk left on the front porch too long in winter. The paper cap and the wrap-around foil seal would be popped off and ride up on a column of cream about two inches high – one of Mother Nature's mischievous magic tricks. When this happened, the milkman said the bottle had tipped its hat.

Another delivery person, somewhat akin to the milkman, was the Home Juice man. He offered a variety of bottled juices that included orange, apple, grapefruit, pineapple, grape and others, as well as non-alcoholic apple cider. No doubt the orange was his best seller. In the days before frozen concentrates, it was a welcome alternative to the laborious process of squeezing several oranges by hand on that little glass "juicer" to produce one small glass of orange juice. (Truth to tell, though, even the best concentrates and bottled products still take second place to that freshly hand-pressed orange juice, complete with pulp and seeds.)

The Home Juice man drove a more conventional panel truck than the milkman and came later in the day. His product did not need to be kept chilled, and he had fewer regular customers with standing orders. He would cruise slowly down the street on an appointed weekday, making his regular deliveries. Most housewives met him at the curb and made selections based upon impulse or the urging of a youngster tugging at their dress.

The juices came in brick-shaped half-gallon bottles with wide mouths centered at the top. A metal cap with a rubber insulator sealed in the fresh natural tastes. It screwed on and off with about a half twist. Empty bottles were perfect for keeping tap water chilled in the "fridge" during summer.

Dry cleaners often had delivery men who came in small trucks about the size of today's minivans. Suits, coats and dresses were hung from rods installed along the ceiling so that they wouldn't be rumpled en route.

Our family seldom utilized this service. My father's factory job did not require him to wear a suit. Except for a few Sunday-go-to-meeting items, most of our clothes were machine washable. When Mom needed anything dry cleaned, she usually dropped it off herself or sent me on my bicycle.

Among my playmates, though, there were fathers who were salesmen, bankers, policemen, firemen, etc. They had items dry cleaned on a regular basis. As one suit or uniform was delivered in its fresh white paper wrapper, another often was handed over for cleaning.

Often dress shirts were included. Most dry cleaners also were launderers. They would return shirts sparkling clean, starched to order and neatly folded into cardboard boxes.

Although the delivery man sometimes received a tip, there was no charge for home delivery. It was provided to incur customer loyalty and encourage more frequent patronage of the cleaner's services.

One of my favorite delivery people usually made just one appearance a year: the coalman. Most families in our neighborhood heated their homes with coal furnaces. In September or October, they would lay in a ton of coal for the cold season. An unusually long or cold winter might necessitate a second load or half-load along about March.

Coal was delivered by truck and stored in a partitioned corner of the basement referred to as the coal bin. Located near the furnace, the bin kept coal from scattering all over and minimized the spread of coal dust.[1]

In the city, most apartment buildings and some well-to-do private homes had covered chutes that came out to the front sidewalk. These made delivery fairly simple. The coal arrived in a dump truck with a trap door centered in its rear gate. The driver and his helper attached a metal slide between the trap door and the open chute. Then the driver tilted the back of the truck, opened the trap door and let gravity do its job. The helper got the unenviable job of climbing into the truck bed and shoveling reluctant piles of coal out of the corners and through the trap door. He also shoveled up stray lumps that bounced off the chute.

Like most of its counterparts, our home had the coal bin located under a window at the side of the house. Our coal had to be hauled manually from the street and dumped through the window.

To accomplish this, the coalman sometimes arrived in a flat-bed truck loaded with sacks of coal. The sacks were of heavy cloth, about the size of a shopping bag, except shorter and fatter. They had double-thick cloth straps which the coalman grasped as he pulled the sack off the truck and hoisted it onto his shoulder. Then he carried it through our gangway and effortlessly tossed it contents through the window. When he dumped the last sackful, he would be as dirty as the coal miners we sometimes saw in movie newsreels.

Another method of delivery was to dump the coal in a pile in the street, or on the parkway if the truck could get close enough. Then it had to be shoveled into a wheelbarrow and poured through the window.

---

[1] Coal dust was the bane of every homemaker. Younger readers who grew up in homes heated with oil or gas can not imagine how pervasively it managed to be tracked or just drift into every room of the house. And burning coal ate up oxygen, which caused everyone's mouth and nose to dry out. Then there were the ashes that fell through the grate as the coal burned. These had to be scooped from the bottom of the furnace (using the same shovel with which you tossed in the coal). Then they were hauled in buckets out to the alley and dumped into the heavy trash cans to be picked up by the garbage man. Among the many chores often assigned to young males, this surely ranked as one of the least favorites.

You could do this yourself or pay a little extra to have it done. If you chose the latter course, the coal usually was dumped by a white driver, who then left. A Negro helper stayed behind to do the heavy work.

In the 1940s, the majority of homes were heated with a coal-burning furnace. The coalman may well have been the origin of the expression: "It's a dirty job, but somebody's gotta do it." (Library of Congress photo)

The black man who did this for us several years running was a source of awe to me. He was a mountainous fellow with muscles like a circus strongman. Sweat poured off him as he worked, but he never seemed to slow down. He seldom spoke, except perhaps to request a drink of water. When finished, he simply laid his shovel in the wheelbarrow and walked away (to another job or back to the coal yard, I supposed), pulling the wheelbarrow behind him.

The man of the house might be ready to leave for the office, but keeping the furnace stoked with coal was a priority during 1940s winters. (Retrofile.com)

The coalman's alter ego, of course, was the iceman. He was already melting into history[2] when I was a boy. Homes in our area all were proudly equipped with those new fangled "electric ice boxes." My grandmother, like many of her neighbors, had a shiny new refrigerator, but kept the old ice box for less frequently needed items (i.e., fewer door openings). Thus, she continued to utilize the iceman's services for several years longer.

The ice company provided a large square card with the numbers 25, 50, 75 and 100 boldly printed on its four borders. When Grandma placed the sign in her window with the appropriate number upright, the iceman delivered a block of ice in the requested size. His supply began the trip in 100-pound blocks, but he was expert at chopping blocks down to the required size.

He carried each block—even the 100-pounders—into your house on his shoulder, holding it in the tight grip of a giant set of tongs. A burlap pad helped protect his shoulder from being permanently frozen. Some dripping inevitably followed in his wake, and housewives were resigned to wiping up after his delivery.

On hot summer days, while the iceman made his delivery, kids would reach across the tailgate and scoop up loose chunks of ice to suck on. The iceman generally tolerated this as long as we didn't actually climb onto the truck. Probably because he didn't want anyone falling off and getting hurt, he drew the line there. When he spotted someone breaking this unspoken rule, we would hear him yell with stern authority: "Get offa there!"

Even before the advent of refrigerators, the iceman had to find other work during the winter. Housewives simply stored items in unheated pantries. Many companies sold both ice and coal, so the iceman often switched hats in the fall and became a coalman.

---

[2] The first gleaming white refrigerators suitable for home use became available in the late 1920s. As mass production increased, they became affordable even for families of modest income. By 1933, in spite of the Great Depression, total sales exceeded a million units. One company dubbed its brand "Frigidaire," and the name became as interchangeable with refrigerator as did Coke and Kleenex with soft drinks and facial tissue.

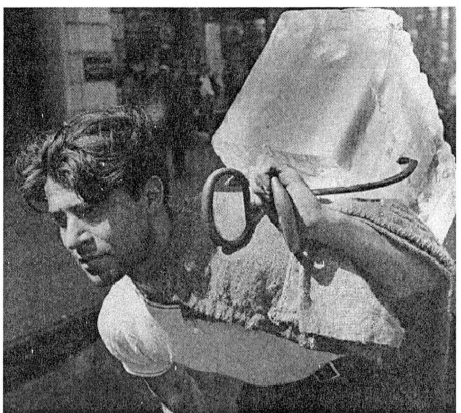

The iceman cometh. If the term had been current in the 1940s, it might have been said of this fellow that he had a cool job. (Photofest/ICON)

Some of the fellows that my cohorts and I watched for were not, strictly speaking, delivery men. There was the scissors grinder who walked up the street pushing (or pulling) his cart with its large iron wheels. When it was in motion, the cart announced his approach by ringing a set of iron bells with a clear, distinctive melody: "Ding, dong, ding. (Pause.) Ding, dong, ding."

Mothers brought him scissors and any kitchen cutlery in need of sharpening. A little wooden seat on the cart positioned him in front of a middle wheel that was actually a large whetstone. Pumping a foot pedal to turn the grindstone, he pressed the scissor or knife blade against it and sent sparks flying left and right.

A traveling scissors grinder, perhaps one of the last, plys his trade in Northfield, Illinois, in the late 1990s. Demonstrating the skill of a true craftsman, he keeps his eye on his work and the blade to the grindstone while his customers clown for the camera. (photo courtesy Mary Fran Purse)

He would pause periodically to test the sharpened edge on his thumbnail. When satisfied, he handed the utensil back to its owner and told her how much she owed him. He had no advertised rates, but housewives always seemed to find his price fair.

The "rags-o-lion" man was different in that he came through the alley and was buying rather than selling. He also was the last mobile merchant in my neighborhood to use a horse-drawn wagon. As this colorful twosome approached, he sang out loudly, "Any rags, old iron?" My pals and I could never distinguish the words from his run-together heavily accented shout. Although we came to know what he was seeking, we still referred to him as "the rags-o-lion man."

He would, indeed, purchase almost any form of scrap iron, tattered clothing, bedding or draperies, even newspapers. Evidently, some things were recycled even in those long-ago days. When someone stepped into the alley with an armload of items, he would check them carefully and, without any negotiation, count out some coins

The Good Humor Man was on break (or perhaps holding the camera) when this photo was taken. On such a vehicle he rode through the author's neighborhood almost every summer day. (Good Humor-Breyers Ice Cream file photo)

for whatever he accepted, usually all or most of it. (As with the scissors grinder, I never saw any housewives—or husbands—dicker with him.) Then he tossed the goods into the wagon, climbed back up and clicked to the horse to move on.

One fellow I never quite fathomed was our ever-smiling Prudential man. He wasn't so much a delivery man as a collector. Once a month my mother paid him a dollar and some change. In return, she received a slip of paper he referred to as "your receipt." It was good for some mysterious product called "insurance."

Doctors routinely made house calls in those days, on an as-needed basis, of course. The paper boy (his more dignified title was news carrier) was the only delivery person we saw seven days a week. But the mailman walked his route twice on weekdays and once again on Saturday. The mailman (or, as some folks called him, the postman), dedicated emissary of the U.S. Post Office, with his sharp uniform and ever-present satchel draped over his shoulder; he delivered birthday and Christmas presents from distant relatives, kids' magazines and

Whether he arrived on a cycle or driving a truck, the Good Humor Man was a summertime hero to kids in the 1940s. But, oh, the agonizing decisions required each time you stood in line to make your selection. (Retrofile.com)

those anxiously awaited radio premiums purchased for ten cents and a sponsor's boxtop.

And then there was the Good Humor man. Bells on his handlebars jingled as he rode his 3-wheeled cycle up the street. A white cooler was mounted on a reinforced axle between the two front wheels. When the Good Humor Man flipped the lid open, a thick vapor escaped from the dry ice inside. With a dime clutched in a grubby paw, each young customer had to make an agonizing choice from the many frozen treats: ice cream bars, fudge bars, popsicles, dreamsicles, fudgesicles, frozen cones, ice cream sandwiches, Dixie cup sundaes, push-ups.

The Good Humor Man was every kid's summertime hero. He deserves a column of his own.

Tune in again next time….

The Neighborhood

How Green Were Our Grocers

The coupon section of Sunday's newspaper contained an offer for an amazing "new" tool. It was a long wooden pole with jawlike metal clamps at one end, controlled by a trigger mechanism at the handle end. The device was described as a "homemaker's *must*" for reaching items on those top kitchen cabinet shelves. Why didn't someone think of this years ago?

Someone did, actually; but not as a boon to housewives. At least as early as the 1940s, a longer, sturdier version of this mechanical arm was in use at Elmer's Grocery Store in my old neighborhood. Elmer used it to retrieve items from high shelves for his customers.

"A box of American Family Flakes," Mrs. Shopper would read off, scanning her handwritten checklist as her finger moved slowly downward. "And a box of Quaker Puffed Wheat..." Elmer shot the arm extender upward and expertly grasped each purchase as it was requested. About halfway down, he released the jaws and let the box plummet downward, catching it in his free hand like Joe DiMaggio snagging a long flyball.

Sometimes, with less clumsy items, such as a can of corn or peas, Elmer would show off a little. Instead of clamping the can, he would gently nudge it off the shelf and let if fall into his large waiting paw. As he plunked it down upon the counter, he raised an inquiring eyebrow to his customer and murmured, "And...?"

Like most of its mom and pop contemporaries, Elmer's store was designed to make maximum use of minimal space. Thus the 12-foot-high shelves. The concepts of stocking selected merchandise at eye level, packaging in subconscious-grabbing color designs and strategically displaying items to promote impulse buying had not yet come into use as psychological marketing tools. These came later, with the advent of so-called supermarkets.

Grocery shopping was a leisurely, almost relaxing activity. Housewives did about 90 percent of it, scarcely any of them being employed outside the home. The grocery store was a place to meet and exchange news and chitchat with neighbors, and with Elmer and his family, all of whom helped in the store.

There were no shopping carts or check-out lines. Shoppers ambled through short aisles of bins and low-level shelves. They selected a few items at a time and accumulated them on the long counter behind which Elmer officiated. In back of him was the glass-doored cooler from which he dispensed dairy items. To his left was a display cooler for lunch meat, sausages and salads. (Unlike some grocers, Elmer did not employ a butcher to sell a full line of meats.)

To Elmer's right, around a corner toward the storage and employees' area, was a freezer chest. Here were kept pint-size "bricks" of branded ice creams, an assortment of popsicles, ice cream bars and the ever-popular push-ups. Those who preferred could have pints of ice cream hand packed from large bulk containers. Kids who were familiar to Elmer's family were allowed to prepare cones for themselves if they didn't get greedy or messy.

Louise Aadland visits with a customer at Lou's Grocery Store. One of many mom and pop establishments in the old neighborhood, it was very similar to Elmer's Grocery, where the author's mother did much of her shopping. Note the high shelves and the Coca Cola poster above doorway. (Aadland family collection)

Next to the freezer was an oblong cooler filled with ice and bottles of various sodas. Besides the familiar big name products, there were root beer, ginger ale, cream soda, Orange Crush and Kayo. (The syrupy sweet chocolate Kayo was a perennial kids' favorite.) Also, you could choose from an assortment of those squat-shaped, wide-mouthed bottles of non-carbonated drinks (Bierley's, I think, was the name brand) ranging from orange to grape to (yuk!) raspberry.

When we kids paid for our sodas, Elmer would ask, "You gonna drink it here?" If we said yes, he would not charge us the customary deposit, trusting us to return the bottles, even though we went and sat outside or perhaps roamed up the block a ways.

There was also a penny candy display case, of course, a staple of most family-run grocery stores. But I need another article to discuss that kids' paradise.

Meanwhile, the lady shoppers gathered their selected items on the counter. Elmer's ornate mechanical cash register had no tape print-out. It simply held cash and registered the total amount of each sale with numbers on little metal flags that popped up when Elmer pressed the typewriter style keys. To tally your purchases, what he did was remove a pencil from behind his ear, lick the point and begin jotting numbers on a brown paper sack. His left hand moved each item slightly to the side as his right hand noted the price. When all the items were regrouped to his left, he took a total. Your groceries went into the sack, which also became your receipt.

I recall once being sent by my mother on an eight-block round trip to confront Elmer with the empty sack because he had made a two-cent error. The rarity of this mistake was evident from Elmer's great embarrassment as he acknowledged it to the young messenger.

Transporting groceries home presented a challenge. There were no two-car families, so Mom was usually afoot. Some moms used shopping bags or those two-wheeled basket carts. Others had it delivered (most stock boys doubled as delivery boys). Moms with infants could stuff several bags next to Junior in the baby buggy.

Since many just hefted the bag in their arms for the walk home, moms often made several trips to the grocer each week and bought just enough to fill one bag. The lucky ones, those with male offspring of the right age, brought them along. Or, worse yet, sent them to Elmer's alone with a shopping list and money wrapped in a handkerchief.

As for those mechanical arm extenders, Mom never needed one in those days. Her groceries were all conveniently stored on easy-to-reach shelves in a little room just off the kitchen – something called a pantry.

A Nickle's Worth Of Memories

In a previous ramble through the past, I reminisced about a local store known as Elmer's Grocery. That discourse undoubtedly prompted a subsequent sentimental journey.

I was relaxing after mowing the lawn at our current abode. The sun was unmercifully hot, but my lemonade was ice cold and refreshing. Under the shade of a tree, I leaned back in a lounge chair and closed my eyes for a moment.

The years fell away. I found myself wearing short pants again, playing junkman in the alley. My mongrel dog, Dinah, accompanied me, sniffing the trash cans as I rummaged through neighbors' uncollected debris.

A broken water faucet made a nifty Buck Rogers ray gun if you gripped it a certain way, but it wouldn't fit into my pocket or set comfortably when I tried to hang it from my belt. I donated it to another barrel farther down the alley.

This one contained a half-full jar of mayonnaise. "Lookit this, Dinah. All those little kids starving over in Europe," I began, echoing suppertime orations of my parents, "and somebody goes and throws away——"

As I gingerly removed the lid, a putrid odor raced up to attack my nostrils. "Eyuck! It's spoiled." I extended the jar toward Dinah's nose for her confirmation, but she declined the offer and scampered away to sniff a suspicious area by someone's alley gate. "Well, I guess even starving kids wouldn't want this," I conceded, dumping it into the next trash can we passed.

Further along someone was disposing of about two dozen 78-rpm phonograph records that had cracks or chipped edges. These would make terrific "sailers" sometime when I was out playing in a wide prairie with Wayne or Bobby. But I'd have to curtail my scavenging to take them home and store them, so I reluctantly left them where they were.

We progressed a couple of blocks down the alley in this fashion before the sun glinted off something on the ground that looked like a bottle cap. I picked it up, rubbed the dirt off on my pants, checked both sides twice to convince myself that it was real. Then I cried out with elation, "Hey, Dinah, guess what. We found us a nickel!"

Dinah's jubilant bark in response to this announcement indicated that she shared my excitement. "C'mon, girl," I said. "We're going to Elmer's!"

In all the years that my family resided in what I now think of as "the old neighborhood," I never really knew if Elmer had a last name. A sign atop the little mom and pop store identified it as "Elmer's Grocery Store." Young and old alike referred to it simply as "Elmer's"

Although it was primarily a grocery store, Elmer's did have several things which appealed to those of us who were not interested in food per se. The pop cooler and ice cream freezer were popular features that I've mentioned previously. By far the most favorite attraction for smallfry, though, was *the candy counter*.

In reality, it was more of a glassed display case, with several shelves accessible only from the storekeeper's side. Each shelf was crowded with trays and open boxes of candies. Except for a few five-cent bars, everything on display was available for just a penny – *one cent*.

In those years just after V-J Day, prosperity was returning. While shopping with their mother, kids usually could beg a penny from her change and purchase something from the candy counter. My playmates and I often had a penny or two to squander. If we had only one penny between two of us, there were plenty of two-for-a-penny items for sharing.

A penny or two at that kids' paradise was a treat. But to be in possession of a whole nickel—a genuine United States Mint five-cent coin of the realm—that was a fantasy seldom realized by anyone not yet in fifth grade.

Finding himself so richly blessed, a boy was apt to be all but overwhelmed at his abundant good fortune. So great would be his elation that, for a moment, he could do little more than press his nose against the display case glass and wave the coin overhead (in a tight, thumb-and-forefinger grip) for Elmer's inspection. Then, lest there be any doubt, he would announce, "I want five cents worth," and begin to point with his free hand.

"Let me have two of those jawbreakers. They're two for a penny, right? Okay, two of them, 'n' a strip of the buttons on the paper. Ummm. Ehh, one whip. No, not licorice; the cherry flavor. Are

Mary Janes a penny apiece? Oh, two for a penny. Good. Gimme two Mary Janes. That's three cents, right? Oh, four cents? Oh, yeah. Well, I changed my mind about the buttons. Put those back and let me have one of those licorice pipes. And one more thing, right? Well, let's see. Ummm. Lemon drops? No. Ummm. Candy hats? No. Ummm. Oh, I got it! A couple of the malted milk balls. And that's five cents, right?"

Elmer would nod his confirmation of the tally as he accepted the proffered coin and dropped the last selection into a tiny paper bag. All of this foot-shifting indecision was endured with long-suffering patience. Occasionally, Elmer might offer a little gentle encouragement. "C'mon, son. I've got other customers waiting, y'know." But the word "other" tempered his prodding, because it indicated that, even with my meager five-cent purchase, I too was a customer.

Anyway, it was to this utopia of childhood greed and euphoria that I now ran, with Dinah scampering enthusiastically ahead. She stopped outside in the shade of the canvas awning, knowing she was forbidden entrance. I slowed to a trot just before charging excitedly through the door.

Overhead, a set of bells jangled to announce my entry. Hurrying toward the candy counter, I noticed that it was much farther away than I remembered, and I was puzzled to hear the bells behind me continue their ringing.

Suddenly, the candy counter dissolved into an open window at the rear of our house. The face of one of my offspring looked out and called, "Dad! Telephone!"

I returned to the present reluctantly. Inside, the editor of this publication was on the phone, asking if I would have an article in time for the next issue.

"Yes," I assured him. "I'm working on a sweet idea that I think I can really sink my teeth into. I just need to sleep on it a little longer."

Hey Valentine, I Ode You One!

Rose are red. Petunias are pink.
Compared to you, a skunk don't stink.

It wasn't much for poetry or grammar, but such verse typified a genre of Valentine card that was popular throughout my elementary school years.

In spite of tongue clicking on the part of mothers, it was the only sort of card a guy could give to another guy. An exchange that would otherwise have been deemed sissy stuff was rendered acceptable by the pseudo-funny insult. (A "red-blooded manly-type greeting," as young Rush explained on one episode of the popular "Vic and Sade" radio program.)

The so-called comic cards were exchanged among buddies and elicited a good-humored chuckle. They also afforded an opportunity for us 97-pound weaklings to tell the class bully what we thought of him, while giving the impression that we were merely including him in our circle of pals.

In those marvelous years of relative innocence, from first through eighth grades, Valentine's Day was akin to our annual Christmas grab bag event. A cardboard box covered with red papier-mache and decorated with hearts stood on a corner table in each classroom. The box was tightly sealed except for a slot at the top. For two weeks beforehand, we deposited our greetings to our classmates. On Valentine's Day, Teacher opened the box and delegated a "postman" from each row to distribute them to the addressees.

Regardless of their printed sentiments, Valentine cards came in a number of forms. Quality cards, including envelopes, could be bought individually for a nickel or a dime. But even a nickel was heavy change for a kid in those days. Boxed assortments, also with envelopes, were economical, but still not cheap.

The popular choice of most school kids was a loosely packaged assortment without envelopes. Since the majority of them would be delivered in person or via our classroom box, one simply wrote "To" and "From" information on the back. Most economical of all was an assortment that came in a series of perforated magazine-size sheets, to be punched out by the purchaser.

Boys could be rather indiscriminate in selecting cards for other fellows. My own criterion was to save the most insulting one for Howie the Zombie, our class' resident gorilla/bully. As a precaution, I gave Howie a big grin when he received the card and began reading. His expression became one of painful concentration as he moved his fingers slowly over the card, sounding out the words of more than one syllable. My grin would be at its widest and beginning to hurt by the time Howie looked up with a half-grunt/half-guffaw, indicating that he had grasped and appreciated the humorous greeting.

Picking cards for girls was a more delicate matter. Here the problem was not a fear of physical punishment. Rather, it involved a more subtle matter of potential social blunders that might cause long-lasting embarrassment. I suppose it was just as touchy for the girls when they had to select cards for us boys. But at least they didn't have to worry that an ill-chosen card for any male classmate might result in two or more boys huddled together, glancing their way and giggling behind their hands.

The majority of cards were relatively safe, at least at face value. A policeman might be depicted handcuffing himself to a lady and pleading: "Police be my Valentine." But to innocent young minds, some cards seemed to border on a proposal of marriage. A few cards from many assortments simply did not get exchanged. Or they might be used in a girl/girl or boy/boy exchange with a friend who would know that they were meant in a spirit of goofiness.

If you had concurrent crushes on more than one young maiden, as I often did, the decision could be (please forgive me) heart-rending. My worst Valentine's Day dilemma occurred the year that my two favorite misses were good friends sitting across the aisle from each other. I finally elected to send them identical cards, lest they compare cards and decide that I had greeted one more affectionately than the other. Even so, I carefully chose a card that could not be deemed "mushy" and risk an open rebuff – or two! (In reality, the girls probably hadn't either one a clue that my heart skipped a beat any time either of them smiled at me.)

The card assortments always included something for one's teacher, but I usually tapped my savings and splurged for a nickel card, because I was privileged to have some really nice teachers. Of course, Mom always rated a special card (no restrictions on schmaltziness for this one), as did grandmothers and a few favored aunts. Dad got one that was corny but not offensive. My two younger brothers enjoyed getting the insult cards, and I had no sisters, which avoided a potentially sticky situation.

As we entered high school, our distribution of Valentine cards was sharply reduced and much more discriminating. Most of us guys, I suspect, gave cards only to girls we were dating or would like to date. The ones we were already dating usually received some candy with the card. (I'll never understand how the Andes Candies chain could have gone out of business, what with all the one-pound assortments I purchased for Valentine's Day, birthdays and other special occasions.)

By the time I was 20, I had developed a better appreciation for the intricacies of the Valentine game. Before departing O'Hare Airport on a trip to California, I passed a machine that dispensed $50,000 flight insurance polices for a buck apiece. I bought half a dozen and mailed one to each of six young ladies I had dated within the past year. At a cost of only six dollars plus postage, it proved to be one of my all-time best Valentine investments.

This Andes Candies store, where super thick malts were mixed at the small soda fountain, was a frequent stop for the author and his pals after Patio theatre matinees. In his nostalgic articles, the author sometimes lamented the demise of Andes. He later was embarrassed to learn that Andes is alive and well and headquartered in Delavan, Wisconsin. During the 1960s, the company elected to vacate the storefront business and concentrate on mass market production. Their Crème De Menthe Thins (inset) are a popular item available in many retail stores. (file photo courtesy Andes Candies L.P.)

The Alley: Avenue Of Adventure

One negative aspect that I've noted about suburban living is the alleys. There are none.

In big cities such as Chicago, business and residential areas always have had alleys. In the early days, they provided a convenient route for delivery and service people. Main streets were left clear for pedestrian, carriage and (later) motorized traffic.

In the days of cheap immigrant labor, rear tenement dwellings were common, and they were easier to service via the alley. Housewives, hanging clothes out on pulley-operated lines, could shout to each other across the alley, exchanging greetings and the latest neighborhood news tidbits.

As the city grew and prospered, alleys became a favorite playground for kids of all but the highest economic strata. Softball games were common, albeit played on an elongated diamond.

Neighbors' back yard gates served as first and third bases. A borrowed garbage can lid marked second. Getting on base required the ability to hit a long ball straight down the narrow field. Balls that were hit over fences into someone's back yard could not be fielded, so that was an automatic "out."

In winter, the alley became a football field. Again, some adaptation was required. The narrow confines put a crimp on fancy plays. Passing predominated, interspersed with a few line charges.

Basketball hadn't achieved its present popularity, but occasional shooting matches erupted nonetheless. The hoop usually was a bottomless bushel basket nailed to a telephone pole. Few kids actually owned a basketball. As often as not they improvised with a sister's volleyball.

My pals and I did our cavorting in an unincorporated village on the northwest edge of Chicago. Our alleys were a bit different. For one thing, they were wider, to accommodate the anticipated growth in the automobile population. They also were unpaved.

Our fledgling village could afford only a thin layer of stones over the dirt. Residents supplemented this with cinders from their coal furnaces. The stones and cinders kept our alleys from becoming quagmires in rainy season. In dry weather, the cinders aggravated the alley's constant dustiness.

To play, run or ride a bike in our alleys was to risk slipping on the crunchy cinders. Those furnace fugitives were murder on bare skin. We suffered countless skinned or bleeding palms, elbows and knees from encounters with those cursed cinders.

A common scene involved a young male running home, a pant leg torn and a knee bleeding through it. As the victim sniffed and fought back tears, his mother examined the damage. After satisfying herself that the injury was minor, Mom would shake her head and say, "I don't know if I can patch those trousers. Why can't you kids play at the school yard instead of running in that dirty alley?"

Why, indeed? We had lots of other play areas. But the alley had its own special attraction.

On dull days, I could recruit Wayne, Chuck, Bobby or some other buddy to go scavenging. The handle of a broken umbrella, stripped down, made a beaut of a fencing sword. Some worn out faucet fixtures were shaped a lot like a Buck Rogers 25th century ray gun. Dry cell batteries, wired to a board with some old oven knobs, made a neat shortwave radio. Or add a buggy wheel and you could imagine yourself seated in the cockpit next to Sky King or Captain Midnight.

Some folk (obviously more well-to-do than most of us) actually tossed out empty milk and soda pop bottles. Those were worth money! The deposit refund on two one-gallon milk jugs and a quart pop bottle would get you into a Saturday matinee at the movies.

One day, as we rummaged along opposite sides of a nearby alley, Chuck called from his side, "Hey, Danny! Look at this!" Next to someone's garbage bin, he had discovered an open grocery store box. Inside were ten of the original dozen jars of Karo syrup. What a bonanza!

Our first thought was to sell it door to door. But we quickly realized that adults would wonder where we had acquired our merchandise. Word probably would get back to our parents, and their questioning would likely lead to some form of discipline. Bad idea.

We considered selling it to neighborhood kids. But they were likely to be less interested, more suspicious and short of cash.

When thoroughly examined, the money-making prospects looked dim. Yet, we couldn't let such a "find" go to waste. Finally, we hauled the box to a nearby prairie[1] that had become an unofficial refuse dump. We set up the jars on empty crates and paint pails. Then we gathered up some stones and had a pitching contest.

Soon we had zeroed in on three jars. As thick syrup oozed through shattered glass fragments, the reason for it being dumped became evident. It obviously had been stored improperly or too long and had spoiled.

Undeterred, we continued bombarding the remaining jars until all were shattered. Flies were now swarming in from seven counties, and a sweet/putrid aroma drifted across the prairie. We departed holding our noses. We felt a bit guilty about our destructiveness, yet glad that we had not tried to peddle the rancid booty.

At times, we simply roamed the alleys, open to whatever distractions might present themselves. It was a change of pace from strolling "out front" on the sidewalk. Observing people in their semi-private back yard activities could give you another slant on their life styles.

Alleys were a welcome detour if you were walking down the street alone and spotted a neighborhood bully on the next block. They also served as shortcuts.

Several of my pals lived on the next street, which shared the alley behind our house. It was an unwritten rule that kids always went to the back door to call one another out to play. So cutting through the alley was a natural course, and faster than going around the block.

In the late 1940s, Robert L. Ripley hosted a daily 15-minute radio version of his famous comic strip series. The program featured seemingly unbelievable stories about all sorts of obscure and fascinating phenomena. It was broadcast during the noon hour, while I was home from school at lunch. Each program's most incredible story was saved for last and would be wrapped up about 12:58p.m.

---

[1] Almost every block in the old neighborhood had one or two empty lots on which no home had yet been built. Just north of us, across Montrose Avenue, a patch of farmland was sometimes left fallow. To my cohorts and me, any such open space, regardless of size, was a "prairie." In my less worldly-wise youth, I thought that "prairie" was a term used exclusively by kids in my neighborhood. Decades later I learned that it was what someone called "Chicago-speak" for any undeveloped land that has been overrun by wild plants. Further investigation might well reveal that the term is even more widely used, but why risk spoiling another childhood illusion?

Standing at our back door, I would hang on every word until Mr. Ripley capped the tale with his copyrighted challenge: "Believe it or not!" Then I'd dash out, down our back porch stairs, through the back gate, down our alley two doors to Bobby's yard. By racing through Bobby's gangway and cutting a diagonal to the James Giles school yard, I could fall in at the end of my class' line as we marched back into the building for afternoon classes.

Without the alley, I'd never have made it.

Not long ago, I needled an old friend who years back had elected to remain a city dweller. "Fred," I asked, "when are you going to leave that dreary city life behind you and join the ranks of carefree suburban homeowners?"

"What?" he retorted. "You mean I should make my family live someplace where people stack up their garbage on the curb in front of their houses?"

Touche, Fred. Touche.

Pranks For The Memories

"Styrt's Drug Store. Hello?"
"Hi. Do you have Sir Walter Raleigh in a can?"
"Yes, we do."
"Well, let him out before he suffocates. April Fool!"

My boyhood cohorts and I harassed various stores with this hilarious phone conversation for several years. We also called grocery stores to inquire if they had Aunt Jemima in a box. While the callee hung up mumbling about "pesky kids," we roared with laughter.

"Phone privileges" were not an issue in those days. Everyone in the family who was old enough to dial and could hold that heavy phone was permitted to use it. This assumed, of course, that you would do so responsibly; i.e., no unauthorized long-distance calls, no tying up the party line (remember party lines?) for long periods.

Had our parents gotten wind of them, our prank calls would have resulted in the telephone being "off limits" to us until further notice. But the lure of April Fool's Day gags made it irresistible to us.

In our short-pants days, April Fool gags usually were limited to close relatives and friends. I'd whisper to Dad that his buttons were unbuttoned. As he hastened to correct the oversight, I'd gleefully announce: "April Fool!" Most times, Mom was wise to what day it was, but she played along when told that her slip was showing.

By age ten or eleven, such innocence had faded. We had moved up to such things as ringing doorbells. Old fashioned doorbells were ideal for inserting a pin. The bell then would continue to ring until someone came out to investigate and removed the pin. The pranksters would be hiding behind a nearby neighbor's porch or bushes, covering their mouths to muffle hysterical laughter at the sight of their victim's consternation.

Window knockers also were popular. After dark, we selected a house with a porch railing close to a front window. While others stood lookout, someone balanced on the railing and stuck tape near the top of the window. A short length of string, with a small nut tied to it, hung down from the tape. The longer length of the string ran to the largest nearby bush, where we hid. Gently tugging on the string would cause the nut to knock softly but insistently against the window.

Some folk would come out onto the porch three of four times, looking up and down the street suspiciously, before discovering the source of the disturbance. At that point, the culprits would all leap out from behind the bush, shout "April Fool!" and depart in a cloud of dust.

A mobilized version of this sport involved bicycles and bean blowers (a.k.a. pea shooters). Riding at a moderate speed down the sidewalk, we could disturb half a dozen or more families per block with a rat-a-tat-tat pattern on their windows. This method was easier but less satisfying because we weren't present to see the startled adults burst through their front doors. Also, I paid for this sinfulness by swallowing many of the yukkie uncooked split peas that we used for ammunition.

Truth to tell, some of this mischief spilled over into other times of the year when we could not excuse our behavior by shouting "April Fool!" Sometimes we simply fell prey to the old "idle hands" syndrome. Fortunately, we did no permanent damage, and most adults were inclined to shrug it off with the "boys will be boys" explanation. (No one ever assumed that girls might be involved and, in our group, they were not.)

Unfortunately, as we progressed (?) to the 7th and 8th grades, our tricks became more …well…more adolescent. Jimmy once put motor oil in all his pals' ink wells at school. David had a miniature spy glass that you looked into and were supposed to see a scantily clad woman. It left a black ring around the viewer's eye.

I had a ring that squirted water from a small rubber bulb concealed in my palm. A lapel button was more effective, because it had a large bulb I carried in my pocket. This enabled me to spray several victims without refilling or give one chump a real bath. The problem with this device was that I seldom wore the right attire for the button to look natural. When I used it in Sunday school once, the story got home before I did, and I spent the afternoon in my room.

Probably my most successful trick involved some hot pepper-flavored gum that I discovered at a shop selling magic and practical joke items. The package would not have fooled anyone, so I removed four sticks and carefully repackaged them in Doublemint wrappers.

(Sorry about that, Gene Autry.) A tiny mark on the fifth stick identified it as the real thing.

All day at school I bided my time. When we lined up to file out at day's end, I looked around with stagy sneakiness and slipped the genuine Doublemint into my mouth, making sure that the kids around me in line could see. Then, while we all watched to be sure Teacher wasn't looking, I passed the peppered sticks to four male classmates.

My timing was perfect. While we marched to the exit, my four victims were able to chew their gum just enough to get a good taste of the peppered flavor. Not until we were safely out on the playground could they spit it out. Then they raced to the water fountain and fought each other for the chance to cool down their singed tongues.

When they recovered, I was still laughing too hard to run, and I became the bottom body in a game of pile-on. But afterward, we all laughed together as they each described how silly the others had looked when their mouths caught fire.

Perhaps the most daring April Fool trick of our grammar school days was the work of a girl. While Miss Hubick was out of the room, the somewhat brash Patsy placed next to her chair a realistic plastic facsimile of that dread substance that was the bane of city walkers until ordinances were passed requiring dog owners to follow their pets with scoops.

When Miss Hubick returned, she halted abruptly at her desk with an expression of appalled distaste. Our snickers were quickly silenced when she slowly surveyed the room and commanded sternly: "The person who belongs to this *thing*, will please come up here immediately and claim it."

Patsy shuffled forward with head bowed and retrieved the offending object. "And now, young lady," Miss Hubick continued, "please take it down to the principal's office and explain how it came to be there." On her way out the door with the "thing," Patsy mumbled to Miss Hubick's stiff back, "April Fool!"

Had she thought about it, Patsy might have foreseen the outcome of her prank. While Miss Hubick was not mean, neither was she noted for her sense of humor. Her long reign as eighth-grade teacher was due at least in part to her straight-shouldered, no-nonsense style in the classroom. Nevertheless, once Patsy had endured whatever discipline she received, she basked in a brief period of recognition as a heroine of sorts. It *was* a pretty original stunt by our standards - and darned spunky for a girl!

My country cousin, Billy, remembers the fun he and his pals had removing neighbors' gates and tipping over—or even carrying off—their outhouses.   One year, the school principal's nameplate disappeared from his desk and was later found mounted above the door of the public outhouse behind the town square.

Later, the principal called all upper grade males into his office one by one to ask if they had any knowledge of the incident. When it was his turn, Billy planned to say, "Sorry, Mr. Gardner, but I'm not privy to that information." However, the principal's stern expression gave him pause as to the advisability of such levity. So he assumed a solemn face and simply mumbled, "No, sir."   Nevertheless, in conferring with classmates later, he could not resist embellishing his report and telling his buddies, "You should have seen the look on the old man's face when he heard that!"

Once, when All Fools Day fell on a Monday, Billy and one of his pals "borrowed" a cow from a local farmer on Saturday night. With an "April Fool" sign hung around its neck, they left the animal in their four-room school house with a day's supply of hay and a bucket of water. The confused, clumsy (and unmilked) bovine roamed the school for 30-some hours, knocking over chairs and desks. Pupils arriving on Monday morning were treated to a break from the monotony of the three Rs, but had to be careful where they stepped.

Only afterward did Billy and his partner in crime ponder the consequences if they had been found out as the pranksters. They knew they'd have gotten what-for, but weren't sure whether the harshest punishment would come from the principal, the distraught farmer or their own parents.

To be fair, the worst of these antics were in excess of our normally harmless rambunctiousness. Nor did we indulge in mischief on a regular basis. During most of the year, it occurred only on those rare occasions when we were totally bored with every other activity. Owing probably to the behavior standards that our parents expected of us, we confined ourselves mostly to pranks that did no damage. And we enjoyed them most when they were legitimatized by a special occasion such as Halloween, graduation day or, best of all, April Fools Day.

I seldom see youngsters today partaking of such high jinks. Are they better behaved than we were, or just lacking in imagination, or perhaps too taken up in their TV-centered world to enjoy such sport?

Perhaps. But I see on the blackboard next to our phone a scribbly message from my son telling me to call a Mr. Sharkey. Don't ask me how, but I happen to know that the phone number under the name will connect me to the Shedd Aquarium.

Juvenile Jobs: They Weren't Child's Play

In addition to the usual three Rs, James Giles Elementary School occasionally gave us lessons in Resourcefulness. Several times a year, there were various campaigns that enlisted students in helping to raise funds for the school. In the fall it was our annual magazine subscription sale.

If my family was larger, I could have made my fortune peddling periodicals. Each year I launched into the drive with a great initial burst of enthusiasm. In no time at all, I had my father and my uncles signed up for *Sports Illustrated* (long before the suspect swimsuit feature), *Field and Stream* or *Esquire* (the latter for my lone bachelor uncle). Mom and my aunts took *Life, Look, Ladies Home Journal, Good Housekeeping* and *Collier's.*

Once I ran out of relatives, though, sales plunged. A few neighbors might order something, but now I was competing with the entire student body. Most folk on our block would give their subscription orders only to kids they knew on the block. But you still had to be the first one to get to them – and half of them had kids of their own involved in the campaign.

Door-to-door sales wasn't really my calling, anyway. But these contests were good training for some of my more ambitious and outgoing schoolmates. Bobby answered an advertisement in a comic book and began selling subscriptions on his own. He earned points which could be collected and turned in for a catalog of "valuable prizes."

Bob may have been inspired by Chuck, who already was selling greeting cards when he was in fourth grade. Chuck's was strictly a cash arrangement. He first invested in a set of sample boxes of cards, using funds borrowed from his father. Chuck's dad, a banker, gave him a thorough quizzing about the business arrangement and his follow-through plans before granting the loan. (Years later, those who knew both father and son were inclined to dismiss Chuck's claim that he had been required to put up his bicycle as collateral.)

Twice during the year, Chuck canvassed the neighborhood with a well-rehearsed sales pitch and took orders for all-occasion assortments. In October, he would start pushing boxes of Christmas cards, long before his customers began seeing them in the stores. The added advantage of being able to shop on your own doorstep was an incentive, and undoubtedly many housewives felt good about helping out an enterprising young salesman from the neighborhood.

Buying from a wholesale warehouse and selling at retail, Chuck made a handsome profit. With little competition, and forsaking a few Saturday movie matinees, he conducted a lucrative business until high school activities put a squeeze on his available free time.

In an era when most parents had suffered through the Great Depression, every kid I knew had chores that he or she was required to perform in return for a weekly allowance. Besides instilling a sense of family responsibility, our folks wanted to teach us the value of money.

I'd say they generally succeeded. Although none of my peers was truly poor, at least three-fourths of them took some sort of outside work while in grammar school.

Lots of fellows had paper routes. Most of the girls were doing baby sitting by the time they were twelve. A few did female chores for old or invalid neighbor ladies.

Grocery stores hired a lot of young fellows as delivery boys. Two-car families were rare (many were still *no-car* families). Busy housewives often called the grocer and gave a shopping list over the phone. The boy filled the order, packed it into paper sacks or an empty box, then loaded it into a bicycle basket and delivered it.

Chain stores such as National Tea Company, A & P or Piggly Wiggly sometimes provided bikes with a small wheel and a huge basket in front. (Have any of these survived? The last one I saw was in a late-night TV movie; might have been Andy Hardy riding it.) At neighborhood mom and pop stores, the delivery boy usually had to have his own bike.

Some customers had accounts with the grocer. Most paid cash. On cash transactions, the grocer tallied the bill by hand, usually on one of the brown paper bags, and the delivery boy collected.

Even if the customer ran a tab with the grocer, prompt and courteous delivery usually earned the boy a tip. Tips were important because the grocer didn't pay much. Between trips, he had to find make-work things for the delivery boy to do—stack milk crates, sort empty pop bottles, sweep floors—just to keep him busy.

With several golf courses just a bike ride away, caddying provided good income for some of my pals. Golf carts hadn't been invented yet. Many golfers willingly paid kids to carry that cumbersome bag of clubs around eighteen holes. A caddy who showed some hustle and learned to anticipate which club the golfer would want next could earn some hefty tips.

I suspect you could only endure as a caddy if you were yourself a budding golf nut. You had to be out at dawn to avoid being assigned last by the starter. Moreover, business was most brisk on sunny days. The prospect of lugging a bag as heavy as me on a hot summer day kept me out of the caddy trade.

In my mind, hot weather and work made for an unwholesome combination. Playing at high energy in the summer sun was one thing. I could engage in fourteen hours of non-stop wild activities with my friends on the hottest of days. But when I was scheduled to mow our lawn, I started as early as possible to avoid the heat. (Mowers were not self-propelled then, you know.)

For kids who didn't mind the sun, several farms in our semi-rural area provided plenty of summer work. There were always jobs available planting, weeding or picking, and odd jobs around the yard or in the barn.

Greg was an experienced field hand. He migrated here from Virginia, where he'd worked on many of the tobacco farms that abound there. However, he recalled his first attempt to find "'bacco work" as an embarrassing disaster.

Greg, then eight years old, joined a group of boys waiting for a neighbor farmer to select the day's crew. Old Mr. Lambert was a gruff man of few words. When he reached Greg, he asked, "Kin ya sucker?"

Greg shook his head. He was pretty sure he couldn't sucker, since he hadn't the faintest idea what it meant.

Mr. Lambert grunted. "Cain't sucker, hey. Y'all better go set in the shade."

Greg thought that he was being ignominiously dismissed. Disgraced, he ran home in tears and spent the day hiding from pals to whom he'd bragged that he was going to find work in the fields. Days later a friend explained that Mr. Lambert had only meant for

Greg to get out of the sun until he could find him some work that required less experience.

Half a dozen riding stables separated the undeveloped western edge of our town from the nearby forest preserve. Just a short bike ride from home, the stables hired kids to groom horses, rake the yard and clean stalls. George loved horses. He wrangled himself a 6-day-a-week summer job at Green Tree Stable. All summer long, George always smelled a little like a freshly fertilized south forty. His mother complained that his clothes had to be washed separately from the rest of the family's things, and even Linco bleach couldn't eliminate the aroma.

Ken and Dave worked several summers at Westlawn Cemetery. Their work was mostly unsupervised and could be done at their own pace. They spent whole days cutting grass with manual rotary mowers. (Motorized mowers were still a rarity, and rider mowers were not even on the drawing boards yet.) They trimmed around grave markers with hand sickles, and plucked weeds by hand. To keep the grass green, they dragged hoses and sprinklers around the entire vast terrain of the cemetery.

Working outdoors agreed with Dave and Ken. They were athletic types who usually worked shirtless. They always had great tans.

For the truly ambitious youngster, there usually was work to be found somewhere. Stop-and-sock golf ranges hired kids to round up balls. Child labor laws were stretched a bit, and boys aged eleven or twelve worked part-time putting up stock on store shelves. Some parents owned their own businesses and would "hire" their offspring.

After trying a few other enterprises, I settled on delivering newspapers as the best preteen job for me. Mine was a morning route. On no-school days, it left the rest of my day free (provided I could avoid being tagged for some task around the house).

The paper route provided a modest but steady income year-round. It paid for a portable radio, a 45-rpm phonograph (and the beginning of my record collection), a toy 16mm movie projector and about twenty of those 100-foot movies produced by Castle Films. It also gave impetus to my youthful writing bug when I was able to purchase a bulky black portable Smith-Corona manual typewriter.

Can you remember the last time you patronized a young entrepreneur selling ice-cold lemonade at a makeshift stand? We

85

should encourage such youthful initiative wherever possible. Jobs for kids under sixteen are still available, but the opportunities are much more limited.

Also, it seems that we post-Depression parents have succeeded in giving our kids a jaundiced view of the work ethic. Several years ago I succumbed to buying a snow blower when I found that none of the local youth was enthused to hire out for an old-fashioned shoveling job. Every one I approached demanded to know if I paid minimum wage.

Made In The U.S.A., By Kids

It must have been his father's idea. Driving home from work one evening recently, I did a double tale and slowed to look more closely. A boy about ten or eleven years old was delivering newspapers on a homemade scooter.

"Kids don't make scooters any more," I protested to the empty passenger seat. Except in late night TV movies, I haven't seen one for 25 years.

They weren't exactly the rage in the neighborhood of my youth. Kids whose families were moderately well off usually had factory-made scooters. But the homemade models were fairly common.

The main component was a pair of cast-off roller skates. This generally meant that some part of one skate had broken or fallen off and been lost. Few things that were repairable were junked in the 1940s, especially during the war years, when many things were in short supply.

Separated halves of a roller skate would be nailed or bolted to either end of a 2-inch by 4-inch board about three feet long. An up-ended orange crate would be centered at one end and nailed in place. Some sort of crossboard was then affixed over the top of the crate to serve as a set of steering handles. This might be a length of thin board (gripable by small hands) or a salvaged section of broken broom handle.

The finished scooter might be prettied up with paint, a white reflector "head light" or other creative ideas. But, essentially, that was it. It was not especially maneuverable, but if the skate wheels were in good condition, it could move straight ahead along the sidewalk at a pretty fast clip.

The homemade scooter was just one of a number of do-it-yourself items that my contemporaries and I rode on or played with. Its big brother was the go-cart.

Go-carts were sit-down vehicles that later fostered a national competition for kids – the soap box derbies. For us, though, they were just another means of having fun and burning off excess energy.

They required a few more materials and a little more mechanical ability than scooters. This probably accounts for the fact that they were more rare than the latter. Generally, they were built as a group project, with various kids providing different parts and lending their particular creative skills. While fathers often contributed materials and some constructive advice, the building usually was done by us kids. Often, however, we got some supervisory assistance from older brothers who had worked on a cart or two in earlier years.

Essential to the project, of course, was a set of wheels and axles. These usually came from a worn out wagon or baby buggy. Sometimes matched sets were not obtainable and one set of wheels would be larger than the other. In that case, the larger set went on the rear of the conveyance.

An orange crate could form the body of the cart. To hold up under rough use, though, it would have to be reinforced with some additional boards. If enough scrap lumber could be found, it was better to make the body of sturdy boards that could withstand occasional crashes.

The wheels and axles were attached to 2x4 boards with horseshoe nails, if we had them. In a pinch, you could use straight nails, hammer them in halfway and then pound them over to hold the axles snug. The board holding the rear wheels could be nailed or bolted in place. For the front wheels, you needed some sort of swivel arrangement that would be bolted through a hole centered near the front of the cart.

Most go-carts had a rope tied to the protruding ends of the front axle. The rider held this rope and pulled it one way or another like reins on a horse to turn the wheels and direct the cart. In a few sporty models, the sides of the body were low or omitted altogether in front. This enabled the rider to position his feet on the front 2x4 and steer without a rope. It was more effective than the rope, but also more likely to result in skinned legs in the event of a spill.

Again, finishing touches might include painting or decals, with red reflectors (usually salvaged from broken bicycle fenders) used as taillights. Empty tin cans were the popular favorite to simulate headlights.

Our neighborhood had no steeply inclined roads that would have been ideal for go-carts, so we mostly pushed each other. Montrose Avenue, the paved road nearest us, had one long gently sloped stretch, and there was little auto traffic then. With a good push to get us started, we could travel six blocks to the bottom (and then pull the cart back uphill).

Occasionally, when two groups of go-carters met, we would improvise a contest. Our smallest driver would be pushed by his two strongest teammates. The other group did likewise. At the top of the slope, the pushers turned loose and the cart that went the farthest before coming to a complete stand-still was the winner. Often the losers would maintain that their cart was in the lead until it began to lose momentum, which helped to save face. Failing this, they could point out that their cart's wheels were in need of oiling.

Because go-carts usually were a group project, they were considered community property by the builders. The only one on our block, built by Wayne, Bobby and Jimmy, might be parked in any one of their yards. It was understood that they all had equal access to it. The rest of us got ample opportunities to use it simply by being on hand when one of the trio needed a partner to take turns pushing. Or the whole gang might assemble to take turns seeing who could push who the farthest down Montrose Avenue.

Not surprisingly, in an era dominated by World War II and its aftermath, much of our creative energy went into forging fine weaponry. Slingshots didn't originate with us, of course. Variants of the ones we constructed had been in use since at least as far back as Biblical times. (Remember David slaying the Philistine giant?) But they were still popular in the 1940s.

All that was required to make one was a strip of rubber (usually cut from a worn-out tire innertube) and a sturdy piece of tree branch that spread out in a "Y" shape. The rubber strip was tied to each upper end of the "Y" and the lower half became a handle. By pulling the rubber back toward your nose and aiming through the "V" at the top, you could send a missile quite a distance toward its target with varying degrees of velocity and accuracy. Almost any small object would serve as "ammunition": stones, acorns, wads of paper, cherries, small apples or tomatoes.

I personally never owned a slingshot. My mother thought (as probably most did) that they were nothing but a temptation for young boys to get into mischief or put each other's eyes out.[1] She hinted at punishment too terrible to put into words if ever I was caught with

---

[1] See the reminiscence titled "You're Gonna Break Your Neck!"

one. Once or twice I was zapped in the back of the head by someone who did own a slingshot. On those occasions the validity of my mother's concern did not prevent me from wishing that I had the means with which to seek revenge.

All of us, on the other hand, possessed one or more rubber guns, which mothers tended to tolerate as foolish but less dangerous than slingshots. Rubber guns also required access to a worn innertube. In this case, strips about an inch wide were cut around the circumference of the tube, producing a supply of intact rubber circlets. These were used both to fabricate the gun and as ammunition.

A piece of 1 x 3 board (or the closest equivalent available) would be cut about 14 or 15 inches long. A wooden clothes pin was braced against one end by stretching four or five strips around the board lengthwise. Next, a large nail was pounded part way into the underside of the board about two inches from the end with the clothes pin. The rubber gun was now complete and ready to be "loaded."

One last rubber strip was placed over the upper front end of the gun and stretched to the back. By pressing down on the bottom of the clothes pin, you pulled it away from the board at its tip and tucked the other end of the rubber strip inside. Then you released your hold on the clothes pin and the strip would be clamped in place, stretched to the point that it strained to be released.

We referred to the nail down below as a trigger, but it really was meant as a grip for a couple of fingers as we aimed. The trigger really was the clothes pin, which we controlled with our thumb. When we pressed the lower half, the pin released its grip on the rubber strip, which zipped through the air toward its target. Unless the target was within five feet in front of you, the rubber "bullet" didn't have much zap when it hit. But it did travel quite a distance, and you could easily tell if it found its mark.

Rubber guns made for great running battles. The "bullet" that had just missed you could be picked up and reloaded on your gun. You could see clearly when your shot found its mark. You hollered, "Gotcha! You're dead!" and there were none of the arguments that went: "Missed me." "Did not." "Did too."

My friend Fred grew up on the northwest side of Chicago and I did not have the pleasure of making his acquaintance until I was beyond such games. Too bad. Fred could have instructed me on the advanced weaponry that his gang used.

With a larger board to form the gun's body, they carved notches at intervals along the top. Five or six rubber strips then were stretched to the rear of the gun. A more intricate arrangement of the "trigger" enabled them to release the strips one at a time or in a continuous volley. In effect, they created a repeating rifle version of the rubber gun.

Among our more peacetime-oriented homemade toys were a variety of boats made from odds and ends of wood scraps. Wayne was rather talented at carving out reasonable facsimiles of sail boats (with popsicle sticks and strips of cloth for sails), canoes and steamers.

My feeble efforts were mostly oblong chunks of wood nailed together with not much nautical imagination. They were invariably top heavy and always tipped over in even the calmest mud puddles or bath tub "lakes."

I was much more successful with a handmade toy that, as far as I know, I invented myself. Kids elsewhere may have had the same idea, but I never saw anyone in my neighborhood duplicate it. (Maybe I should have gotten a patent.)

With four pieces of string cut to equal lengths, I tied the corners of a handkerchief to one of my lead soldiers. Then I carefully rolled the cloth around the soldier and tossed him as high into the air as I could. The handkerchief would open and my soldier would become a paratrooper and gracefully descend to the ground.

Sometimes I threw from an open window in our attic and the parachute soldier had an extra long ride down to the vacant lot next door. But this meant running outside and back upstairs for each flight, which quickly grew tiresome.

Even this seemingly innocent activity eventually got me into trouble. Occasionally I was careless about where I launched the parachutist. One of the soldiers ended up in a rooftop gutter and another got caught in the upper branches of a tree in our back yard. I tried to knock it loose with a clothes pole, but to no avail.

One day, my mother, who knew how many handkerchiefs I should have in my dresser drawer, demanded to know: "Is that one of your good hankies hanging in our tree out back?" Even in the 1940s, do-it-yourselfism had its drawbacks.

About that boy delivering the newspapers, though. On closer inspection, I observed that the wheels of his scooter had come from a skateboard, the rubber-gripped handlebar from one of those large-wheeled tricycles. The box portion, in which the newspapers were so symmetrically arranged, consisted of two of those plastic storage crates that come in all colors from Wal-Mart and Target.

I ask you: Would a hi-tech 1990s kid have dreamed this up? It had to be his father's idea. Maybe the father was just up-dating a well proven design. Or perhaps he was following the time-honored practice of using the materials at hand. Either way, he probably enjoyed a nostalgic kick out of applying modern technology to the skills and ingenuity of a long-ago boyhood.

And who knows? It could become the next big juvenile fad, and his son will be "the first in his neighborhood" to own one.

Happy Birthday Memories

Strictly speaking, it is a federal offense to put anything but genuine mail items into anyone's mailbox. If the U.S. Post Office had enforced that rule, most of my friends and I would have spent time at Leavenworth for stuffing unstamped birthday party invitations into mail slots and boxes.

In a two-block radius of my boyhood home there were at least fifty kids who played together on a fairly regular basis. Scarcely a month went by without each of us being invited to someone's birthday party.

Selecting the invitees could be a traumatic experience. Despite all pleas, mothers usually limited the guest list to between 10 and 12. (After all, Mom was going to be chief planner, hostess, coordinator, clean-up person – and nurse, if some kid got sick.) Decisions about which friends to omit were earthshaking by our youthful social standards. By comparison, that later business of trimming down the wedding guest list was a piece of cake.[1]

Given their limited size, birthday parties also were remarkable for their consistently co-ed make-up. Thank Mom for that, too. It was no use protesting, "Aw, Ma, I don't want any *girls* (or *boys*) comin' to my party!"

Once the list was drawn, invitations were prepared. Some mothers encouraged their offspring to be creative with colored paper, scissors, streamer tissue, crayons, paste, whatever. Usually, the invitations were cute store-bought cards, about 4 by 6 inches, with plain white envelopes. Mom would carefully fill in time and date on the cards and you got to mark the envelopes. First names only were sufficient unless you invited two Jimmys or Shirleys.

Addresses weren't necessary either, because you would deliver the invitation yourself. First class postage was three cents, and for 36 cents Mom could buy a loaf of bread or a quart of milk. Besides, kids had a surplus of idle time. Playing mailman would keep you out of mischief for half an afternoon.

Some kids rang doorbells and personally handed the cards to Mary or Johnny. I thought that was a give-away that it was an

---

[1] Alright, I know it's a groaner, but cut me a little slice—eh, slack. Okay?

invitation (as if my cohorts regularly received unstamped letters delivered without the benefit of addresses). It seemed to me that somehow spoiled the fun of receiving mail, albeit illegally delivered mail.

Birthday invitations from my best friends were always welcome. Others I received with mixed feelings. Most birthday parties were held on Saturday afternoon – hallowed time for preteen boys. The parties usually were fun, but they meant skipping a Saturday movie matinee, going swimming at the "Y" pool, etc. With so many parties throughout the year, the trade-off had questionable merit.

Two exceptions were Peter and Judy's parties. Peter was an almost-best friend, and Judy was his acceptably tomboyish younger sister. Pete and Judy's father subscribed to *Esquire* magazine. The most recent issues always could be found in a magazine stand next to his easy chair. At some point during the party, while the girls were occupied elsewhere, the boys would gleefully thumb through portraits of scantily clad woman, comparing favorites, and smirking over cartoons that we really didn't understand but instinctively knew must be risqué.

Even for best friends, choosing a present could be a problem. Mom would say, "I'll give you a dollar, but see if you can find something for about fifty cents." That eliminated most of the more elaborate toys and games. The absence of a nearby five-and-ten-cent store didn't help. Most of our purchases came from the rather limited selections of games and toys that could be found in local hardware and drug stores.

Model kits, especially airplanes, were popular gifts. Not the pre-formed plastic variety sold today, but balsa wood models that had to be cut out, glued together and painted. They were in the right price range and looked really neat in the illustration on the box. Among us boys, probably hundreds were exchanged as birthday presents. But few of us had the talent or the patience to ever finish assembling one.

Better liked, I suspect, were planes that actually flew. A glider model required little more assembly than sliding wing and tail pieces through pre-cut slots in the fuselage. This model you just tossed into the wind. On a breezy day, it would do several loops and dives or just coast on the wind for up to fifteen seconds. Sometimes it would glide to a smooth landing on a flat surface, but if it nosedived and crashed the nose was protected by a metal plate.

A propeller model was powered by a rubber band that you twisted. It had wheels and could take off from a smooth surface and fly for 30 seconds or more – if you spent five minutes winding the rubber band almost to its breaking point.

Other gifts included bags of marbles, lead soldiers or cowboys, miniature pinball games, kites (not easy to wrap), decals (either wet-n-stick or iron-on) or "tattoos" of comic heroes. Girls often received doll stuff and books.

A few kids were able to give more expensive gifts, such as board games, baseballs or footballs. By unspoken but universal agreement, one present no one ever received at kids' parties was clothing.

Birthday parties usually began with a lot of clowning and milling around in the living room while Mom counted heads to see if everyone had arrived. Then a series of games began. One involved kneeling on a chair and dropping clothes pins into a quart milk bottle. You were supposed to hold the pin right under your nose and aim, but some kids always tried to reach down and get closer. Loud protests of "No fair!" and "Cheater!" were guaranteed. At this point, the hostess was obliged to step in and re-establish the rules.

A junior version of Spin The Bottle called for players to perform silly stunts. "Pick a partner and wheelbarrow through the house." Or: "Imitate a singer with the hiccups." Because we shared an exaggerated sense of our comic talents, Chuck and I excelled at this nonsense and always picked each other for partners.

Ring Toss was an indoor version of Horseshoes, usually played in teams, which generated lots of competitive excitement. If Mom played the piano or the family had a phonograph, she might lead a game of Musical Chairs. The winners of each game received prizes such as rubber balls, bubble blowing kits or dot-to-dot books. Some mothers, probably hoping to encourage reading at whatever level, awarded the popular Big Little Books. (Wish I had all the ones that passed through my hands, now valuable collector items.)

Game time wound up with the all-time favorite that was played at *every* birthday party: Pin The Tail On The Donkey. Catcalls and howls of laughter greeted blindfolded players who pinned the detached appendage to sofas, lampshades or, with comparative accuracy, somewhere near the donkey's ear. Expressions of disbelief were common when contestants were shown the results of their fumbling efforts.

Finally, the games concluded, the birthday girl or boy got to open all those enticing looking packages. Then our hostess steered us to the gaily decorated dining room table. Next to our plates were party favors – frilly paper cups of assorted candies, boxes of Cracker Jack and snap tubes with prizes inside.

Before going to the kitchen for the cake and ice cream, the hostess started us on a game of Telephone Gossip by whispering something in one guest's ear. That person giggled and "passed it on" by whispering to the next person. The last girl or boy to hear the gossip would relate it aloud. Then the first person told how the story had been heard originally. The two versions usually were miles apart, causing shrieks of laughter from all.

With the cake on the table and candles lit, we sang "Happy Birthday" to the guest of honor. He or she then made a wish, blew out the candles and had to wait a year for each candle left burning.

In spite of my sweet tooth, eating was my least favorite part of birthday parties. Because it was a festive occasion, most mothers— even the ones who were super bakers—served bakery cakes decorated with little figures and candy flowers. Instead of the simple chocolate I craved, they were 80 percent cream and frosting and usually filled with yukkie stuff like strawberries.

To satisfy the varied tastes of youngsters, Neopolitan was the most commonly served ice cream. I always tried to get someone near me to trade their chocolate section for my strawberry, but I seldom got any takers. So I compromised by eating little bites of the vanilla and strawberry together and saving the chocolate for last.

Some parties continued informally for awhile with games in the back yard or basement. Mostly, we just sort of dispersed homeward, with awkward thank-you's to the weary mother-in-charge. Twenty minutes later, when quizzed by our own mothers, we'd have trouble remembering who all was there, what presents were received and what games we played.

Those parties are history in more ways than one. In the 1960s, many parties consisted of trips to a ball game, the zoo or some adventure park. During the 1970s and 1980s, at-home parties were in again, but instead of games to entertain the kids there were hired clowns, ventriloquists, puppeteers or magicians. More recently, I'm told, there has been a trend to prepackaged birthday video tapes. Soon, I suppose, the guests will receive their invitation via e-mail, they'll purchase gifts from and have them delivered by e-tailers, the entertainment will be beamed to them at home over the internet and the refreshments will be delivered by Fed X.

Having reached my AARP years before hesitantly purchasing a VCR, I may be just a bit crotchety about all our new technology. If I could be eight or nine years old again for one more birthday, I'd waive all that modern sophisticated stuff in favor of an old fashioned party with funny hats and silly games. I wouldn't try to trade my strawberry ice cream for chocolate. I'd eat the gooey cake with relish. Heck, I'd even spend 37 cents to mail the invitations.

Afterthought: When this piece was originally published, several readers wrote to comment that cake with relish sounds like a rather strange dish. (Hey, I'm just reporting what *they* said. Don't send me any poison pun letters.)

Dan McGuire

Confessions Of A Juvenile Don Juan

February presents an opportunity for even the most reticent of us to express our feelings for the guys and gals we hold special. For those with a nostalgic bent, Valentine's Day also may trigger some warm recollections of early loves.

I lost my heart for the first time (fittingly enough) in the first grade at James Giles Elementary School. At the door of Room 101, I realized that my mother—she with whom I would entrust my life; even my Lone Ranger whistle ring—really was going to *leave me* with this mob of unknown children. Along with three other youngsters, I began to shed tears of desperation and betrayal.

The 32 other kids were taking opening day pretty much in stride. They probably viewed us as babies. Not so Miss Taylor, the first grade teacher. She gathered us around her in a semi-circle and spoke soothingly of the fun things we would do in school. As mothers tiptoed out behind us, she patted our cheeks and brushed tears away with Camay-soft hands.

Miss Taylor won my confidence that morning. Within a month she had won my heart as well.

She was the youngest teacher at Giles School, probably fresh out of teacher's college. She was the most beautiful grown-up lady I'd ever met up close. When she called on me in class, her smile told me that I was special to her. Gradually, I came to realize that one day she would take me aside and whisper, "Danny, this must be our secret. I love you more than anyone in the world. I can barely wait until you are grown up so we can be married!"

Somehow, the opportunity for Miss Taylor to actually make that revelation never arose. At the end of the school year, she marched my class across the hall to meet Miss Atterberry, who would be our teacher for second grade. When she glanced my way and I could not catch her eye, I knew that she was as heartsick as I over our missed rendezvous.

I vowed to grow up quickly and fulfill our destiny, Miss Taylor's and mine. For a week, I was listless and withdrawn. (My mother thought I had a summer cold.) Then the lure of vacation activities engulfed me. Somewhat guiltily, I felt my heart healing.

When school resumed in September, I sometimes met Miss Taylor on the playground at recess. We exchanged hellos and she, too, seemed to have recovered from her heartbreak. Later, I learned that she had become engaged during the summer. That hurt a little. It was good that she had accepted the impossibility of our romance. Yet such a swift and compete recovery seemed to me a bit callous.

Perhaps that episode hardened me against women for a time. For I was ten years old before Cupid succeeded in zapping me again

Dorothy sat across the aisle from me in fifth grade. She laughed at my jokes and exchanged answers with me on homework assignments. After school, we walked together for the distance that our paths overlapped. (Walking her all the way home would have resulted in certain ridicule by my male peers.) Our conversations revealed many shared interests: movie serials, radio programs, bike riding, Big Little Books.

We lived several blocks apart and had different playmates. But I met some of her friends when she invited me to her next birthday party. Thereafter, if things got dull on my block, I wandered by Dorothy's house and often could join a game already in progress.

Bike riding enabled us to pop in on each other. If she found me alone on my porch, we might shoot marbles or play soldiers. (I could barely beat her at marbles. She may even have tossed a few games to avoid seeming too domineering.) With my metal soldiers, she became as engrossed as I did in setting up elaborate battles in our back yard rock garden. But at some point the war always would be halted by a cease fire to allow time for a nurse and a wounded soldier to fall in love.

Dorothy was not a tomboy, exactly, but she was good at a lot of things usually done well only by boys: running, jumping, climbing, riding a bike no-hands. All this made it easy for me to accept her as a solo playmate. It also led to the curtailment of what may have been a budding romance.

One afternoon our back yard game prompted some playful pushing. The pushing gave way to wrestling that began with laughter but escalated to an earnest contest. It ended with Dorothy sitting on my chest, pinning my arms and demanding, "Give up?" When my continued struggles did not unseat her, I was forced to mumble, "I give."

Our play resumed with Dorothy apparently putting the incident behind her; but my pride had taken a blow. I was thankful that none of my boy friends were around to witness my humiliation. I took a closer look at Dorothy and realized for the first time that she was pretty, but also rather…well…husky.

Her boyish behavior has attracted me, but it now represented a threat. Women's lib was a quarter century down the road. I dared not fall in love with a girl who could out-wrestle me.

After that day, I remained friendly with Dorothy but minimized our contact and avoided one-on-one play altogether. She persisted for awhile, but gradually got the message. She probably never realized what had short-circuited our relationship. I hope not. Despite my cautious retreat, I still thought she was a very nice girl and would not have wanted to hurt her feelings.

Hindsight proved my decision wise, though. Dorothy grew heavier each year. I remained a 98-pound weakling well into high school.

Most of my boyhood crushes were hampered by a tendency to become enamored of older women. Wayne's sister, Shirley, was a high school freshman while we were still in sixth grade. Shirley had a friend named Meg who came by to visit frequently while I was playing with Wayne at his house. I found Meg irresistible, possessed of a bubbly personality and the wholesome beauty of a farmer's daughter. She reminded me, in fact, of Jeanne Crain in the movie "State Fair."

In her presence, I strained to appear older and more sophisticated than my years. I broke off from games with Wayne to involve myself in the girls' conversation. Meg was polite and friendly. Shirley, who knew me well from my long association with her kid brother, appeared puzzled. Wayne was just disgusted. Privately he told me, "She's got three boy friends and she's almost engaged to one of them."

Even so, I persuaded myself that Meg shared my attraction and was waiting for me to close the age gap. It was, after all, a much less formidable gap than the one that had separated Miss Taylor and me.

At night, I dreamed Meg and myself into scenes from Errol Flynn movies. She was the princess captured by pirates. I was the bold adventurer boarding their ship with my men to rescue her with dazzling swordsmanship. Instead of a climactic kiss, those dreams dissolved into a big "The End" when Meg began wearing the ring of a high school classmate.

At least three baby sitters broke my heart. Margie, in particular, left it in pieces. She was fifteen and in an advanced stage of what adults then referred to as "blossoming." She had long silky brunet tresses and was allowed to wear a trace of light red lip rouge.

There was an upright piano in our living room. When Margie sat with my brothers and me (actually just Alan and Dickie, because I was 12 and certainly didn't need a baby sitter!), she would entertain us by playing our favorite songs. Sometimes we sang. Sometimes we just listened, tapping our feet and marveling as she flawlessly rendered "Malaquena" or "Bumble Boogie."

I was allowed to stay up later than my brothers, and Margie taught me to play the bass half of duets on "Chop Sticks" and "Heart and Soul." As we played, seated together on the piano bench, she sometimes put her arm around my shoulder. A casual gesture? Just a practical place to hang a loose limb? Perhaps. But to me it was a signal that this lovely creature, a mere three years my senior, responded to my adoration and looked forward to our time alone together as much as I did. Yet when she asked what I'd like to hear, and I picked the most romantic tunes in our Golden Book of Favorite Songs, Margie never took the hint.

Lopsided love wasn't always the problem, though. Even my well balanced matches had a Romeo/Juliet quality to them.

Susan and I hit it off pretty good in seventh grade, but her parents prohibited dating until high school (a fairly standard attitude at the time). To see a movie together, we plotted to meet at the Patio Theatre. She would tag along with her older sister and some friends. We would meet "by chance" in the lobby and she'd tell her sister, "My friend is alone. I'm going to sit with him." I couldn't buy her ticket, but I'd treat her to a soda and popcorn.

We had worked out all the details – except for the part where her sister gets sick and they both stay home. I nervously paced the lobby, sneaking occasional peeks through the theatre doors to catch snatches of the two cartoons, previews and Chapter 12 of "The Monster and the Ape." When I finally gave up and went inside to watch the feature film, Abbott and Costello weren't as funny as usual.

During my thirteenth summer, I attended a church camp. I knew there was a God when a gorgeous female of my own age and faith took to me as spontaneously as I to her. For two weeks, we were as inseparable as camp restrictions would permit. Our parting was one of epic poignancy, but we exchanged phone numbers and vowed to reunite.

Then geography reared its ugly head. She lived on the far south side of Chicago and I lived in a suburb on the northwest fringe of the city. Much too far by bicycle. Even the streetcar would have required two hours or more and multiple transfers each way.

We kept in touch by phone and letter. We resigned ourselves to meeting again at camp. But absence does not always make the heart grow fonder. In the spring, we met at a downtown Chicago youth rally. A few hours together made it clear that the spark was gone. We parted friends. I attended a different camp that summer.

In those tender years when all emotions are felt most keenly, I perhaps thought I had cornered the market on unrequited love. Now, I realize that many of my pals were afflicted as badly as I.

Jimmy nursed a barely acknowledged crush on Wanda through 7th and 8th grades. He frequently recruited me to go bike riding with him and steered us down her block. If Wanda was sitting on her front porch or playing out front with a girl friend, we would make repeated circles around the block. Each time we passed Wanda's house, Jimmy would perform some daredevil trick for her benefit. To disguise his intent, he cleverly hollered: "Hey, Danny, watch this!"

Wanda usually appeared to not even notice us. But on rare occasions, when Jimmy embarrassed himself by sprawling in the street, she and her friends would first gasp and then cover their mouths to muffle giggles as he dusted himself off, laughing in a vain attempt to retain his dignity.

When we advanced from grammar school, Wanda selected a different high school than Jimmy. Only then was he convinced that his affections were not returned in kind. To his credit, Jimmy recovered admirably and became quite a ladies' man in high school.

Between 6th and 8th grades, Roger used a generous allowance to treat at least half the girls in our class to sodas, carnival rides and movies. After graduation, we had an outing attended by most of the class at Riverview Amusement Park. Roger blew a wad trying to get every girl to accompany him on the roller coaster rides, the Chutes water ride, the Pair-O-Chutes, the Mill of the Floss (a.k.a. Tunnel of Love) – anything that offered an opportunity to put an arm around them and maybe steal a kiss.

Roger was neither an athlete nor a Mr. Personality type. The girls mostly tolerated him or took advantage of his efforts to buy their affections. I confess that I joined most of the other guys in snickering behind his back.

Ol' Rog eventually triumphed, however. In junior college, he met a plain but nice gal from a well-to-do family. After C.P.A. school, he married her. They adore each other and her father set up his egghead son-in-law in a very profitable business.

For us boys, at least, one comfort in those early romantic encounters was knowing that there always was one female who really cared. If some insensitive girl shattered your heart and your ego, you could depend on that original sweetheart who spent a third of her life in your kitchen. When every other female spurned you, Mom was always thrilled to be your valentine.

So, call it puppy love if you will. For girls and boys alike, those painful childhood crushes helped prepare us for the more tempestuous affairs of the heart that awaited us in our teenage and young adult years.

These Films Made Pupils Brighter

Regular readers of this column are aware that movies were a key ingredient of the "formative years" for my buddies and me. Throughout our grammar school period, Saturday matinees were a given on most weekends. In our early teens, a Friday or Saturday night movie, followed by a stop at the malt shop, was a favorite choice of couples savoring the first joys of unchaperoned dating. When we were old enough to have access to "a set of wheels," drive-in theatres had a major role in the getting-to-know-you process.

Yet another type of motion picture comes to mind, unlike anything we saw at the commercial movie houses – except, perhaps, for some segments of newsreels. I'm talking about movies that we saw at James Giles Elementary School. They were called educational films.

The original James Giles Elementary School: eight classrooms for eight grades, with combination gym and auditorium in basement.

A dozen or more small local companies produced a wide variety of such films back in an era when Chicago still was a hub for commercial filmmaking. The vast majority, however, were produced by two giants of the trade, Coronet Films and Encyclopedia Britannica Films.   Some of the wildlife and African tribal documentaries had a *National Geographic* quality to them, but I don't specifically recall any of the films beginning with a declaration that "National Geographic Films presents...."

One that did make a lasting impression on me was a rare departure from comedy shorts by the Walt Disney studios. It dealt with the epidemic of malaria among the workers who built the Panama Canal. I vividly recall a lot of four-fingered men pausing in their labors and roused from their sleep to swat vicious looking mosquitoes.

The typical educational film dealt with almost any subject we might study in school, including some the textbooks barely covered or omitted altogether. Hygiene films instructed us on the proper way to blow our noses and how germs were spread if we did not cover our coughs and sneezes. One showed us the correct way to brush our teeth. Then it followed a brother and sister on a visit to the dentist. They both smiled throughout, demonstrating that this was not an ordeal to be avoided, but a sort of adventure.

Another film dealt entirely with good manners. In one scene, young Ted and Mary are at dinner with Mother and Father. Ted begins to make a comment and Father abruptly cuts him off with: "Ted! Don't talk with your mouth full!" Father speaks rather harshly, actually; but Ted probably deserves it. He looks to be in his early teens and certainly should know better. Andy Hardy would have.

Even back in the 1930s and 1940s, educational films were giving kids more information about the birds and the bees than most parents did. Many films dealt with the nesting habits and family lives of birds. We never actually saw Mr. and Mrs. Robin being intimate, but we did see Momma Robin sitting on her eggs and the chicks eventually breaking out. Later we watched the babies being fed sqwiggling worms and being urged out of the nest to test their wings.

Bees and ants had their lives documented so intensely that it's a wonder they didn't rise up and attack the snoopy photographers. In these insect societies, we witnessed the parallel to human civilization as great hordes of workers labored on behalf of the upper classes. It never impressed me much that one queen ant or queen bee laid all those eggs and was waited on by her faithful drones. What fascinated me was how the filmmakers got their big cameras into those little nests and life went on as normal among the bee and ant colonies.

The sweeping range of the educational films' topics was incredible. Science films covered everything from the formation of volcanoes to building a simple compass with a straight pin and a dry cell battery. Geography films took us on journeys down the steamy Amazon River and to the frozen Arctic region.

During World War II, there were War Department films instructing us on air raid procedures, warning us that loose lips sink ships and demonstrating how the scrap iron, rubber, paper and fats that we collected and turned in would be used in the war effort. Every year, just before Fire Prevention Week, there would be a film on potential fire hazards in the home. Chief Schoenfeld, of our local volunteer fire department, would be on hand to introduce the film and urge us to help keep our homes firesafe.

Generally, the films ran between 12 and 20 minutes. Anything longer tended to make the lower grades grow restless. Eighth graders often felt they'd already absorbed enough education. In the semi-darkness of the school basement, they occasionally were tempted to tell jokes or aim wadded gum wrappers at their friends. However, their attention span was aided by the sharp eye and stern voice of Miss Hubick, strategically seated midway behind her class. If she found it necessary to speak to anyone, Miss Hubick would rise and stand against the wall, where she could watch the film and still observe every movement within her group.

Educational films were big on summarizing. Any film with a "how to" format concluded with the narrator doing a recap. On the screen, a house is engulfed in flames, and the narrator says, "So to prevent *your* home from becoming a victim of fire, remember..."

Abridged scenes from the film reappear as he enumerates:

"One. Don't let old newspapers accumulate."

"Two. Never use gasoline or kerosene for cleaning."

"Three. Keep flammable liquids in tightly sealed containers and stored in well ventilated areas."

"Four. Dispose of oily or greasy rags in a sealed metal container...."

Talking to a friend who grew up in Chicago, it surprised me to learn that educational films were somewhat of a special event for most Chicago public school classes. Not so at Giles Elementary.

Every other Friday, our teachers marched us, by grades, down to the basement assembly hall. Wooden slat folding chairs would be set up in theatre style rows. The smaller kids in the lower grades sat in the front. Succeeding grade levels filtered into the rows farther back.

With time out for changing reels, two or three films usually ran about 45 minutes to an hour. Our arrival was timed so that the program would end around our 3:15 dismissal time. In warm weather we brought our books and satchels with us (with instructions to stow them neatly under our chairs[1]), and we were turned loose directly from the hall, again being dispersed in order by classes.

John V. Leigh, our beloved principal, was film selector, overseer and projectionist for this celluloid segment of our education. When the regular films' length permitted, Mr. Leigh loved to slip in a little "extra added attraction." Usually, these were vintage black and white cartoons (Oswald Rabbit, Mutt and Jeff, Krazy Kat), sport shorts or animal films that were more entertaining than strictly educational.

A unanimous favorite was the sing-along series that flashed each song's words on the screen and helped us stay together by bouncing a black dot over them. ("Just follow the bouncing ball.") Mitch Miller was never blessed with a more spirited sing-along audience. Even the teachers joined in, and some had very pleasing singing voices. Most enthusiastic of all was Mr. Leigh's rich tenor as he upped the volume a little to carry over the whirr of the projector.

With or without the "extras," our Friday afternoon films were a good way to wind down as pupils grew restless for the weekend break. Though we often viewed them as an escape from classroom drudgery, many of the films dealt with subjects we were studying and helped to reinforce what we had learned.

A suburban teacher tells me that many of these same films are available in school film catalogs, although seldom used. Most schools have made the transition from 16mm films to video. Much easier to use, they also lend themselves to viewing in single

---

[1] Where, of course, classmates' feet would, accidentally or otherwise, kick them out or drag them backward so that we could not reach them when we got up to leave.

classrooms; thus, subjects can be selected based on a class' current study.

Some of those old films are available on video, I'm told, but teachers would need to choose carefully. The science films are likely to present space travel as "something to be looked forward to in the not-too-distant future." Geography films might present a Berlin before the rise and fall of the infamous wall, or refer to Istanbul as Constantinople.

It would be great fun, though, to get a roomful of Giles alumni together for a day-long film fest of those dated educational flicks. If we could bring back Mr. Leigh to lead us in some sing-alongs, I'll bet it would draw an S.R.O. crowd.

The Ghosts Of Halloweens Past

An incident that occurred when I was eleven years old vividly illustrates why I flunked out as a juvenile delinquent.

It is two days until Halloween. Bobby and I are suffering from terminal impatience. Bobby says, "I know what. Let's get us some soap and decorate a few windows tonight."

"Yeah, let's," I agree. I dash home, burst through the back door and into the kitchen. My mother stands at her ironing board, a basket of damp laundry on a chair beside her. Still panting, I ask, "Mom, do you have any bars of soap you're about done with?"

My mother completes a stroke, tilts the iron upward and looks at me suspiciously. "What for?" she asks.

Too late, I realize that a would-be vandal does not ask his mother for the tools with which to do his mischief. Stalling, I exaggerate my breathlessness as I rack my immature brain for an answer: "Ummm...me and Bobby...puff!...are gonna give...puff!...his dog a bath."

"Um hmm," my mother replies as she picks up another item from the basket and resumes her ironing. "Have you cleared that with Bobby's mother?"

I do not get the soap, but I am content to be sent on my way without being trapped by my own dumbness. I tell Bobby that I could not find any soap.

He shrugs and says, "Me neither." Weeks later he confesses that his mother caught him snooping around her laundry area and sent him packing. He was lucky not to be confined to his room.

We decide instead to get an early start on our trick-or-treating. After supper, we meet and don our masks – the only part of our costumes that we can smuggle past our parents. We do not begin ringing doorbells until we are eight blocks from home – beyond the radius we are likely to cover on *the* night.

This is a precaution against being recognized. Schools discourage students from bothering neighbors ahead of time. Most parents agree with the policy, but a few kids always get started a day or two early. Bobby and I haven't done it before; but we know it's best to work in an area where we aren't known, lest word get back to our parents.

Most folks have already stocked up on goodies in anticipation of the horde of smallfry that soon will be ringing their doorbells. The trick is to get them to part with these treats two nights early. Almost as one, they ask, "You boys are a bit early, aren't you?"

We have our answers ready. Bobby has to be at his grandmother's birthday party on Halloween. My story earns me a few extra portions. "I'm having my tonsils out tomorrow. I'll be in the hospital."

A few people insist that we come back on the right night. The majority are more lenient, and we make a pretty good haul. We eat a lot of it as we go. The rest gets hidden in Bobby's garage. It won't do to carry it into our houses tonight.

The next night we hike eight blocks in another direction and repeat the performance. One night early, hardly anyone refuses a treat. We munch discreetly, remembering the queasy stomachs we experienced this morning – and dared not mention to our parents as we forced down our breakfast. Most of this night's goodies get hidden along with the earlier booty.

The afternoon of Halloween is a special occasion at James Giles Elementary School. We wear our costumes to class. The principal, Mr. Leigh, visits each classroom and admires our get-ups. He gives us a little lecture about having a good time but not embarrassing our parents or our school tonight.

No one sits in his or her assigned seat. One by one, we stand up front and the class tries to guess who we are. Shirley the Showoff identifies most of us right away. Later she admits that she memorized everyone's shoes that morning.

A little after two o'clock, our principal sends word around to the teachers that it's about time. Each classroom lines up and marches out to the schoolyard. The teachers form us up by grades. Then Mr. Leigh leads us in a parade that circles around the two square blocks that comprise the school grounds. Knowing the tradition, neighbors line the sidewalks to cheer all the cowboys, cowgirls, clowns, bums, ghouls, pirates, princesses, comic book characters and what-have-you.

Teachers, directing and monitoring, are sometimes overheard joking among themselves. "Floyd is certainly in character today, isn't he?" Floyd is dressed as a devil.

Students march around James Giles Elementary School in the 1959 Halloween parade. Begun by Principal John V. Leigh in the 1940s, the parade became a tradition that has continued into the new millennium. (photo courtesy Izetta Giles Castiglia)

We parade back into the school and return to our classes. Masks are removed for a headcount. Then it's time for dismissal and the mad rush home. We are already in costume. It is only necessary to check in with mothers. "I'm home, Mom. We're going trick-or-treatin'

For many years, Mr. and Mrs. Leigh's dog, Schnauzer, joined the school kids, in costume, to lead the annual Halloween parade. (photo courtesy June O. Orten)

111

now. Bye." An admonition to be home for supper follows us out the door.

Wayne, Chuck and I form a threesome. Optimists all, we each carry a shopping bag[1] to be filled with loot. We cover the blocks nearest home first. Mindful of parental displeasure, we refrain from munching and are home on time for supper.

On this night, supper is an inconvenience to be endured and gotten through. Back on the street, we widen the area of our beggerman activities. We trade information with passing friends about places to be sure to hit because "They're giving out really good stuff."

Mr. and Mrs. Johnson, who live a block away, own a mom and pop grocery store. They are famous for giving out nickel candy bars. We hit them early. Later, we trade parts of our costumes in a diabolical ruse to avoid being recognized – and we go back again! Although he gives us a long quizzical examination, Mr. Johnson drops another candy bar into each of our bags. Our greed is rewarded!

Around 8:30, most porch lights are lit, and we can no longer pretend that "It ain't really dark yet."

Reluctantly, we head home. We have exuberantly walked several miles today – half of it up and down stairs. Tomorrow we will drag our feet wearily if our mothers send us four blocks to Elmer's Grocery Store.

After we report to our folks on our night's adventure, a quick hot bath insures that we will sleep the minute our heads hit their pillows.

Tomorrow, the booty we've collected will be sorted into three piles: our really favorite stuff; the just okay stuff; and the stuff we'll try to trade off – but nobody else will want much of it either.

Months later, Bobby and I will remember the stuff that we hid in his garage. Some of it may still be edible...if we're really, *really* hungry.

---

[1] Every mother had an ample stash of shopping bags. Emblazoned with store advertising, they were liberally dispensed by retail chains such as Wieboldt's, Montgomery Ward's, Woolworth's – now all a memory.

You're Gonna Break Your Neck!

The neighborhood of my youth was inordinately quiet that day. People and animals alike were seeking shade and minimizing activity on an especially sultry summer afternoon. Suddenly the stillness was shattered by a terrified shriek as Wilbert came running frantically up our alley with his pants afire.

In a prairie at the end of our block, Wilbert had discovered a small trash pile burning unattended. The day's heat was no deterrent to a young boy's fascination with fire. Wilbert added a few leaves and twigs, then some larger branches. While kicking the fire into a more sizeable blaze, he discovered a flame creeping up his right pant leg.

He burned his hands trying to pat it out. When the flames persisted and spread to his left pant leg, Wilbert panicked. He did precisely what our school safety films told us not to do. He ran.

Across the alley, Mr. Fornell, a volunteer fireman, was cleaning his garage. He intercepted Wilbert, pulled him to the ground and rolled him in the dirt of our unpaved alley.

Wilbert sustained severe burns that left both legs scarred. After a long recovery, he walked with a slight limp on the right leg. But his luck was not all bad that day. Had he run in any other direction he might have been engulfed in flame before anyone came to his rescue.

In the fashion of kids, we deemed Wilbert a minor hero for surviving his near disaster. To the neighborhood's mothers, he became an example to hold up before any errant offspring caught playing with matches. Hands on hips, speaking with the voice of doom, they would demand: "Do you want to end up like your friend Wilbert?" (Dramatic pause.) "Or *worse!*"

Mothers were unanimously militant in their dire warnings to sons about their foolhardy activities. Daughters were not immune from this, I'm sure. But until the dating age, they generally received relatively milder and less frequent exhortations.

Slingshots, bean blowers and BB guns headed the long list of items that mothers universally viewed with alarm. "That thing will put your eye out!" was the interchangeable warning.

A BB or a missile shot from a slingshot also could make a considerable indentation in the back of your head or raise painful welts on bare arms or legs. Kids who owned bean blowers (or did you call them pea shooters?) were more likely to suffer self-inflicted agony from accidentally swallowing a mouthful of split peas or snuffing up a bean stuck playfully into a nostril. Yet the fear of every son's mother was that we would shoot out each other's eyes.[1]

Comedian George Carlin recalls his own and other mothers shouting at kids to stop this or that wild activity "before you break your neck." The possibility of a fractured skull, twisted ankle or broken collar bone never seemed to occur to maternal parents. Whatever you were jumping on, climbing up or leaping over, the cry of imminent danger inevitably was: "You're gonna break your neck!"

My mother forecast this fate regularly when she observed me climbing the cherry tree in our back yard. Unlike a sturdy oak or elm, it was not built for my make-believe Tarzan games. But Mom's prediction was faulty, nonetheless. What eventually broke was the branch on which I was hanging in my famous possum imitation.

I landed on the second softest –and best padded—portion of my anatomy. Only my dignity was damaged; although sitting on one of our hard wooden chairs at supper was a bit painful. Having already been chastised for the damage I'd done to the cherry tree, I wisely kept silent about my discomfort.

Our mothers undoubtedly experienced some bumps and bruises when they were children. That seemed only to reinforce the instinct to protect their young. Fathers took a more fatalistic view, accepting as preordained that no kid escapes childhood unscathed.

My gang's experience supports this view. Our list of injuries was legion. Most resulted from mishaps that our parents could not have anticipated.

Chuck's brother, Kenny, prevailed upon their father to let him have a "safe" bow and arrow set. The arrowheads' rubber suction cups were designed to stick on a tin bull's-eye target. The manufacturer assured hesitant parents that this made the toy harmless.

---

[1] In the movie "A Christmas Story" (based upon author Jean Shepherd's recollections of his Indiana boyhood), one frustrated but determined young male campaigns relentlessly to acquire a genuine Red Ryder 200-shot Carbine Action Air Rifle, in spite of his fearful mother's objections. This classic comedy appears somewhere on TV every holiday season. If you've never seen it, make it a "must" on your viewing schedule.

A week later, one of the "harmless" arrows hit Chuck in the mouth and knocked out a front tooth.

Our dog, Dinah, gave birth to puppies in her box under the kitchen sink. Their eyes were barely open and Dinah was still feeling protective when my brother, Dickie, reached in to pet one. Reacting instinctively, Dinah took a neat bite out of Dickie's hand.

Did I mention that girls weren't immune?

Wayne's older sister, Shirley, had just recently endured the painful ordeal of being fitted with braces on her teeth. The gang organized a peggy-move-up game in our street. Shirley was pitching to me. Our battered 16-inch softball usually could have beaned someone and not even dazed them. But just this once I really connected.

It was a line drive to the pitcher, who did not get her hands up fast enough. It caught her smack in the mouth, making a mess of her orthodontia. Shirl's immediate pain was nothing compared to the prospect of having those braces redone.

I felt pretty terrible myself. More than once I asked God, "Why, oh why, couldn't I have just hit a pop up to center like I do almost every other time?"

Ball games fostered lots of injuries. Jimmy was "on deck" when someone got a hit and tossed the bat too hard. Jimmy's left leg stopped it, and he limped for three or four days afterward.

Georgie was pitching a solid new 12-inch softball when a line drive caught him in the worst possible area. He was sidelined for two innings. When he could stand up straight again, he finished the game as plate umpire.

Once I slid into third base on our makeshift diamond at the vacant corner lot. A chunk of broken glass jabbed into the soft flesh of my palm. I thought I would bleed to death as I rushed home with the hand clamped under my armpit.

The gash probably deserved a few stitches, but emergency rooms were only in hospitals then, and we did not own a car. Dad poured alcohol over it to prevent infection. (That dang stuff hurt worse than the cut.) Mom fashioned a bandage with a huge mound of gauze padding.

Eventually, the bleeding subsided. A small scar below my thumb still reminds me of that incident.

Just as in professional sports, the game stopped only briefly for such mishaps. Something serious like a broken limb might have caused us to disperse. Otherwise, there was a brief time-out while those closest to the injured player made sure that he or she was okay. Then the game continued. As I ran off the field that day, I heard a teammate volunteer to take my place on third base.

When we graduated to league ball, several kids got beaned by wild pitches. David had his glasses broken during one of his turns at bat. In that instance, he *was* lucky not to have had his eye put out.

The most ordinary activities sometimes went awry. One day Bobby gave Tommy a ride on the handlebars of his bike.

Yeah, I know. Today, kids have bicycle safety classes, and two on a bike is a no-no.

Anyway, Tommy got careless and his right heel dangled into the spokes. Both riders went sprawling. When they dusted themselves off and examined the damage, several spokes of Bobby's front wheel were bent. The back of Tommy's shoe was split open. A large chunk of skin hung through what was left of the heel of his stocking.

Someone once observed that occasional broken bones are part of the standard currency in the economy of childhood. As a kid, I would not have understood that. As a parent, I agree, but under protest. None of the injuries I sustained in my own youth was as painful as the sight of one of my children running home bleeding and crying.

As for broken bones, I cashed in on that childhood currency at the Lake Michigan beach. We were playing a roughhouse game that the lifeguard would have broken up if he had seen us. One kid lies on his back and pulls his legs up over his chest. A buddy sits on his feet, and the first kid catapults him through the air. Theoretically, the sand provides a soft landing. It was great fun until, on one of my turns to be tossed, I landed with my left arm twisted under me. It snapped in two places.

That time, I did end up at the hospital. Unfortunately, the break was not set well. A week later the doctors X-rayed it and decided that they would have to rebreak and reset it!

What hurt most, though, was the fact that this happened right at the start of summer. Thus, it didn't get me out of any school work, and it put an awful crimp in my vacation activities.

Then there was my classmate, Harold. Harold broke his right arm in March. Poor Harold. The whole class ooohed and aaahed over him, signed his cast and did him favors. Because he was a "rightie," Mrs. Greig made concessions for him in class and on written homework assignments.

Some kids got all the lucky breaks.

A Treasure House Of Songs

Thursday afternoon at James Giles Elementary School

Miss Fingerhut is concluding our Geography lesson and having us clear our desks as Mrs. Brockway sweeps into the classroom with her armload of musical materials. After a brief exchange of pleasantries between the two teachers, our class is turned over to Mrs. Brockway. Now begins one of my favorite periods of the school week: Music Appreciation.

Our weekly music classes took many forms. Sometimes, we performed on instruments such as rhythm sticks, tambourines or black plastic flutes (later up-graded to the more glorified name "recorder").

We might listen to a recording of "Peter and the Wolf" or some other children's classic, with enlightening background information supplied by Mrs. Brockway. Several times a year we rehearsed songs for a schoolwide program to be presented for parents. Today, we will spend an undemanding hour singing songs from *The Golden Book of Favorite Songs*.

The Golden Book was a digest-sized compilation of perhaps 150 pieces of music. As its name implies, the cover was a golden yellow, embellished with borders of fancy scrollwork. Published by Hall & McCreary Company in Chicago, its contents mostly (or perhaps all) were in the public domain. Thus, it could be published very inexpensively, and was used in many schools.

Indeed, little advertisements appeared as footnotes throughout the book: "If bought separately in sheet form, these songs would cost you 10 to 50 cents each. You get all of them for but a few cents. Why not tell others about this big value."

The Golden Book ran the gamut of vocal music, from religious tunes to fun songs, folk music, patriotic and period pieces. A section up front, for instance, offered "Dixie" and "Battle Hymn of the Republic" back-to-back, followed by "John Brown's Body," "Tramp, Tramp, Tramp (the boys are marching)," "Keep the Home Fires Burning" and other Civil War songs.

We enjoyed the lively tempo of "Dixie," little caring (or knowing) that it was a Confederate marching song. "Battle Hymn" was stirring, but what did we understand of "tramping out the vintage where the grapes of wrath are stored"? (Years later, still without comprehending, we made a vague connection when we saw Henry Fonda starring in the film based upon John Steinbeck's famous novel.) On the other hand, we sang "When Johnny Comes Marching Home" with gusto, for it had been revived as a chin-up propaganda song for folks on the home front during World War II.

Half a dozen Stephen Foster songs followed. "Old Black Joe," "My Old Kentucky Home" and "Old Folks at Home" were among our favorites. Too young to analyze, we did not realize how much of Foster's music was a lament for home, family and friends of a life left behind – even the hard life of a slave.

"Darling Nelly Gray" and "Carry Me Back to Old Virginny," by other composers, were in the same vein. Mrs. Brockway didn't attempt to explain the inherent sadness of these lyrics. For now, it was enough that we be exposed to these traditional favorites and become familiar with their wistful, lilting melodies. Later, when we had matured some, we would appreciate the poignancy of Robert Burns' "Flow Gently, Sweet Afton," and comprehend the mournful meaning of such lines as "My Mary's asleep by thy murmuring stream."

"Auld Lang Syne" and "Comin' Thro' the Rye" were Burns pieces (actually his poems set to music by others) more to our liking – even though the former's lyrics[1] were equally mystifying. They led into a section of "old airs" from various countries: "Wearing of the Green" and "Believe Me If All Those Endearing Young Charms" (Irish); "Drink To Me Only With Thine Eyes" (English); "Juanita" (Spanish); "Santa Lucia" (Neapolitan) and others.

There were several dozen just-for-fun songs, like the rounds "Are You Sleeping? (Frere Jacques)," "Lovely Evening" and "Row, Row, Row Your Boat." For "Rueben and Rachel," Mrs. Brockway would have boys and girls sing alternate verses. At our prepubescent ages, we all got a kick out of the idea of "what a grand world this would be, if the men were all transported far beyond the Northern Sea."

---

[1] Long into my adult years, I finally came across what was described as an "English translation" of the complete text of Burns' poem. Thanks to his heavy use of what might be termed Scottish slang, large portions still would have been incomprehensible without lengthy explanations. The spirit of the song certainly makes it appropriate as a New Years classic; but my guess is that not one person in a hundred would understand what he or she was singing if it ever progressed beyond the familiar first verse.

In "Robin and Chicken," the two birds of the title taunted each other about their respective talents. In conclusion, "each thought the other knew nothing at all," an object lesson that even we were not too young to grasp. Years later, my first-grade daughter received a record album of children's songs. A lump formed in my throat one evening when I overheard her singing this tune along with Burl Ives.

"A Capital Ship" was one of my favorites. A rollicking old English tune in the Gilbert and Sullivan manner, it praised the captain and crew of the Walloping Window Blind, who were so wacky as to be impervious to the dangers of their seafaring life. The gunner, for instance, "fired salutes with the captain's boots in the teeth of the booming gale." As for the captain, we were left to judge for ourselves whether his response to the fiercest storms at sea was one of bravery or something else. For "it often appeared, when the gale had cleared, that he'd been in his bunk below."

In the miscellaneous category were such songs as "Good Night, Ladies," "Little Brown Church in the Vale" (with its chant in the chorus of "Come, come, come, come, come to the church in the wildwood"), "The Old Oaken Bucket," "When You and I Were Young, Maggie" and Brahms' "Cradle Song." Negro spirituals were represented by "Go Down, Moses" and "Swing Low, Sweet Chariot." And regardless of more contemporary entries, I will always consider our state song to be the one that begins "By thy rivers gently flowing, Illinois, Illinois."

Half a dozen pages were devoted to ecumenical religious favorites, followed by a mix of religious and secular songs for Christmas. "Jolly Old Saint Nicholas," and "Jingle Bells" got many hearty renderings by our class every December. When we sang "Up on the housetop, click, click, click," Mrs. Brockway had us snap our fingers in time to the clicks, and we obliged with glee.

As she directed us from the piano bench, Mrs. Brockway apparently felt a calling to have us learn a new song about once a month. She fulfilled her mission well.

During the Christmas holidays last year, we entertained friends and someone dug up our tattered copy of *The Golden Book*. My wife was recruited to play the piano, and a song fest ensued. I found myself transported back forty years to Room 5 at James Giles School. To my great delight, I discovered that I still remembered about two thirds of the tunes selected and immensely enjoyed singing them again. Mrs. Brockway would have been proud of our little impromptu singing group.

The Golden Book of Favorite Songs apparently has gone the way of the "Dick and Jane" readers. At least, I have been unable to locate copies at book stores or the library.

Our copy is missing the cover and eight pages, front and back. Now that I realize what a treasure it is, I plan to create a new cover of construction paper (golden yellow, of course). In bold block letters, I'll print the title, and use my school compass to draw some scrollwork around the borders. To protect it from being torn or soiled, I'll put on a second cover of brown wrapping paper. In the upper right hand corner, I'll hand print: "Danny McGuire, Room 5." Then I'll seal it in clear plastic and stash it in our safety deposit box along with my old comic books.

2 Wheels Are Better Than 3
(A Recycled Memory)

Is there anyone in the AARP age bracket who does not have fond memories of his or her first 2-wheeler? What a driver's license was to the older teenagers, that first bicycle was to the preteens and young adolescents of my generation.

THE NEW
MONARK
Super Deluxe
...A GREAT BIKE!

America's most beautiful bicycle! Stronger ... safer ... easier riding! Super streamlined air-flow design ... new "Air-Wing" head shield ... new "Kronegard" rear bumper ... new sponge rubber padded saddle with weather-resistant plastic-type cover ... new heavy-duty luggage carrier with chrome plated automobile-style grille ... new rust-proof and chip resistant finish ... and dozens of other exciting new features. Boy's and girl's models. Regular and junior sizes. For sale by better stores everywhere.

For anyone who grew up in that era, the manufacturers' names have about them an almost mystical quality. *Elgin. Monark. Hawthorn. J. C. Higgins.* And, for the lucky kid with well-to-do parents or a rich uncle, the ultimate in non-motorized transportation: *Schwinn.*

There came a time when we roller skated only occasionally and had outgrown wagons, scooters, even the largest of tricycles. Though we yearned for the freedom and mobility of bicycle ownership, parents often responded to our pleas by saying, "Umm, maybe next year, when your legs are longer." Unless an older sibling had a bike you could practice on, you walked everywhere and impatiently cursed your short legs throughout that limbo period.

Wayne's older sister, Shirley, was the first on our block to move up to a 2-wheeler. Her popularity immediately increased, as every kid in our gang begged for rides – the guys just as eagerly as the gals. (Boys with short legs were not too proud to get in some practice on a girl's bike, which did not have the troublesome upper support bar in its frame.)

Shirl's father recognized a potential problem and used some homespun psychology to head it off. He began running "time trials" every evening, giving each of us a turn to go around the block while he clocked us with a pocket watch. Shirley cringed nervously as she watched us gangly boys race recklessly around corners on her beautiful (and, as yet, unscratched) new bike. But she endured it patiently and took her turn at being clocked, too. Eventually, our interest lagged, the races ended and Shirley breathed a sigh of relief as she repossessed her bicycle. Meanwhile, the rest of us resumed the seemingly interminable wait for bikes of our own.

My first 2-wheeler was a Christmas present when I was eleven. For months I had importuned my parents. I really *needed* a bike; not just for frivolous pleasure riding, but for business purposes – I planned to get a paper route. The folks took me seriously, I guess. The bike I found next to our tree was second-hand, but it was a 28-inch model with an oversized front basket.

Never before had Spring been so slow to arrive and melt the ice and snow. At last, I was able to bring my new treasure outside. Riding it was another matter. Its size offered a real challenge.

Even with the blocks that my father attached to the pedals, I could barely reach them in the down position while seated on the saddle. Because I had to stretch so far that last inch going down, I took to reaching for the opposite pedal with my toe, pulling it up into position to be pedaled downward. Sometimes I misjudged, and when I stepped down the pedal turned backward – which applied the brake.

At best, this method made for leisurely travel. To get any speed, I had to forget about sitting and straddle the top bar, actually standing on first one pedal, then the other, to achieve maximum thrust.

Just getting started required some ingenuity. I wasn't tall enough to straddle the bar and push off from a standing position. My initial technique was to lean the bike against a fence or building, with one pedal at 12 o'clock high. After gingerly climbing aboard, I pushed off and started up with a mighty stomp on the raised pedal.

Later, I copied the style of a cowboy mounting his horse. With my foot on the left pedal (at about 10 o'clock), I gave the bike a push

Dan McGuire

and leaped astride in one motion. The bike would take off and stay upright just long enough for my right leg to clear the saddle and my right foot to find the other pedal…usually.

My bike's handlebars were the wing type, ver-ry wi-ide, with rubber grips that had finger indentations. They reminded me of motorcycle handles and I was proud of them. But they presented their own hazard – like bumping handles with pals who rode too close beside me. After a few spills, most of my buddies took to riding behind me or in front.

The entrance to the gangway between our house and Wayne's was enclosed with a small section of fence and a gate. With the gate swung wide, I had about an inch of clearance for the tip of each handle. Before I mastered that kind of precision steering, I regularly skinned one or more knuckles weekly. Sometimes I'd remember to grip the handlebars a little farther in, but after a few safe passages I'd get careless again, and pay for it.

My bike and I took so many spills that the pedal arms became bent inward. One clanked against the chain guard on every rotation. The other rubbed against the rear frame and actually began wearing a slot into it. I bent the arms outward with a crowbar numerous times, but it was a losing battle.

Eventually, the S-shaped pedal crank arm assembly had to be replaced. That meant a trip to Alley's Hardware and Bike Repair, the only shop within miles that worked on bicycles. It also meant a 12-block walk home and a week without a bike.

Fortunately, I was growing and the bike wasn't. By Fall, when I got my paper route, my feet met the pedals even when I sat on the saddle. Steering with one hand while tossing rolled newspapers onto porches probably improved my skill at handling the over-sized bike. Many of my peers got their early practice on a girl's bike. Others had older brothers or pals who let them ride their bikes and ran beside them holding on. We did not ask fathers to do this. After all, most of us were 10 or 11 years old when we started riding. It would have been humiliating to have Dad hold us up. Rather, we would prefer to fall a dozen times and personalize our first bikes with distinctive dents and scratches.

124

With his father at the wheel, Alan McGuire gets his first ever ride on a 2-wheeler.

In our hands, bikes took much abuse. The "balloon tire" type could take it. Chuck's first 2-wheeler was the "skinny tire" style. I don't know why he asked for that, since skinny tires usually were chosen only by serious cross-country riders. Maybe he liked the little extra speed he could get when racing a balloon tire bike.

One day, Chuck and I were racing along Cullum Avenue, a neighborhood side street generally free of auto traffic. He was in the street. I was pedaling parallel to him on the cinder path that served as a pedestrian walkway. Chuck was half a length ahead of me when he shouted, "I'm going to cut you off at the alley."

"You'd better not," I called back. "I'm not going to stop."

Well, that was practically a double-dog dare. So, of course, Chuck had to follow through. I really did try to stop as his bike loomed in front of me, but cinders provide little traction. The collision sent both of us sprawling. As we picked ourselves up, we first compared cinder burns on hands, elbows and knees. Then we checked Chuck's front wheel. It had eight spokes knocked out or loose. The next day, we balanced the wheel in my basket, Chuck sat on the crossbar and I rode him up to Alley's.

I'm not sure how Chuck explained that accident to his folks. But a week later I was wandering down our alley and overheard part of an over-the-fence conversation between his mother and a neighbor lady.

125

Riding 2-on-a-bike through muddy creek water was not what our parents had in mind when they gave us our bikes. But the combination of youthful exuberance and a 2-wheeler brought out the daredevil instincts in even the best behaved kids. (Library of Congress photo)

It was something about "Chuck's beautiful new bicycle" and "that wild McGuire boy."

One ungodly hot summer day Chuck's bike was parked in his yard and both tires simply exploded. That week, Wayne and I were feuding with Chuck over one of our periodic boyish disagreements. He suggested to his father that we might have planted firecrackers under the tires. Mr. Schaden considered the idea, but a few pointed questions led to an admission by Chuck that he had filled his tires at Sell's Service Station that morning. Although the recommended air pressure for his tires was 35 PSI, Chuck had filled them to 60 pounds because it resulted in a much smoother ride. Following this revelation, Chuck received a short physics lecture on the effects of air under pressure and heated by the sun.

While such blow-outs were rare, flat tires were a common occurrence. The tubeless puncture-proof tire was a couple of generations ahead on the bike trail. Almost any sharp object was capable of poking a hole through both tire and innertube as your wheel rolled over it.

Bike riding was an all-inclusive activity that could break down gender barriers. Anyone with a 2-wheeler could join in, even a big sister. Of course, if she couldn't keep up with the guys... Well, too bad. (Library of Congress photo)

All bikers were equipped with a standard tire repair kit. The container was shaped like a toilet tissue roll and made of similar paperboard, but sturdier and a tad larger. The bottom and the screw-on cap were metal. The cap also doubled as a small grater. Inside, the kit contained rubber patching material, a squeeze tube of glue and a piece of chalk. There is nothing quite like the mingled aromas of rubber, chalk and glue that greeted your nostrils when you opened the repair kit.

To repair a flat tire, you first had to locate the hole in the innertube. Large holes could be found by pumping up the tire and running a hand over it or just listening for the hiss of escaping air. Small holes sometimes required submerging the tube in your mother's basement wash tub and watching for bubbles. (Emergency field repairs sometimes were accomplished with spit.)

127

Once the puncture was chalk-marked, the rest was relatively easy. Roughen the area with the grater for a good bond. Apply a thin layer of glue. Press on a patch about an inch square. Let dry. Remount tire, tube and wheel. Reinflate tire.

The hazards to bikes—and their riders—were numerous. Pant legs got caught in chains – even with chain guards, rolled up pants or rubber bands around cuffs. Chains slipped off sprockets. Chain links broke. Kick stands loosened and bikes fell over. Or the bolt fell off and the clamp was lost, making the stand useless. Handlebars became loose – not good for steering. Pedals became bent, stopped turning or broke off. Fenders became bent and rubbed on tires.

The clamp that secured my coaster brake assembly to the rear frame fell off. When I pedaled backward to apply the brake, nothing happened. I resecured it with picture wire many times, but whenever I attempted an urgent stop the wire would snap. This resulted in several bumps and bruises and many near collisions.

We accepted such minor inconveniences as the price of owning a 2-wheeler. As our riding skills improved, we suffered fewer accidental spills. To compensate, we increased our daredevil antics. Remember the old kids' gag?

"Look, Ma, no hands.

"Look, Ma, no feet.

"Look, Ma, no teeth!"

Most of us survived to possess a second bike. It was more likely to be purchased new. Usually we had more of a hand in selecting it, and we adorned it with a variety of widely sold accessories: speedometer, rear-view mirror(s), headlight, taillight, foxtail(s), saddlebags, horn, bell, etc.

Yet, however much it may have paled by comparison, we always retained a special appreciation for our first 2-wheeler.

Afterthought: In 1895, on the near west side of Chicago, Ignaz Schwinn and Adolph Arnold founded Arnold-Schwinn & Co., which later became the Schwinn Bicycle Company. In 1936, U.S. bicycle production exceeded the million mark and Schwinn was a major producer. By the 1950s, one in every four U.S. bikes was built by Schwinn.

Long considered the Cadillac of the bicycle industry, the company encountered trouble from both within and without in the 1980s. Slow to pick up on new trends such as mountain bikes and exercycles, Schwinn saw many new, cheaper brands, often foreign-made, move into these areas and the basic bike market. Meanwhile, Schwinn struggled with an excess debt problem.

After closing several plants and shifting much of its remaining manufacturing overseas, Schwinn filed for protection under Chapter 11 on October 8, 1992. The company changed hands several times during the 1990s, but managed a come-back along the way. It posted a profit in 2000. In July, 2001, the company announced it would be bought by Huffy Corporation for $60 million. Although less predominant in the bicycle market, the Schwinn brand would continue to be manufactured.

Thus, in spite of some rough roads, an American icon rolled proudly into its third century,

Dan McGuire

Yesterday's Paperboys: We Delivered!

For five dollars, Ken "sold" me his paper route. On the day he resigned, he introduced me to the news agency manager. There were always more applicants than routes, and kids recommended by faithful carriers generally were given preference.

The agency manager was busy with other boys turning in their collections and being brusquely informed of customers' complaints. My "interview" was conducted in a 2-car garage, half of which had been converted into an office of sorts. Standing behind a makeshift counter, the manager received the paperboys' weekly collections, checked the amounts against their route books and handed back the portion that constituted their earnings. In spurts between one carrier and the next, he quizzed me through teeth clenched on a dead cigar.

"Got a bike, kid?"

"Think ya can get up at six?"

"Can ya deliver on Sundays?"

In spite of Ken's earlier assurances, my palms were wet and my knees were shaky. Still, in my best Gary Cooper imitation, I answered with a stoic "Yep!" to all his questions. Finally, with a gruff "Hmph!" as preface, he asked, "Okay, when can ya start?"

I started the day after Thanksgiving, a holiday. That gave me three days to get acquainted with the route without having to worry about getting to school on time. The previous Saturday, I had ridden with Ken and learned to roll the papers.

My route covered twelve blocks on each of three north/south streets. It required a lot of doubling back so as to avoid being twelve blocks from home after delivering the last newspaper. I had about 120 customers. That was too many papers to carry in even the oversize basket mounted over my bike's front wheel. At the far end of the route, about half my papers were dropped off in a grocery store doorway. I stopped there to roll them and stuff them into the basket before starting back in the general direction of home. The store was never open at the hour that I arrived, but the recessed area gave some shelter from bad weather.

Not all paperboys had baskets on their bikes. A bag over the shoulder would suffice if there were few customers on the route. Otherwise, though, it could require several trips home to refill the bag. Note the accessories on this lucky kid's bike: siren style horn, headlamp, speedometer and (probably) a taillight on rear fender. (Retrofile.com)

Each customer's name and address were printed on a 3-by-6-inch card, strategically sequenced on a large snap ring. The ring slipped over your bike's handlebar. As you tossed a paper onto the porch at 3421 Oriole Avenue, you flipped the card to see who was next. The cards indicated who were the 6-day, 7-day and Sunday-only subscribers. There was also room on the card for the agency boss to note such reminders as: "Deliver to back porch," or "Put paper inside door."

I conscientiously tried to accommodate such requests, and in all cases I strived to get the paper up onto the porch. If I didn't at least hit the steps, I would return and toss it up. In rain and snow, I made a special effort to find dry spots. Protective plastic wrappers were not yet in use.

On the other hand, after memorizing the route, I grew lax at times about using the flip cards, and sometimes missed a stop as a result. (I had a good memory, but it was short.) Arriving home with one paper left, I had no way of knowing where it belonged—until I got a terse note from the boss, tucked into the papers that were dropped off for me the next morning. Fortunately, most customers didn't make a big fuss over one missed newspaper, and I would be extra careful not to miss them again.

Two weeks before Christmas, each carrier was given a supply of calendars for the people on his route. We were told to deliver them personally, and separately from our paper deliveries. I naively accepted the explanation that the calendars were an expression of our gratitude to subscribers.

It quickly became evident to me that this actually was a ploy to solicit seasonal gratuities. Almost every customer returned my wishes of happy holidays and responded with a tip. The amounts mostly ranged from fifty cents to a dollar. With 120 customers, I made a handsome haul. A couple of ladies knew the routine, anticipated my visit and presented me with boxes of homemade cookies.

Actually, all my customers were kind to their paperboy. Some tipped me frequently for little extra services, or just for dependable service. I broke three or four windows during my career. All the victims accepted my embarrassed apologies with no demand for reparations.

One dear grandmotherly lady made cookies for me frequently. Sometimes she was up to greet me when I delivered the paper and would invite me in for a cup of hot chocolate. I always declined with thanks because I had half the route yet to deliver. Years later, it occurred to me that she may have been a lonely widow seeking a little company, and I regretted not having taken the time to share a cup of kindness with her.

I survived almost two years of fair and foul weather as a paperboy. Generally, I could get up at 6a.m. and be done about 8:30—time enough to rest awhile before school started at 9 o'clock. Slow going in Winter made it necessary to arise at 5a.m. There were some tension-filled mornings when bad weather made the boss late dropping off my papers. Plenty of spills on icy sidewalks took a toll on my bike and occasionally dumped me into a snowbank.

Commencing high school forced my retirement from the news carrier business. We started at 8:15 and had a long bus ride to get there. The week before Labor Day, I sold my route to a younger pal for ten dollars, thus making a profit even as I handed over my route cards.

In our suburban area, I still see kids delivering newspapers. But they toss them from the back of station wagons or minivans driven by a parent. Maybe that's the only way to cover the more spread-out routes. It probably doesn't build much character, but I suppose it avoids a lot of colds, spills and saddle sores.

Having A Field Day At James Giles School

Toward the end of each Winter in the years when I attended James Giles Elementary School, our principal, John V. Leigh, kept a watchful eye on the landscape outside our classrooms. As Spring's first warm rays of sunshine began melting the last resistance of caked snow mounds, his thoughts turned to planning the annual Giles Field Day.

Field Day was one of many special occasions organized by Mr. Leigh in which students would demonstrate various talents for parents and neighbors. In this case, the accent would be on physical and athletic skills.

Preparations began in the school's basement assembly hall, where indoor gym classes were held. Individual and combined groups began practicing coordinated calisthenics, tumbling and marching together. The school band started rehearsing some favorite march tunes and learning a few new ones.

As the weather improved, we went through our paces in the huge field, encompassing almost two square blocks behind our school. We used regular gym periods and frequently stretched these to an hour as the practice progressed. Field Day was an all-day affair, a big event in our school calendar, and Mr. Leigh reminded us that we would all want to be at our best when we performed for family and friends.

Mr. Leigh scheduled Field Days for late May, when the weather usually could be counted on to be warm but not sweltering. We had a couple of cool, breezy Field Days, but during my eight years at Giles, he had a perfect record of never being rained out. (I've never been quite sure whether to believe Mr. Leigh's claim that he always picked the date by consulting the *Farmers' Almanac*.)

Our school did not have uniforms, and white gym suits were not yet in universal use. To achieve an appearance of uniformity, girls and boys dressed in dark skirts and pants with white blouses or shirts. Boys were permitted to wear white teeshirts in lieu of dress shirts and, if it proved to be a hot day, most chose this option.

About 9:30 in the morning, the band led us, marching, out of the building. Stretched out several rows deep in a starting formation, we faced the rear of our school from the place where a gravel play area ended and the grassy open field began. On either side, space was marked off for visitors, many of whom came early to reserve front row positions and establish themselves on blankets or folding chairs.

Principal John V. Leigh oversees the 1948 "Field Day" exercises at James Giles Elementary School. Note wires strung across basketball net to hook up the school's vintage public address system. (photo courtesy June O. Orten)

A vintage public address system was stretched from the basement via a long extension cord. Its two large speakers, each about two feet square and encased in wooden housings, were mounted on stands at far left and right. A bulky microphone sat atop a shiny metal post with a heavy base. Over this somewhat squeaky sound system, Mr. Leigh welcomed all our visitors and called upon everyone to stand at attention to join in the Pledge of Allegiance and singing our National Anthem.

We turned slightly to face Old Glory waving atop our school flagpole, and placed our hands over our hearts for the Pledge. The audience included a few policemen, firemen and servicemen, who gave the military salute. Then, still at attention, with the band leading us, we joined in a spirited rendering of the National Anthem, typical of the unreserved patriotism that was shared by all in the 1940s.

Mr. Leigh, his voice occasionally augmented by the public address system's trills and squeals, gave a few introductory remarks, informing our audience of what we had in store for them. Then the band struck up a Sousa tune and we marched with precision to our individual class sites on the field. Rather than proceed directly, we demonstrated our marching skill with a little mass drill that wove us in and through each other's lines en route to our assigned areas.

Each class formed itself on several rows of white marker lines provided the day before by Parent-Teacher Association volunteers. Shorter pupils were positioned in front and taller ones in back so that families and friends could identify everyone. Half the school turned north and the other half south, facing the spectators.

With Mr. Leigh counting cadence over the P.A. system, we demonstrated about a dozen gymnastic exercises. To get our blood flowing in the morning coolness, we did "jumping jacks." Standing with hands at our sides, on the count of "*One*," we leaped up, slapped our hands together over our heads and came back down with feet wide apart. On the count of "*Two*," we leaped up again, swung our arms back down and brought our feet back together.

In the "trunk twister," we stood with feet apart and arms outstretched at shoulder level. Alternately, we twisted at the waist as far as we could go, first left and then right. From above, we must have looked like one of those "cast of thousands" dance scenes from a Busby Berkley movie.

Families and neighbors gather for "Field Day" at James Giles Elementary School. On next street (Ottawa Avenue), author's family lived in white house, third from corner. Dark house next to it was pal Wayne Cleghorn's home. On other side, partially hidden by tree, is long-time buddy Chuck Schaden's home. At far end of block, facing highway, is Norwood Park Township Volunteer Fire Department. Note open areas north of school that were still being farmed in mid-1940s. (photo courtesy Vera Fulhorst)

There were deep knee bends, sit-ups, push-ups, etc. During practices, we may have moaned and eased up some at times, but for our attentive audience we did everything with great enthusiasm. (Wouldn't it be great today to be able to bend down and touch our toes twenty times – and not have to be helped into an easy chair by our grandchildren?)

After our calisthenics exhibition, we were allowed to sit in place and rest as the band played a couple of numbers. Then there was a sort of informal intermission as delegated upperclassmen brought out gym mats and spread them near the edge of the field. Teachers gave their classes leave to go in small groups to the washroom.

When the mats were ready, Mr. Leigh announced that we now would have an exhibition of tumbling. Each class would participate, beginning with the lower grades. Students would perform their own choice of stunts, including some that involved two or more tumblers at once.

Classes waiting their turns could relax and watch, talking quietly among themselves. We gave polite applause to all the performers and a big hand to anyone who did anything the least bit difficult, such as a series of cartwheels or walking on hands. Our little brothers and sisters received big "Hurrays!" even for a simple somersault.

There were a few kids who showed real talent. Some of the upper class girls formed a human pyramid. Some boys and some girls (no co-ed stunts allowed in those days) gave each other rides on shoulders.

The finale was two eighth grade boys, one standing (a bit shakily, it's true) on the other's shoulders. After walking the length of the mats, they fell forward and did synchronized somersaults. This earned them whistles and cheers with the applause, and some friendly jibes from male classmates.

Observers from the P.T.A. took notes and turned in a list to Mr. Leigh. At the end of the performance, he gave out prize ribbons to the best tumblers in each class. There were first, second and third place ribbons for girls and boys in each class. Naturally, this called for more applause and cheers from the audience and classmates.

The band struck up again and our classes marched to positions a little farther back on the field. This made room for the competitive events that would fill the remainder of the day. These started off with relatively unheated group contests. The first grade class divided into two lines and played a game of keep-it-up with a volleyball. There was a tug-of-war between second grade girls, then another among the boys. Each grade level had two runnings of the 100-yard dash, again one for girls and one for boys.

The races would bring us close to noon, when we took a break for lunch. Students were free to join families and friends on the sidelines or mingle with classmates.

Many relatives came with picnic baskets. For those who didn't, there were tables set up alongside the school and the P.T.A. ladies sold sandwiches, hamburgers, hot dogs, French fries, chips, cookies, hot and cold drinks. Items that had to be cooked or kept cold were passed up by co-workers through the window of the teachers' lunch room in the basement. The food sales added a festive touch to Field Day and brought the P.T.A. some modest revenue that eventually would benefit our school.

After lunch, the competitive events continued throughout the afternoon, with an occasional rousing tune from the band while equipment was moved about. The fourth and fifth grades had a soccer game. There were standing and running broad jumps for all grade levels. Then we started over with the first graders and had high jumps. By the time our champion eighth graders had their turn, the pole was set up at what, to me, seemed an amazing height.

In all the contests, there were ribbons galore being presented. With honorable mention and runner-up awards, Mr. Leigh's strategy seemed to be that *everyone* would earn a ribbon for something before the day was over.

The final event of the day was a volleyball game between the seventh and eighth grades. Although everyone may have been tiring by then, it was a spirited match. The seventh grade was determined to beat their upper classmates, while the eighth grade was equally motivated to defend its honor by not letting these young upstarts defeat them.

Whatever the outcome, Mr. Leigh had warm praise for both sides. In his wrap-up of the day, he would observe that we again had been blessed with a sunny day and that his unadorned bald head no doubt would be sunburned tomorrow. He thanked all the parents, village officials, P.T.A. people, relatives and friends whose presence had made this an extra special occasion for all of us.

Then he congratulated "all of you wonderful girls and boys for your long hours of practice and the good sportsmanship and school spirit you've demonstrated for us all here today." However pooped we may have been at day's end, we left the field with our chests puffed up by our principal's high praise.

Long before any President's Council conducted in-depth studies of the matter, Mr. Leigh understood the importance of physical fitness to a child's overall development. He and his staff of dedicated teachers strived for a balanced curriculum that encouraged young people to adopt good physical health habits as well as educating and improving their minds.

I don't know if Giles School continues to hold a Field Day. With so many organized sports in schools today, perhaps it has given way to various individual events since Mr. Leigh retired.

Even the expression "having a field day" is not as commonly used as it once was. Young people hearing it these days probably think in terms of some outing such as a trip to the zoo or Chicago's Art Institute or Field Museum.

For me and many other Giles School alumni, it will forever evoke warm memories of being surrounded by hundreds of schoolmates, parents and neighbors, and hearing Mr. Leigh declare at the end of the day: "This has probably been our best Field Day ever!" He said it every year. But, you know, he was never wrong.

Kiddie Park

In the first half of the 20th Century, the term "theme park" was unknown. In Chicago, Riverview Amusement Park (where they invited you to "Laugh your troubles away!") was the Six Flags or Great America of its day. Less populous areas often had smaller amusement parks, usually geared mostly to children.

Our unincorporated semi-rural community was privileged to enjoy its very own modest-sized amusement park. Its attractions were almost exclusively kid-size, and it was called, aptly enough, Kiddie Park.

It occupied a square block on the eastern boundary of town, along State Route 42A (Harlem Avenue). A small buffer area of undeveloped grassy field separated the park's west side from our first residential street. About a block south was Irving Park Road, the main link to our big neighbor, Chicago. Just beyond Kiddie Park's northern perimeter, the farmlands began.

Buses on the Harlem route brought a few visitors from outside the area. There was token parking along the shoulder for families who came by car. But most of Kiddie Park's patrons were local folk who lived within a dozen blocks. Ankle Express was the predominant mode of transportation. Most families would walk over together. Kids coming with friends sometimes rode bikes, but usually walked; it prolonged the anticipation of the day's adventure.

Visitors could enter from any direction. There was no gate, since no admission was charged. Stumps of telephone poles were planted just beyond the shoulder of Harlem Avenue. They prevented cars from driving into the park proper and slowed the arrival of reckless bike riders. Over the main entry was a decorative archway. Large block letters, in a halfmoon shape, spelled out: "KIDDIE PARK."

In our pre-teen years, Wayne, Bobby, Chuck and I visited Kiddie Park numerous times each summer. A typical scenario would find Wayne and me sitting in the shade with no immediate plan for our afternoon's entertainment.

Wayne picked up a leaf and absently split it down its center stem. "You wanna go to Kiddie Park?" he asked me.

"Ain't got enough money," I replied. "I spent most of my allowance at the show."

Wayne nodded. "Me too. Think you can beg some off your mom?"

I shrugged. "Dunno. But I'll try. How 'bout you?"

Wayne grinned and jumped up, saying, "I'll take a whack."

We separated. As I entered our house, I paused to ascertain that my mother wasn't too deeply absorbed in something where she would not appreciate being interrupted. Then I blurted out, "Mom, can I have fifty cents to go to Kiddie Park with Wayne?"

My mother appraised me with raised eyebrows. "Fifty cents?" she said. It was a hefty sum for a boy in short pants. "What happened to your allowance?"

"I spent most of it," I admitted with downcast eyes. "I've only got a quarter left, and that's not enough for Kiddie Park." The confession weakened my case, but I'd carefully avoided mentioning that Wayne was equally poverty-stricken. Parents who had lived through the Great Depression hated to see their offspring deprived, even as victims of their own spendthrift nature.

"Very well," Mom agreed. "I'll add a quarter to yours, but you'll have to earn it with some extra chore this week."

Neither my inept bargaining skills nor whining was likely to get me a better deal. I accepted the coin with a hasty "Thanks" and dashed out to meet Wayne. He triumphantly flashed a half dollar at me before snugging it down into his pants pocket.

We were still a few years away from owning two-wheelers. But we had most of the afternoon at our disposal, so the ten-block walk was no challenge to our enthusiasm. Along the way, we stopped to exchange a few jibes with schoolmates playing in their front yards or lounging on their porches. This enabled us to evoke envious looks when we parted and said, "Well, so long, *we're* headin' to Kiddie Park."

The first thing you were likely to observe upon arriving at Kiddie Park was the train. It was the familiar miniature-size steam engine, probably modeled on an early 1900s 10-wheeler. The engineer wore authentic garb, but he had barely enough room for his legs in the abridged "cab."

All the passenger cars were uncovered and had room for two medium-size people in each seat. Seats were non-adjustable, unpadded wood, with a choice of facing forward or backward. The caboose had a roof and slightly less cramped seating. Parents usually sat here with children who were too young to ride alone.

There was a station platform, complete with benches, from which you boarded the train. A uniformed conductor collected tickets and called out the familiar "All aboard!" Then he climbed into the last seat of the caboose and signaled the engineer to proceed.

Circling the outer rim of the park twice, the train gave us a pretty good ride for the money. Just before reaching the station, we went through a long, dark tunnel. Signs at the station and at the tunnel entrance cautioned riders to stay seated and keep hands and arms inside the cars. Entering the tunnel, the engineer would give a blast of the whistle to warn anyone who might be crossing the track up ahead. Where the train crossed the park's walkway, there were miniature crossing signals, complete with bells and flashing red lights.

Along the walkway was a booth where we bought tickets for five cents each. Just beyond this, a circus style wagon served as the confection stand. Here you could buy pop corn, soft drinks, taffy apples, ice cream and a variety of candy bars. Except for the economy size pop corn, everything was a nickel.

Legend had it that the taffy apples were made with crab apples. This apparently was a rumor passed down by one generation of kids to the next, and probably untrue. However, few of the pint-size customers were willing to risk five cents to find out.

Because it catered to smallfry, Kiddie Park had a number of rides that were pretty tame. An assortment of miniature cars, trucks and fire engines, for instance, accommodated one rider each. Spoke-like rods kept them spaced safely distant from one another as they moved sedately around on a smooth pavement. Similarly, a fleet of two-seater boats made scarcely a ripple as they floated in a circular metal moat containing about a foot of water.

The airplane ride was a bit more exciting. Steel arms stretched out from a motorized axis with the planes suspended by chains. Centifugal force caused the planes to swing outward in a gentle arc as they "flew" around. It was not a lump-in-the-throat sort of thrill; more akin to riding in a fast-rising elevator.

The Kiddie Park ferris wheel was only about two stories high. Its seats were completely enclosed by wire mesh. Once the operator latched the door from outside, a kid could not fall out if he tried.

Thus the ride lacked that sense of danger, even when your seat was stopped at the top, swinging in the wind.

Two rides were actually adult size: the merry-go-round and the Tilt-a-Whirl. The carousel had the usual high-backed benches in which adults often rode with babes in arms. Preschoolers could opt for the stationary horses, camels and unicorns. Us big kids naturally preferred the ornately decorated horses that rode majestically (albeit slowly) up and down on poles that poked up through the carriage floor.

The Tilt-a-Whirl, long a staple at most carnivals, has been overshadowed in recent years by more awesome rides. But it continues to be an exciting ride even today. Each crescent-shaped car spins completely around on its own metal rail. As the entire platform revolves with increasing speed, individual sections undulate, resulting in three separate and simultaneous motions. If several riders synchronize leaning their weight into the car's rotation, they can produce some really neck-straining spins.

Riders had to be 12 years old unless accompanied by an adult. Wayne and I would have tried to pass for 12, but the Tilt-a-Whirl operated only on evenings and weekends. There weren't enough qualified riders on weekday afternoons.

That left the pony rides as the top choice for me and most of my buddies. Behind the main park stood a rickety stable and an elliptical bridle path. The latter was surrounded by a white railed fence and looked like a midget race track.

Real live ponies could be ridden around the track for the price of one ticket. The critters were rather swaybacked and moved at a very leisurely pace. Older teenagers or college boys home for the summer escorted each rider around. This was partly for the riders' safety. The grooms always warned kids to keep their hands away from the ponies' faces because they liked to bite.

But a guide was also necessary because most of the ponies needed some leading. They tended to stop and gaze off across the field or nibble grass growing through the fence. On occasion, when no adults were nearby, we could persuade the groom that we had ridden these beasts "hundreds of times," and they'd let us start out unassisted. "But mind you," they'd warn us, "don't gallop these colts."

Fat chance. Often as not the pony would take us about halfway around the track, then realize that we had no escort and turn around, or just stop and refuse to budge. The groom would have to catch up with us and tug our reluctant mount around the rest of the circuit.

For all that, us would-be cowpokes loved those ponies. From the moment we put our left foot in the stirrup and swung up into the saddle, we became six feet tall and assumed the persona of Roy Rogers, Gene Autry, Hopalong Cassidy or whoever was our favorite Western star of the silver screen. If we were lucky enough to be paired with a pony that demonstrated some spirit, we would reach into our pocket for another ticket at the end of the trail and say, "I'll ride again."

When our families visited Kiddie Park, we'd ride anything that our smaller siblings tried. Otherwise, we'd have to just stand and watch, itching to move on to something we really wanted to ride. In spite of frequent reminders that "Money doesn't grow on trees," parents could always be counted upon to buy a long string of tickets.

By ourselves, with only fifty cents apiece, Wayne and I would be more selective. We'd probably head straight for the ponies first. Then a ride on the train. Ten cents probably would go for ice cream and other edibles. The carousel and the airplane were worth one ticket each. Occasionally, when we were old enough to pass for 12, we'd go on a Saturday and take multiple rides on the Tilt-a-Whirl.

Weekdays, though, we'd usually spend the bulk of our loot on alternate pony and train rides. Sometimes we actually returned home with a nickel or a dime still in our possession. But not often.

In the early 1950s, the land on which Kiddie Park was located became too valuable for such a modest enterprise. A shopping mall was going up a block south. Farm land on the east side of Harlem Avenue had been cleared for the construction of a drive-in movie theatre. At the end of the summer, instead of just closing up, the park was dismantled. The following spring, new buildings started sprouting up. Kiddie Park was history.

Fortunately for kids growing up today, some such parks still exist around the country. In Maywood, another northwest suburb of Chicago, a somewhat larger park has prospered for many years with a wider assortment of rides that appeal to all ages. (Its proximity to

145

Maywood Park, a popular harness race track, probably attracts patrons from other areas.)

Theme parks are great fun, but they usually entail a major trip (and major expense) for the family. The small local amusement parks that continue to thrive are a super treat for little people who haven't yet fallen prey to the Electronic Age.

At a recent lunch with my lifelong pal, Chuck, the conversation inevitably turned to nostalgia.

"I had a terrific dream last night," Chuck told me. "My mother was having some lady friends over for a luncheon, so she gave me a dollar and told me I could spend the afternoon at Kiddie Park."

"Wow, that sounds like a great dream," I agreed. "Now me, I had an awful dream last night. I was home alone and the doorbell rings. When I open the door, I see Marilyn Monroe and Ava Gardner standing there in tight-fitting, low-cut dresses. They both burst in and start trying to make mad, passionate love to me."

Chuck looked puzzled. "You call that awful?" he asked.

"Sure," I explained. "Here's these two gorgeous Hollywood stars wanting to make out, and there's only one of me."

"Well, gee whiz," Chuck protested. "I'm your best buddy. Why didn't you call and invite me over?"

"I tried to. But your mother answered and told me you were at Kiddie Park."

Ba boom! (i.e., The End)

Making Christmas Happen

The first Christmases that I recall with particular clarity are those we celebrated during the war years. It so happened that I reached my sixth birthday during this period and was duly enrolled in grammar school. No doubt the latter milestone, coupled with the impact of World War II, made all special occasions more memorable for me.

Still, my entry into the world of the three Rs exposed me to a whole new aspect of Christmas. Until then it had been a holiday primarily orchestrated by adults.˙ I was enlisted in some token assistance here and there along the way. But my major contributions were gleeful anticipation (which included much thumbing through and marking of the Sears, Roebuck "wishing book") and exclamations of delight (which brought satisfied smiles to adult faces) when I opened my presents on Christmas day.

In my first year at James Giles Elementary School, it was revealed to me that many hands and a great deal of preparation were required to make Christmas "happen" at school. Indeed, we began preparing on the very Monday that we returned from our Thanksgiving holiday.

The order of business included both presents for our parents and decorations for our school tree. Except for tinsel and colored lights, every ornament on our school tree was made by the students at Giles.

Construction paper was a vital raw material in this enterprise. It was cut, folded and pasted into a variety of shapes. A lot of that bottled white paste was used in the process.

Teacher supplied the paper. We each had our own jar of the sickly sweet-smelling paste. It was applied with short metal-handled brushes. These tended to get lost or broken, or eventually became so encrusted with dried paste that they were unusable. No matter. You could dip your finger into the paste and use your fingertip as a brush.

A sheet of construction paper might be curled into a tube shape and the overlapped edges pasted together. Next we flattened the tube and cut slots about one third of the way in from either edge. Then we reshaped the tube and pushed the slots in. A strip of paper pasted over the top became a handle. The result was a reasonable likeness of a colored lantern.

Literally thousands of thin strips of construction paper were curled and pasted into rings about an inch in diameter. Each one was looped into the next to form an immense chain. Eventually, it encircled our school tree from top to bottom.

A more intricate folding technique resulted in a tall pyramid shape. Two of these, pasted bottom-to-bottom, would create a diamond that was hung by a piece of thread inserted through one peak. To achieve the desired symmetrical shape, this design had to be folded with precision. My pyramids usually looked more like the beak that appeared some years later on TV's Garfield Goose.

Less intricate folding and some cutting was required to form little cubes about an inch and a half square. These were decorated with Christmas wrapping stickers of Santa Claus, angels, elves, snowmen, Christmas bells, etc.

To create snowflake designs, we began by making multiple folds in a sheet of white construction paper. With our stubby, semi-sharp, round-nosed scissors, we cut out random patches in square shapes, triangles and half moons. When the paper was unfolded, no two snowflakes were alike.

Mrs. Atterberry, one of my favorite teachers, furnished us with templates in the shape of familiar holiday figures. We used these to trace and cut out silhouettes on various colored paper. Santa Claus was red, of course. Snowmen and doves were white. The tree had to be green. Reindeer were brown. Elves could be many colors. This enabled us to use most of the scraps from other cut-outs, making us feel patriotic during that period of shortages when folks on the homefront were being reminded to avoid waste.

Around Thanksgiving and Christmas, bowls of assorted unshelled nuts were set out in many homes. We brought to school all the walnut shells that our families succeeded in separating into two unshattered halves. These we glued back together with a loop of thread pressed in between. Then we covered them with glittery gold or silver paint.

We wadded tin foil (much of it painstakingly peeled away from inside chewing gun wrappers) into five-pointed shapes that loosely approximated stars. Like many of our creations, these were hung by means of a loop of thread passed through one of the star's points.

Stringing pop corn required not only needle and thread, but a degree of dexterity. To avoid a lot of pricked fingers among the younger kids, this handicraft usually was delegated to upperclassmen. Even though the pop corn was dry and unsalted, teachers had to supervise closely. Otherwise, much of the raw material never made it onto the string.

In addition to our mass production of ornaments, we always had some project that involved making a gift for our parents. One year we simply folded sheets of construction paper into the size of greeting cards and decorated them with our own original artwork and greetings. Another time we covered homemade cards with silhouettes, using the same templates from which we had fashioned tree ornaments.

One year we cast both our palm prints in plaster. It wouldn't surprise me if hundreds of these matched sets survive yet today, stored in parental treasure chests.

The traditional angel that topped our tree was a different one each year. It would be contributed by one (or a group) of the more talented girls and boys in the eighth grade.

The Giles School Christmas tree stood in the main hallway for about two weeks before our holiday vacation began. We filed past it several times a day as we marched into and out of the building or assembled for activities. Each time we observed it, we could take pride in the collective results of our classes' handiwork and our own individual contributions.

Even more special was the pleasure of presenting our parents with the Christmas gifts we had crafted in school. Some of us had the means to afford a modest store-bought gift as well. But parents always seemed to take an inordinate joy in receiving the gifts that we had clumsily but lovingly made with our own small hands.

This aspect of Christmas, like its many other mysteries, does not change. Years later, I experienced it again from the perspective of a proud parent. No doubt my offspring will one day enjoy that experience as well.

When we are young, our appreciation of Christmas tends to be self-centered. Everyone and everything seems to be intent upon making this the merriest and most exciting of holidays for us. In the innocence of youth, it is right and fitting that we simply accept and enjoy this.

But, as in all of life, the greatest joy of Christmas is to be found more in giving and sharing than in receiving. As we become active participants, making Christmas happen for others, we begin to reap the richer rewards of the holiday spirit. What a debt we owe to those church and school teachers and other adults who guided us in making the transition.

It's been a few years since those carefree school days. I've seen some lavishly and elegantly decorated Christmas trees here at home and in other parts of the world. Yet none ever outshown the one that my classmates and I adorned with our own handcrafted ornaments in the hallway of James Giles Elementary School.

Snow Is A Four-Letter Word

There was a time when I actually viewed snow as a welcome sight. Anticipation of wintertime fun overweighed even my dread of clearing sidewalks. The only snowthrowers then in use were young boys, teenagers and fathers.

For my school-age peers and me, the first heavy snowfall was a source of especially great excitement if we woke to it on a Saturday morning. Shoveling could be deferred until the last flake fell. Breakfast was an occasion both of fueling up and self-debate over which activity to partake of first.

In my case, something involving sleds usually won out. A trip to the basement was required to retrieve my Flexible Flyer from a storage area. A new length of rope would have to be sized, cut and tied to the steering handles to replace the one that had frayed and snapped last season. A quick waxing of the runners and I was ready to go – once I passed my mother's inspection.

Mothers were uniformly dutiful about insisting that we leave our houses wearing hats with turned down flaps or earmuffs, gloves or mittens on our hands and galoshes with our pant legs tucked inside. Yet we always returned with snow inside our shoes, pant legs out and soaked to the knees, gloves and seats snowcaked. Our fingers, ears and noses would be frozen; the latter dripped, as well, and we wiped vainly with sopping wet hankies.

As soon as two kids were bundled up to their mothers' satisfaction[1] and got outside with their sleds, they could begin taking turns pushing or pulling each other. Pulling usually involved going over every curb and pothole, swinging the rider within inches of street signs, fire hydrants or parked cars, and eventually dumping him by going sideways over a steep incline or by making a high-speed 180 degree turn.

Pushing was more tiring for the pusher, but proportionately more fun for the pushee. The rider clung to the sides of the sled and steered

---

[1] For a vivid illustration of what this entailed, watch the movie *A Christmas Story*, based upon a book by Jean Shepherd about his memories of growing up in Indiana. An annual TV holiday offering, it contains a hilarious scene in which the hero's younger brother struggles to negotiate down the street wrapped in twelve layers of clothing.

Two kids, two sleds and a street covered with well packed snow. A busy day of winter fun awaits. (Retrofile.com)

with his feet braced on the two protruding handles. You placed your hands on his stiffened shoulders and began pushing until you were running at top speed. Then you gave one last full-force shove before falling to your knees, panting.

The rider could simply steer a straight course and see how far your push would carry him. Or he could do some wild zig-zags, or even risk trying to hop curbs or small snowpiles. A favorite stunt was to attempt a sharp turn at a cross street. If the sled had any real momentum left at this point, this usually resulted in a spill.

Belly flopping was popular because it could be done solo. You held the sled chest high, got a good running start and then just fell on top of the sled. To gain some degree of steering control, you had to immediately move your hands to the outer ends of the movable front handle. At the same time, you needed to raise your head and feet to see where you were going and to avoid dragging your toes.

I once belly flopped eight blocks over to Harvey's house. The last block, I hit a patch of salted sidewalk. The sled stopped instantly, but I kept going. I arrived at Harvey's with a split lip and a loose tooth.

There were plenty of group activities, of course, as more of the gang appeared on the street. Building a snowman or two was almost an obligatory activity if the snow was good packing. Good packing snow almost guaranteed, as well, that an impromptu snowball fight eventually would ensue.

If the snow was too powdery, our snowman project quickly would dissolve into throwing handfuls at our pals. Soon we'd be putting snow down each other's collars. Finally, everyone having been wrestled to the ground, it was only natural that we roll around in the snow a bit, creating snow angels or odd shapes randomly sculpted, which we would then try to outdo each other in identifying.

Sledding often was a group activity, too. I still recall with admiration Marvin the Marvelous. Marv, the biggest preteen in our gang, liked to tie sleds together and see how long a "snow train" he could pull. He once tugged seven medium to large peers almost a block before pooping out. Admittedly, it was a long, slow ride, but it still was an impressive feat. No one but Marvin could have dragged us half that distance.

Inspired by seeing the movie *Call of the Wild*, Wayne once tied his dog, Blackie, to his sled and sat two large boys on it. Standing about 25 feet ahead, Wayne called, "Here, Blackie. C'm'on, boy!" Blackie was a fairly large dog, but he was no Yukon King.[2] In response to his master's summons, he gave one tentative lunge forward. The sled did not budge. Blackie sat down to rest.

It was no better when one boy got off, or when the second boy was replaced by someone's 6-year-old brother. Having made that initial unsuccessful effort, Blackie apparently concluded that playing Huskie was not his thing. As his master continued to call hopefully, Blackie cocked his head and gazed at him with an expression that seemed to say, "Are you kidding?"

---

[2] Blackie was a laid back animal who would endure most any indignity at the hands of his master. Wayne sometimes held his collar, straddled him like a horse and asked anyone who hadn't heard it before: "Know what this is? Wayne on the woof!" (Hey, Wayne said it, not me. Don't send me any poison pun letters.)

Disappointed but forgiving, Wayne finally came back to untie his pet. Before he could undo the rope, a neighborhood dog that Blackie evidently disliked wandered past across the street. Blackie growled menacingly, then burst out barking and took off, dumping his small passenger in the snow. The other dog gave a frightened yelp and ran. Blackie gave hot pursuit, the sled bouncing and careening left and right behind him. Down streets and alleys the two animals raced, a dozen kids trailing behind and calling for Blackie to come back.

Only when the sled overturned and became dead weight did Blackie give up the chase. We were four or five blocks from home. Wayne freed Blackie and pulled the sled himself as we trooped wearily home. Blackie was a new neighborhood hero.

Probably the favorite group sled activity was sliding down hills. There always was a building site somewhere around the area with a dirt hill now covered with snow. Very quickly, it would have at least three paths worn into its side. There was a slow slope for the little kids, a fast track and the daredevil cliff – almost straight down. I suspect the heavy layers of clothing we wore was all that saved us from suffering many broken bones.

The magic of Winter faded for me when it became necessary to take long bus trips into the city for high school and the jobs that preceded my first automobile. In recent years, I have rediscovered some measure of Winter's enchantment as I played with small offspring. I confess, though, that I was more relieved than hurt when they declared that they no longer needed me to pull the sled or hold them up on the skating pond.

These days, my idea of a pleasurable Winter afternoon is to sip a cup of hot chocolate on the warm side of a picture window and enjoy the esthetic beauty of a Winter landscape. One highlight of which is the sight of my teenage son demonstrating his skill with the snowblower.

The Great Christmas Tree Bonfire

CHRISTMAS TREE BONFIRE
December 30 Saturday 4:00 PM
Sponsored and Supervised by your Nor-
wood Park Township Volunteer Fire
Department. Keep your home safe.
Bring your tree to the station, corner
Montrose and Ottawa, any time after
9:00 AM Saturday.
Hot Chocolate   Coffee   Cookies

If my observations from both perspectives are accurate, there are two distinct attitudes concerning the week that follows Christmas. Between brief fits of tidying up and putting things away, the adults breathe a sigh of relief. It is a period of relative calm, a welcome respite from the exciting but frenzied weeks of preparation. Mom and Pop share the post-holiday pleasure of kicking off their shoes and slumping into an easy chair with their feet up on a hassock.

For youngsters aged twelve and under, it is an anti-climactic time. After weeks of almost unbearable anticipation, The Big Day arrived and passed with sudden and blinding speed. All those wonderful gifts are still treasured, of course. Yet, once they've been played with a few times and displayed for friends, they surreptitiously begin to merge with other possessions. By December 28th, there is an uneasy sense of things returning to normal.

Taking a mental survey of the friends who shared their preteen years with me in the 1940s, I'm convinced that we all were affected by this vague ennui. Not for us the anticipation of New Years Eve parties enjoyed by adults and some privileged teenagers. (If we whine enough, possibly the folks will wake us for ten minutes at midnight to join in the tooting of horns and shaking of noisemakers.)

With school out, we've had a week or more to burn off our excess energy with outside winter sports. To combat our growing boredom, we now resort to reading books and listening to radio programs such as "Front Page Farrell" and "Just Plain Bill." (Though aimed at adult listeners, these shows occasionally have some worthwhile plot involving a murder or an escaped criminal.) Our restlessness is such that we almost—not quite, but *almost*—look forward to school reopening.

As we sink lower into this limbo of lethargy, the Norwood Park Township Volunteer Fire Department comes to our rescue. Their crack team of high school boys and retirees invades the neighborhood, sticking fliers inside every door with an important announcement. The department's Christmas tree bonfire will be conducted on the New Years weekend. All village residents were urged to attend and bring their trees to be added to the blaze.

Except for Chief Schoenfeld, our firefighters were all volunteers. They received a modest stipend for attending training sessions and for each actual fire they helped combat. Previously, when a fire was reported, the chief would corral his driver, who lived two doors away, and they would head for the fire site with the engine. Mrs. Schoenfeld, meanwhile, would begin a round of phone calls to alert as many volunteers as she could locate.

During World War II, however, the Civil Defense people donated a large siren to be placed atop the firehouse. Its piercing alarm could be heard well beyond the ten-block radius where most of our firefighters resided. If they were in the area, they checked in with the chief's wife and arrived at the scene much more quickly.

Early in December, the N.P.T. Volunteer Fire Department had distributed another flier with reminders about fire safety during the holiday season. "Keep Christmas trees well watered; check wires on strings of lights," etc. It was especially appropriate for people who liked to put up trees early, but it applied to all of us. There were not yet any plastic trees that looked so much like the real thing. The only artificial trees were silver colored metal novelties. Most of us had the genuine article produced by Mother Nature. No matter how much they were watered, they did dry out and become highly combustible.

The great Christmas Tree Bonfire had become an annual event, so my pals and I knew that it was coming. We just needed to be reminded. Now we had one more special event to look forward to before the holidays were over.

The bonfire usually was held the first Saturday after Christmas. If the 25th came late in the week, it would be deferred until the following Saturday so folks could keep their trees up a few days longer if they wished. By then, most families removed the decorations from their trees and put them in the back yard to await the bonfire.

Early Saturday morning, a stream of kids from every direction began delivering evergreens of every variety, shape and size to the fire station. They dragged trees by the stump or by ropes tied to the stump. They pulled them on sleds or wagons. Big kids delivered them alone. Smaller kids worked in teams.

Like Hansel and Gretel improvising with green toothpicks, we left a trail of thousands of pine needles along our streets and sidewalks. If there was snow on the ground, it would be decorated with a montage of footprints partially obliterated by the branches dragged behind us.

At the firehouse, we were directed across Montrose Avenue to a farmer's field, now bare except for a light covering of snow. Several volunteers accepted the trees and tossed them onto a growing pile. As the day progressed and the stack grew, the firemen would climb tall ladders to toss the trees higher. By midday, the pyre would be about 40 feet across and at least 20 feet high.

My pals and I gathered at the station around three o'clock to claim our cocoa and two cookies, dispensed by ladies of the Firemen's Wives Association. The homemade cookies were always scrumptious, but the hot chocolate was a challenge.

Scooped out of a large vat that bubbled around the edges, the hot cocoa was served in uninsulated paper cups that were almost impossible to hold. We walked across Montrose, blowing on the steaming brew, which caused gobs of scum to accumulate on one half of the surface. Our first sips resulted in near third degree burns to our lips, tongues and the roofs of our mouths. By the time we dared risk another sip, the winter air had gotten to the cocoa. Now we had to gulp it quickly, scum and all, to finish before it was ice cold.

As Christmas trees are being stacked up for a bonfire across the road, kids line up for cookies and hot chocolate being dispensed by wives of the volunteer firemen. (Norwood Park Fire Department photo collection)

All the volunteer firemen were there by then, and they roped off the bonfire area. Chief Schoenfeld patrolled inside the ropes, puffing on his ever-present cigar and giving occasional instructions. More trees continued to arrive, and the greenery eventually towered two stories high.

Parents now began to join their offspring. Many neglected the winter dress rules that they enforced on their children and stood blowing on cold hands or rubbing cold ears. They drank steaming coffee from the same unwieldy paper cups. Some added a sprinkle of snow to cool the brew. It was rumored that male adults could pop into the firehouse kitchen and one of the firemen would add a dash of spirits to help keep their blood circulating.

Chief Schoenfeld supervises the bonfire as kids watch in awe. (Norwood Park Fire Department photo collection)

As usual, stragglers arriving with yet more trees delayed the 4p.m. schedule. Soon, though, with kids and grown-ups alike milling impatiently, the chief signaled for his men to begin. Torches were lit and used to ignite the bottom layers of trees all around the circle. Then they were tossed to the top of the pyre.

It took but a moment for the flames to whoosh through the mound of tinder-dry evergreens. Fingers of fire raced to intertwine throughout the piney mountain until it was engulfed in a glorious crackling blaze. A murmur of awe-inspired "ahhh's" rippled through the crowd. Parents could be heard lecturing to wide-eyed youngsters: "You see why we must be so careful of fires?"

Evening comes early in the Midwestern Winter. By the time the fire reached its apex, the area all around was almost dark. But this patch of field was alight with a red and yellow glow. Hot sparks danced wantonly in the air. Fathers held infants up for a better view, while small boys, and some girls, sat atop their older brothers' shoulders. Thirty feet away from the bonfire, we could feel the heat penetrate our layers of winter clothes and toast our cheeks.

159

More rapidly than seemed possible, the giant blaze began to run out of fuel. Its size quickly diminished as the topmost trees crumbled down into the burnt-out center. We crushed our paper cups, leaned over the cordon ropes and tossed them into the flames. Then we joined our parents and friends as they turned and started home. The few folk who lingered were treated to a display of fire fighting equipment as the volunteers extinguished the last smoldering embers.

Many adults paused to congratulate Chief Schoenfeld for the spellbinding show and the public service provided by his men. Nodding his appreciation, the chief studied his cigar and replied, "What was it that Shakespeare said? 'Tis a consummation devoutly to be wished'."

Afterthought: About half the Christmas trees displayed now are plastic, firesafe, realistic and conveniently easy to assemble, disassemble and store. For those who prefer to be traditional and put up a real tree, most communities provide an after-holiday curbside pickup service. There may still be organized bonfires in some rural areas. I know of none in my territory.

In 1994, the city of Waukegan, a few miles north of Chicago, decided to have one more. Until about 1980, it had been a part of the town's Twelfth Night celebration dating back to the 1940s. Officials reported that literally thousands of trees were burned, many probably contributed by residents of surrounding towns.

Those who had never before witnessed an organized Christmas tree bonfire must have found it an awesome event. For the older attendees, it surely provided a nostalgic glimpse back to a bygone era. The American Lung Association, however, called attention to the danger for people with respiratory ailments. This concern also may have contributed to the tradition being generally discontinued.

Attention, Graduates: Ready, Set, Commence!

The fellow who said "Everything is relative" certainly knew whereof he spoke.

For folk over thirty, 365 days can whiz by all too rapidly. While from a six-year-old's perspective, one week often seems an eternity to wait for some special occasion.

Aware of the difference, our parents tactfully made no reference to a time frame when they enrolled my classmates and me in our first grade class. Our area had no junior high. So this new adventure would occupy us for *eight years*!

Trusting innocents all, we approached our first day with nervous excitement. Could we have envisioned the scope of our commitment, no doubt we would have rebelled *en mass*. Picture 37 male and female tykes throwing themselves prostrate, pounding small fists on the polished wood floor and wailing: "Mommy! Daddy! How can you sign me up for *eight years?* I haven't even *lived* eight years yet!"

Nevertheless, as happens in those card games in the *Mutt and Jeff* comic books, Time passes. One day there comes a momentous revelation. Not only have we entered our teen years. We are now the eighth grade class. Those eight years are mostly behind us, and a fateful event looms. *Graduation*!

It was formally known as a "commencement exercise." But the formal phrase was seldom used except on invitations and tickets and in our principal's speech.

The James Giles Elementary School year was divided into two semesters. Rather than being referred to as January and June classes, all our grade levels were designated as A (upper) and B (lower). Thus, regardless of the month, the 8A group always was the one about to graduate. A major portion of that semester was spent in preparation.

In February, soon after my class moved up to 8A status, Miss Hubick began collecting payments toward class ribbons, class pins and a class gift to the school. The cloth ribbons were about an inch wide by fourteen inches long, with a W-shaped cut at the bottom. One was gold, the other dark blue (our school colors). They were joined into a bow at the top. A safety pin device facilitated pinning them to lapels, dresses or shirts.

Without exception, everyone in the class ordered two ribbons. One would be tucked neatly into a drawer at home to save for graduation night. The other would be initialed by each of our classmates.

Early in March, Mrs. Brockway, the school's music teacher, and Principal John V. Leigh agreed upon two musical selections to be sung by our class. Mrs. Brockway began rehearsing us on a Stephen Foster medley and "America the Beautiful" (all four verses). After a month or so, she pronounced herself pleased with our performance. Regular music classes then resumed their varied format, with just one run-though of the two graduation pieces each week.

In April, we received scripts for what was called a choral recitation. It was a sort of pageant in words. A typical choral recitation would highlight the history of our "Sweet Land of Liberty" from the landing of the Mayflower through the Civil War.

We began gathering to rehearse once, sometimes twice, a week. Seated on the "auditorium" stage in our school's basement, in roughly the formation we would assume for graduation, we followed Mr. Leigh's direction as he explained where to put dramatic emphasis. Gradually, he designated small segments to be recited by girls only, boys only, a small group, individuals, left side, right side, etc. The effect was rather riveting.

A photographer arrived in April to take class pictures, This was a yearly ritual for all grades, but for us soon-to-be graduates it took on a special significance. Instead of ordering one copy for the family albums, most parents would distribute copies to grandparents and other close relatives.

By the end of April, Miss Hubick had tallied everyone's grade averages to determine who would be our valedictorian and salutatorian. These two students would work with her to prepare and deliver short speeches at the ceremony.

Since I had an above-average scholastic record, it occurred to me that I might qualify for one of these supposedly coveted roles. If so, I knew—not just feared the possibility, but *knew* beyond any doubt— that on the most important night of my young life, I would: 1) choke up and become speechless; 2) throw up; 3) wet my pants; 4) faint; or 5) all of the above.

Fortunately, Garrison Keillor's observation proved correct, at least in my case. God does look out for shy people. At least one girl and one boy proved to have grade averages superior to mine. Thus, they earned both the honor of addressing our parents, other relatives and friends— and my undying gratitude.

By May first, things really began fulminating. We spent less and less time on classroom work, more and more on rehearsals and other preparations.

Our class ribbons and pins arrived and were distributed. Girls, who always knew how to do these things, helped boys attach the class pins to the center of their ribbon's bows. The pin was no bigger than a dime. It bore the school's name and emblem and the month and year of our graduation.

We had all acquired autograph books by now. These little imitation leather-bound books were about the size and appearance of a diary, with pages of many different colors, all unlined and blank. As we circulated our extra ribbons, acquiring classmates' inked initials for posterity, we also penned remembrances in each other's autograph books.

Except for some mushy messages to close friends, the sentiments were mostly lighthearted or plain goofy.

"Marilyn: Best wishes for your high school years and beyond. May all your troubles be little ones. Ha, ha! Love, Barbara."

("Little ones." Kids. Get it? Because we were all very family oriented, everyone caught on and this one always brought a few snickers.)

"Eddie: Roses are red, Grass is green, Stovepipes are hollow, And so is your bean. Your classmate, Nancy."

"Charles: When you get married, don't marry a fool. Just marry a girl from James Giles School. Wanita."

(Was that a proposal?)

"Robert: I love you a little. I love you big. I love you like a little pig. Shirley."

"Roger: I better hurry and write on this page. For the keepers are coming with your cage. See you at the zoo. Harvey.'

And, at the bottom of the last page of my book: "Danny: By hook or by crook, I'll sign last in your book. Your pal, Eddie."

Eddie really wasn't one of my regular pals. I just tried to be nice to him at recess because he was kind of goofy and none of the other guys every wanted to play with him. (Years later, I learned that Eddie thought that it was he being a nice guy for playing with me.)

One of the girls got really ticked off at Eddie because he wrote the same clever verse on the inside back cover of her autograph book after someone else had already filled the last page. Covers were sacrosanct and not to be mutilated.

Early in May, every store that sold kids' clothing had a graduation sale. Anyone who did not already have an outfit laid by found himself or herself on a streetcar with Mom, heading for Sears, Wieboldts, Goldblatts or some other favored department store. Boys, especially, had to shop early, since their suits would require fitting and a return trip.

Harold, the self-appointed class weirdo, owned a wild red plaid sport coat that he wore to parties. Harold informed all of us that he would attend commencement exercises wearing that jacket with a pair of striped pants, a checkered shirt and a polka dot tie.

Apparently he neglected to apprise his mother of this plan. On the big night, Harold showed up in a dark gray double-breasted suit, white shirt and conservative tie. At that, he managed to stand out among the crowd of navy blue suits that predominated.

On the last couple of weekends in May, there were numerous pre-graduation parties. These were boy/girl affairs held in streamer-decorated basements of kids' homes. They featured snacks, soft drinks and dancing under dimmed lights to music from a 78rpm record player. There were enough parties to insure that even the class deadbeats and wallflowers were invited to at least one. I was.

Finally, June arrived. Now we were rehearsing complete run-throughs of the graduation ceremony. We no longer counted weeks. We were down to counting days.

On Wednesday of *the week*, we were treated to a luncheon by ladies of the Parent-Teacher Association. Tables were set up in the half of our school basement which served as assembly hall, indoor gym and movie hall. Our lunch period was extended so we could partake at leisure and hear a few congratulatory comments from our principal, teachers and the PTA president.

For graduation night, our janitor arranged seating by lining up neat rows of square-shaped wooden slat folding chairs. Tickets were required and had been distributed equally, based upon class size and seating capacity. My class received five tickets each. That enabled Mom and Dad to invite Grandma and Grandpa Farr. Aunt Evie, a school teacher who would appreciate seeing her oldest nephew graduate, was honored with the last ticket.

A very young John V. Leigh (with an almost full head of hair) poses with the James Giles School graduating class of June, 1939. (photo courtesy Izetta Giles Castiglia)

The organizational experience of our principal and teachers, and our countless practice sessions, paid the desired dividends. The actual event went quite smoothly.

We marched up the center aisle to the tune of "Pomp and Circumstance" (played on an upright piano by Mrs. Brockway) and found our assigned seats without confusion. The salutatorian and valedictorian remembered to speak slowly and clearly and not stop if they occasionally flubbed a line. One of our classmates presented the class gift to a representative of the 8B class.

Mr. Leigh gave the main address. He had been almost bald since the day I entered first grade. In his opening greeting, he apologized for his head reflecting the stage lights into the eyes of guests in the front rows. It was a well worn gag, but always got a laugh.

Mr. Leigh, as the author and his classmates knew him, poses with the graduating class of June, 1948. Miss Hubick, the eighth grade teacher, stands at right. The author's pal Chuck is in second row, last boy on right. (photo courtesy C. Schaden)

Becoming serious, he congratulated us on the accomplishment of reaching this momentous goal in our lives. He thanked our parents for their support in making it possible. Speaking to the class, he touched on some of the challenges and opportunities that lay before us. In conclusion, he gave his twice-a-year assurance to relatives and friends in the audience that "I believe the fine group of young people on this stage tonight is probably the best graduating class we've ever had at James Giles School!"

As always, this prompted an enthusiastic burst of applause from proud families in the audience. Then, almost before we realized it was happening, we departed James Giles School for the last time. Proudly clutching our rolled-up diplomas, most of us accompanied parents home for one more party, this time with aunts, uncles, cousins, grandparents, et al.

It would be a while before the elation subsided. Eventually, we would pause to reflect upon our triumph. An 8-year commitment—nearly two-thirds of our young lives—had been successfully completed.

Ahead loomed the greater challenge of high school. But we were no longer children. We were teenagers now. And high school would require only four years. "Greater challenge?" Are you kidding?

Dan McGuire

The Big, Wide World

Voyage Beyond The Three Rs

Oh, the glory of being a grammar school grad!

Proud families granted us favored status. Younger schoolmates envied and idolized us. Summer vacation took on an added glow in the aftermath of our triumph.

Alas! As with all things glorious, the day of reckoning arrived. Our high school careers began, and once again we were "the new kids."

Our semi-rural unincorporated suburb was years away from having a high school of its own. Because we were on the northwestern fringe of Chicago, the district regulations permitted us to attend any Chicago school we chose (subject to enrollment limits). During our last semester at James Giles Elementary, we received sign-up sheets and information about various high schools.

Several girls and boys elected to attend Schurz or Taft, two well-regarded Northwest Side schools. A few of our athletic males chose Lane Technical High. It was a long way into the city (near the famed Riverview Amusement Park), but boasted some of the city's best inter-scholastic teams for the sports-minded. For those thinking ahead to their working years, it also offered numerous shop courses.

After studiously evaluating all the school materials given to us, I selected Steinmetz High School for two very significant reasons. 1: Most of my classmates were going there. 2: It was the closest one to home.

Distance was not a trivial factor in this decision. Kids under eighteen didn't own cars, and there was no fleet of school buses or parental car pools dropping students at the school door.

At Giles, some kids rode bicycles to school. Most of us lived close enough to walk. Our trip to Steinmetz would take an hour (in good weather) and involve three Chicago Surface Lines buses.

I walked four blocks (less than some of my friends) to Irving Park Road, our nearest arterial route into Chicago. A motorized shuttle bus was scheduled to arrive every twelve minutes. It took us to Neenah Avenue, the western end-of-the-line connection for the Irving Park trolley bus. If the trolley bus was ready to go, we boarded and rode a mere two blocks to Narragansett, where we transferred to a southbound sister bus. If the Irving Park trolley wasn't there or was just turning around, we could walk the two blocks faster. Then, however, we risked encountering a grumpy Narragansett driver who would demand: "How come your transfer's not punched?"

On this last leg of the trip, the bus became crowded with other students. In heavy traffic, on a narrow street, it proceeded at a turtle's pace. Many mornings we poured off the bus half a block from the school with just minutes to spare before class.

Other Steinmetz alumni, who transferred at points about five blocks from the school, lament how they frequently despaired of the bus ever arriving. They would begin walking briskly, run the last block or so, and arrive at school panting and sweating. Often as not, the tardy bus passed them when the campus was in sight.

Whatever your starting point, the scenario was worse in bad weather. Chicago winters tended to make a mess of bus schedules, so adding ten or fifteen minutes to your anticipated travel time was a wise precaution.

Newly arrived freshmen were apt to be awed by the immense size of most Chicago high schools, Steinmetz included. Giles Elementary graduates were products of a square-shaped building with classrooms on each of two floors – just enough rooms for eight grade levels.

Steinmetz High commanded a full city block. It stood three stories tall, with wings extending back to the alley on each of the east/west side streets. At its center, a partial fourth floor (used by band and orchestra classes) and twin towers lent a fortress appearance.

Stairways at Giles were wide enough for us to march in or out five abreast without crowding. Here they were twice as wide. Yet, with the student population close to 3,000, stairs were designated "Up" or "Down," with large red arrows posted for those in need of remedial reading courses.

The disoriented "freshies" were easy to spot. They were the ones being buffeted left and right by a tide of young humanity as they struggled to go up the stairs marked "Down."

Finding assigned classrooms was a challenge until you became acclimated to the numbering system. On city streets, even numbers are on one side, odd numbers on the others. Here, even numbers were in the south hall of the building, odd numbers in the north. If you forgot that some rooms hid around the corners in the two wings, you might travel a hallway several times, fruitlessly rechecking numbers. By the time a sympathetic hall guard steered you to the room, other students had evaporated into their classes and you already were being marked "absent."

Students relax on the campus of Chicago's "Best in the West," Steinmetz High School. (photo courtesy C. Schaden)

Between bells, we had five minutes to depart one class, ("in an orderly fashion, please, like young ladies and gentlemen") and reach the next, making washroom stops as needed. Suppose you left Room 120 bound for Room 317. You joined the herd and walked at as brisk a pace as possible past slowpokes and loitering socializers (how did they have the time?). After fighting your way up two flights on the "Down" stairway, you paused to remember if you must go left or right. Heaven help you if you'd forgotten a book and had to detour to your locker.

Lockers! Now there was another revoltin' development. No more girls' and boys' cloak rooms. You paired up with a buddy or girl friend (same sex, please) and shared one of the hundreds of metal lockers embedded in the walls between classrooms. Hardware stores did a land office business on combination locks the month before school opened. You needed another lock for your individual locker in the gym class, too.

The author and his pal Wayne try to out-cool each other as they strike poses at their shared locker on the second floor of Steinmetz High School. The pin-up photo was the author's current sweetheart. (Yeah. Sure.)

For weeks you carried the locker combination on a slip of paper in your wallet. After you had opened the locker a dozen times without consulting the note, you figured you had the "combo" memorized, so you threw the note away. Two days later, as you spun the dial, your mind went blank. You attended several classes minus the proper books and homework papers until you caught up with your locker partner and he or she refreshed your memory.

During our relatively stress-free years at Giles Elementary, at least three-fourths of the pupils lived close enough to walk or ride bikes home for lunch. At Steinmetz, probably 85% of the student body ate at school, while another 10-12% patronized the neighborhood "slop shops."

Several of the latter were located near most high schools. They tended to attract the self-styled tough crowd and other minors who had taken up smoking. The schools would have liked to eliminate them, but they were legitimate mom and pop operations, offering sandwiches, shakes and a "hang-out" where the aforementioned "delinquents" could safely light up. (But all smokes were hastily snuffed when the local beat cop popped in for his occasional look-see.)

Those of us who were lunchroom patrons had two choices. You could bring a brown bag lunch. Or you could buy a lunch at the cafeteria. To be fair, if you selected judiciously, the cafeteria offered well-balanced, nutritional meals. But let's face it. High school, college and army chow is generally bland at best. At its worst, well.... If I didn't have a sack lunch, I usually played it safe and ate plain hamburgers with fries, both liberally doused with ketchup.

Knowing that swimming was part of gym class, some freshman boys brought swim trunks. Surprise, fellas! Boy swam nude. A few of the kids were embarrassed by what passed for humor in the rowdy locker room atmosphere. I was prepared, having been exposed to this practice at the "Y."

("Exposed to this." Get it? Yuk, yuk! That's a joke, son.)

Girls got to wear tank suits, albeit drab, ill-fitting ones. They used safety pins and chains to keep them from falling off. Rules were a little looser for girls, too. They sat out swim sessions in the bleachers when they had the monthly "female trouble." Some girls who really hated swimming were able to convince their P.E. teachers that they had "trouble" three or four times a months.

Female freshies took a giant step forward in the fashion area. They began wearing nylons and using make-up. These were grown-up privileges that most girls enjoyed only on very special occasions (if at all) while in grammar school.

We experimented with a raft of new styles in high school. Cashmere and angora sweaters, penny loafers (with coins inserted in the flaps), poodle skirts and pony tails (on girls only in those pre-beatnik days). For guys, there were hip-hugging jeans, pegged pants, turned-up collars, crew cuts, cleats on shoes – and the infamous D-A haircut.[1] We could devote a whole column to the fashions and fads – and how they evolved over a mere four-year span– but it's almost time for classes to let out.

Even with staggered class schedules, going home was a mob scene. Hundreds of teens streamed into the streets at the same time – all trying to board a few buses already half-filled with adults who wished they had traveled earlier or later. We didn't all get on the first

---

[1] Young readers will have to ask their elders what D-A stood for. I'm not allowed to spell it out in this family oriented publication

bus, of course. Even on the third or fourth, we were wedged in tight, falling over seated passengers when the bus swayed.

Kids who rode just a short way had to start almost immediately negotiating their way to the rear exit door. Don't drop a book or you might never see it again. Those of us who rode long distances eventually found a seat and could stretch our legs and relax. Some kids actually would break open books to begin reading homework assignments. Geez!

High school took a big bite out of our free time. In grammar school, we attended classes from 9a.m. until 3:15p.m. I could walk to Giles School in under two minutes. Steinmetz classes started at 8a.m. Now I rose at six o'clock and was seldom home before 4:30p.m.

All these unforeseen adjustments (and others) were among what our grammar school principal alluded to at graduation as "new and exciting challenges." But Mr. Leigh was equally on the mark about opportunities that awaited us as the scope of our world expanded to a phenomenal degree.

Some of us, once we got the hang of it, were reluctant to leave those hallowed halls after only four short years.

We Could Have Danced All Night

In a previous episode, gang, we reminisced about those magical high school years. Because of limited space, I skipped over one high-interest topic: The Prom.

Actually, most high schools had both junior and senior proms. Steinmetz held its Junior Prom in the gymnasiums. For 17-year-old attendees, the gym presented a safe locale, close to home and easily policed by chaperones.

A prom committee (volunteers from the junior class with teacher supervisors) decorated both gyms with balloons, ferns, streamers and hanging lanterns. The boys' gym became an impromptu ballroom. Each prom had a theme, such as "Orchids in the Moonlight," some aspect of which was woven into the decorations.

Couples danced under dimmed lights to music provided by "live" musicians. Ray Ponds' and Dan Belloc's bands were among the favorites. Though not quite the equal of touring "big band" groups, they were smooth professionals who were popular and much in demand locally. The closest thing we had to a "d.j." was the male teacher/chaperone who piped in "Top 50" recordings over the public address system during the band's breaks.

The girls' gym was transformed into a lounge, where a photographer snapped couples' pictures. The over-priced, unretouched photos highlighted every blemish. Guys often passed on ordering a print for themselves, but felt they had to give one to their dates. A wishing well reappeared every year at one end of the gym. A brief pause there to toss in a coin and make a wish was mandatory for couples who were "serious" about each other.

Every young lady was lovely, of course, in her full-length "semi-formal," her hair freshly permed and a beautiful corsage pinned to her dress or tied around her wrist with a bright ribbon. Their handsome escorts wore suits, white shirts and ties. The 1951-52 Steinmetz yearbook attests that loose-fitting double-breasted were "in" during that period.

Precious moments from the Steinmetz junior prom, as captured in the school's yearbook.

Not many juniors of that era had a driver's license, much less "a set of wheels" of their own. Most couples were driven to the Junior Prom and picked up by a parent. Those lucky few who owned or could borrow a car might stop at White Castle or a pizza joint for a midnight snack. Their incongruous attire aroused knowing smiles from other patrons. Otherwise, the excitement and weeks-long preparation notwithstanding, the Junior Prom was generally a Cinderella-style occasion.

Senior Prom was more elaborate and elegant. We were more mature by then and we were, after all, *seniors*. Those who did not have a "steady" began lining up dates months in advance so as not to be left out in the cold. Guys then dashed to Gingiss Bros. to be fitted for and lay away a rental tuxedo. Girls began shopping for a new— possibly a first—really formal gown.

The fellows then started a campaign of begging for use of the family car. If that wasn't an option, they needed to team up with a buddy who had his own car or was better at parent negotiations. Sometimes the arrangement hinged on your date wanting to double-date with her best girl friend. The girls also would begin planning group activities for before and after the prom itself.

The big night began with a "cocktail party" at Mary's house. Her mother served hors d'oeuvres and punch. Her father took a zillion snapshots with a camera that required a new flashbulb after each picture. Often the bulb didn't flash unless he rubbed the contact on the bottom of his shoe and/or licked it before inserting it into the flash unit. The subjects were then required to freeze in place as he ordered: "Wait! Wait! Don't move. Let's try that pose again."

Couples exchanged corsages for the girls (orchids and camellias were popular) and buttonnieres for the fellows. Guys graciously attached their dates' wrist corsages. Girls helped each other with the pin-ons. Party poopers!

Tam O'Shanter Country Club and the Edgewater Beach Hotel were favorites of the Steinmetz prom committees. (These and several other popular prom locales have long since fallen victim to the monetary lure of land development.) My class opted for the Edgewater, and an elegant evening it was!

The fellows looked suave and mature, in spite of sagging cummerbunds and crooked ties. The ladies were uniformly lovely, their hair perfectly coiffured, their dazzling gowns exposing soft white shoulders and backs. To this, add a pair of fluttering eyelashes and a bewitching smile that outshined the multi-colored overhead lights. Many an escort surrendered his heart on the dance floor that night of nights.

Prom music was meant for dreamy ballroom dancing. Rock 'n' roll had the night off. (A bunny hop and a polka or two usually did slip in somehow.) Between dances, we sipped punch, greeted the sponsors and prom committee, and posed for those unflattering photos. Some couples managed to elude chaperones and take a romantic stroll along the moonlit shoreline of Lake Michigan (whence the Edgewater took its name).

The author's class gave their prom committee high praise when the Edgewater Beach Hotel was selected for the senior prom. The Edgewater (far left) took its name from the nearby Lake Michigan beach. An elegant hotel, offering multiple choices of dining and live entertainers, the Edgewater was a favorite of visiting Hollywood stars and other well-heeled patrons who chose to go first class. (Lake County [IL] Discovery Museum, Curt Teich Postcard Archives)

When the music stopped (was it only midnight?), we bid everyone goodnight and headed in small groups to such places as Mr. Kelly's or the London House, both noted for their jazz entertainment. At the Top-of-the-Rock, one could view the beautiful Chicago skyline in the beam of a revolving searchlight atop the Prudential Building (later to become the Playboy mansion). My group chose the sometimes risqué Chez Paree.

Chicago nightclubs knew when high school proms were scheduled. Their menus and entertainment were adjusted to accommodate the groups of teens who were living high for one night on limited resources.

Scenes from the Steinmetz senior prom. In above picture, at center stage, the author's lifelong pal, Chuck, waltzes his date around the ballroom. At left, almost out of frame, fishing buddy Wayne dances with his future wife, Carol.

Our first misgivings came with the rickety elevator ride up to the famed nightspot. Our table for four was checkerboard size. Pseudo cocktails cost a dollar. The $4.50 prom night special, served with frugal portions of potato and green veggie, was Salisbury steak about a gram larger then the Steinmetz cafeteria's burgers—and very similar in taste.

But the stage show was lively, if forgettable. The resident comic's somewhat ribald routine was a revelation to us; and, to adolescent male eyes, the high-kicking Chez Paree Adorables were truly gorgeous.

In the wee hours, the girls were all delivered to their front steps. A porch light was sure to be on and, in most cases, a mother would be only half asleep listening for the sound of the key in the lock. Guys who were just prom dates would be rewarded with a discreet kiss. Steady couples mushed it up for awhile, then reluctantly said goodnight.

We were beginning to drag a little by then, but no one was about to admit it. At seven the next morning, ten of us met at Beverly's house. Her mother sat us around the dining room table and served up a round of pancakes, bacon, muffins, juice, coffee and questions as we recapped the previous night's extravaganza.

Rested (sort of) and nourished, we then set off for a two-hour horseback ride on tired nags rented from one of the many riding stables which then thrived near the forest preserve bridle paths. Next came a picnic at Bang's Lake. Matt drove his Merc convertible so the girls with us could enjoy screaming and struggling to tie on babushkas as the wind whipped their hair every which way. The afternoon was devoted to swimming, boating, tanning, cooking hot dogs, making out on beach blankets and catching little catnaps when no one was looking.

When the food ran out, we packed up and drove home to shower and change clothes. Around 7:30p.m., about a dozen of us reconvened at Pat's house. The two-car garage had been cleared out and decorated with streamers and balloons. A cooler held soft drinks. A card table held snacks, a 45-rpm record machine and a stack of records. Determined to prolong the prom-induced spirits of excitement and romance, we rock 'n' rolled until midnight.

When that hour arrived, our eyes were drooping and our bodies sagged. Yet we feigned regret that the party could not go on through the night. Still, most of us made it to church together the next morning.

Sunday afternoon, we downshifted and rejoined our families. At dinner, we gave them a complete report of the glorious prom events that would enrich our high school memories for years to come. Monday morning, the halls of Steinmetz High School buzzed with shared tales of the year's foremost social event.

Most high schools now permit kids to go stag to their proms. That's good. No one should miss his or her prom for lack of a date, as inevitably happened to some in the 1950s. By dating one girl from a class behind me and two from other schools, I had the pleasure of attending four senior proms. Each one provided its own precious memories, which I've tucked away for the time when my legs will no longer support me on the dance floor.

"We're Loyal To You, Steinmetz High..."

NEWS ITEM: Steinmetz High School will hold an open house on Saturday, May 19, to commemorate its 50th year.

Okay, guys and girls, everybody on your feet, and let's sound off with a rousing rendition of our school fight song:
> We're loyal to you, Steinmetz High.
> We're with you forever, and aye!
> We'll do all that's best for the school in the West,
> And for you we will always fight. Rah! Rah!
> So, fight boys, push on for our school.
> Come on, team, we're with you to rule.
> Keep bright the silver and the green,
> The colors of the greatest team.
> For Steinmetz we'll ever be tr-OO-oo!

Steinmetz High School marks its golden anniversary this year. I hope my alma mater won't ban me from the celebration. My scholastic efforts won no prizes, but they provided me with five memorable years.

Designed to accommodate 2,500 students, Steinmetz opened on September, 17, 1934, with an enrollment of 3,373. By 1938, the number peaked at 4,225. By then, a 3-shift schedule had been initiated. The opening of the Sayre Branch and three nearby parochial schools brought a gradual decline in numbers. By the early 1950s, when I attended, enrollment had leveled off to a manageable 2,854.

Arriving at Steinmetz fresh from my elementary school of eight rooms and eight grades was an awesome experience. The reddish brick edifice, with its twin towers and tall smokestack, stretched the length of the 3000 block on North Mobile Avenue and occupied a square block of campus. I wandered the hallways in the pre-class pandemonium and one thought dominated: Run!

Fortunately, upper classmen were friendly and helpful. One fellow sold me a map that highlighted boys' johns, the lunchroom and designated smoking areas. From another, I rented a locker on the less-trafficked fifth floor – and he threw in an elevator pass gratis.

An orientation assembly and directions from division room teachers cleared up lots of confusion. After a few days, only a handful of "freshies" were still going up the down staircase or looking for Room 241 at the even end of the building. We stopped carrying our printed class schedules, and remembered which books we needed for each class period. I found that I really could leave Room 359, stop at my locker and get to Room 148 in the five minutes between class bells.

We had our good and bad subjects. I did well in Math and English. (Mrs. Boughton's encouragement of my early writing efforts is gratefully remembered.) Latin and History were stumbling blocks. A non-athletic type, I never once made it even halfway up the rope that hung from the gym ceiling. I passed four years of mandatory P.E. classes largely on the basis of turning in superior Health tests and written reports.

In the gym, I risked bodily injury each time I vaulted the horse or tried to get my feet into those hanging rings. When we went outdoors in shorts and tee shirts after the first Spring thaw, my goosebumps had goosebumps. The indoor pool was neat-o, in spite of icy, over-chlorinated water. But why did boys have to swim nude?

Girls at least got to wear those drab gray tank suits that fit so loosely they had to pin the straps together in back "to avoid embarrassment." Rumor had it that a favorite pastime in girls' P.E. was peeking through the crack of the locked shower room door at the boys' swim class.

Steinmetz was a paradise for joiners. Just-for-fun groups included the ethnic clubs: French, Spanish, Polish, the "Cholly Chermans" – even the "Latin Lovers." There were also Library, Future Teachers, a chess & checker group and The Key Club. The Saddle Bouncers mounted up at Happy Day Stables, a short walk from my home in the boonies (now long gone, since the town grew, prospered and moved outward).

Fun and service merged for Green Curtain Players, stage crew, Steinmetz Star (newspaper) staff, cheerleaders and majorettes. There were committees for everything: prom, yearbook, Christmas decoration, social dances, civic tickets. Student Council, N.H.S. and Dardanelles required some scholastic achievement. Hall guards had to be certified as either sadists or masochists (extra credit if you qualified in both categories).

Musical types could join concert, R.O.T.C. or dance bands, orchestra; girls' or mixed chorus for the vocally gifted. Male jocks went out for football, baseball, basketball, swim and track teams. Precursors of women's lib included girls' bowling and *rifle* teams.

Members of The Sparkies gather outside a local ice cream shop. Because they were not an officially sanctioned school club, members were not allowed to wear either the school name or the club name on their jackets. Their distinctive caps helped to set them apart from the many similar groups. (photo courtesy Nancy Gisselbrecht Simandl)

Those who preferred to join gangs congregated in little stores behind the school known as hang-outs or slop shops. Gang fights were said to be an almost daily occurrence, and the girls were reputed to be more combative than the guys. (Bert's place was an exception. Bert attracted all types with his great homemade fudge, but he tolerated no rowdiness and had the beat cop pop in frequently in case anyone got out of line.) I suspect the stories of gang fights were mostly concocted to keep non-members away. I ventured in a few times to buy supplies. It was noisy enough, but the greatest danger seemed to be asphyxiation from smoke inhalation.

Steinmetz provided an environment where we could blend in anonymously with a multitude of other girls and boys making that awkward transition from prepubescence to almost-adult. Together, we endured the pain of skin blemishes, crotchless Levis, dateless weekends and turning blue while we waited for C.T.A. buses during the winter. In spite of numerous teenage trials, for most of us, the good times dominated. Our worlds expanded as we formed many new friendships—even future wives and husbands—and learned that teachers (well, some teachers) are people, too.

A portion of the mural that once adorned the firewall on the auditorium stage at Steinmetz High School. The mural depicted Steinmetz, some of his achievements and how they affected people's lives. (photo courtesy Sheldon Kruger)

Charles Proteus Steinmetz (1865-1923) emigrated to America from Germany in 1889. He secured his reputation at the age of 27 by defining the law of hysteresis. (*Don't ask me, class. Look it up!*) It revolutionized the development of A.C. motors and generators while Thomas Edison was still concentrating on D.C. But Steinmetz then had to give lectures, teach and write textbooks until more average engineers began to comprehend. This gentle hunchback genius, with the rimless glasses, goatee and ever-present cigar, would surely have been pleased to know that our school was named in his honor.

That wonderful W.P.A. mural depiction of Steinmetz and his achievements no longer adorns the stage firewall in our assembly hall. Fluorescent lighting has been installed throughout, and a modern public address system has replaced those great old squawk boxes that hung on the wall in every classroom. But the fortress-like façade is unchanged and, inside, today's students are even now forming tomorrow's fond memories of our/their school.

There have been over 30,000 stories in the annals of Steinmetz High School grads. I'm glad that mine was one of them.

Afterthought: Charles Steinmetz was a bona fide genius. An oft-told story epitomizes both his eccentricity and his brilliance.

Steinmetz was retired after having worked at General Electric for many years. A complex and costly piece of equipment at GE's plant was malfunctioning. None of the GE engineers could determine the problem, so the company asked Steinmetz to return and have a look.

Steinmetz walked around inspecting and testing various parts of the machine for a long time. Finally, he took a piece of chalk from his pocket, marked an "X" on one part and told the GE people to replace it. When the part was replaced, the equipment worked perfectly.

A week later, General Electric received a bill from Steinmetz for $10,000. Thinking the figure rather high, they requested that he itemize his charges. Steinmetz obliged with a new bill that read:

Making one chalk mark............................$ 1.00
Knowing where to place mark.....................$9,999.00

General Electric sent a check by return mail.

NOW SHOWING: DRIVE – IN NIGHTS!
Starring: You And Your Steady
With: All The Gang —— And:
Supporting Cast Of Thousands

"Remember the drive-in movies?" Dropped into an already nostalgic dinner conversation, the question had a momentary stop-action effect.

Did we remember! Raised forks and glasses halted in midair. The eyes of a dozen almost-seniors glazed over as adolescent memories rushed back and decorated each face with a smile, a smirk or a blush.

Drive-in Movie. To anyone who was a teenager or young adult in the 1950s or 1960s, the words have an almost historical significance.

Operators of the drive-ins preferred to refer to them by the more dignified term Outdoor Theatre. The teenagers of my era simply called them "the drive-in." Away from parental ears, we used nicknames such as "passion pit" and others less refined.

Dusk at the drive-in. As darkness descends, the show (and, for some, the romance) soon will begin. (Photofest/ICON)

In the cramped front seat of his jalopy, many a teen couple made their first clumsy attempts at heavy necking. Frequent interruptions were a part of the ritual, as refreshment vendors passed by or knees banged against the glove compartment or the steering column.

Girl friends and buddies frequently compared notes on their drive-in dates. Among the boys, this usually involved exhilarating tales of romantic conquests. The girls' versions generally were considerably less steamy. "Right in the middle of this *groovy* kiss, I had to stop and tell him, 'Hey, I don't do *that!*'" No doubt the truth lay somewhere in between, with the males' stories leaning more heavily on fantasy.

More casual couples would often double-date. A girl receiving a first-time invitation for a drive-in date was apt to suggest that they double with her girl friend and her date. She did this as a security measure, but she'd make it sound as though the evening would be even more fun that way. Most guys got the message. Say yes, or no date.

Double-dating imposed a measure of decorum, but it could still be cozy and fun. It also afforded the guys with a built-in cop-out when they regrouped with their buddies and reported on their weekends. "Geez! Babs and me was wantin' to make out, but we couldn't do *nothin'* with Marty and LuAnn watching in the back seat."

Not all drive-in outings were couples, of course. Some cars arrived with 8, 10 or a dozen teens packed inside. Convertibles were favored for these occasions, since most of the group would have to sit somewhere *on* the car to watch the movie. No matter; the real object was just to party.

Admission to the drive-in was not based on a flat rate charged per car. Rather, there were adult and child admission rates for each occupant. Tickets were dispensed from a booth, but intermediary ticket attendants stood at the entrance, stopped each vehicle and looked inside to count heads. They then calculated and announced how much the total would be, took your money over to the ticket vender, returned with tickets and change and motioned you to proceed.

The attendant had to be alert for hot rods with the rear end dragging. Often these contained a couple up front and two or more friends hidden in the trunk. Before back-up lights were standard equipment, some teenagers became adept at stealthily backing in without lights via the nearby exit lanes. Managers quickly caught on, though, and began posting lookouts and saw horses until the main feature began.

Although teenagers usually made up the majority of the drive-in audience, they certainly had plenty of company. Married couples often saved the cost of a baby sitter by bringing kids along. After the cartoons, preschoolers would curl up with a blanket and a pillow on the back seat. Many an infant was changed there and then given a prewarmed bottle.

Parents didn't hesitate to bring school-age children when so-called family films were the norm. Some outdoor theatres provided playgrounds for kids who became restless. For families and adult couples of all ages, the drive-in was a convenient way to see a movie without dressing up or being disturbed by talkative patrons nearby. A speaker that hung inside your window delivered the soundtrack. So by the same token, if you chose to carry on a conversation, you would not disturb the folks in the car parked next to you.

A fellow named Richard Hollingshead is credited with starting it all. The story goes, he tested the idea by projecting a film onto his garage door while sitting in his car with the windshield wipers flicking away simulated rain from a lawn sprinkler. That same summer he opened the Hollingshead Outdoor Theatre in Camden, New Jersey. The year was...(let's have a little drum roll here, please)...*1933*. As Robert L. Ripley would say: "Believe it or not!"

The concept was a bit slow in taking hold at first. Automobiles were a luxury in the 1930s and well into the 1940s, especially during the war years. But in the 1950s, burgeoning suburbs spawned multi-car families. To "have wheels" became a key element of the rites of young manhood – even if you had to beg Dad to borrow the family vehicle.

Drive-ins multiplied rapidly, often built by theatre owners or chains that already operated conventional movie houses. In 1958, their numbers peaked at over 4,000 nationwide.

In my small suburban town on the northwest edge of Chicago, the Harlem Outdoor Theatre typified most single-screen drive-ins. Its pie-shaped acreage was bordered by Harlem Avenue, running north/south, and the diagonal Forest Preserve Drive. A block south, Irving Park Road ran east/west. These main arteries formed three busy intersections that ran close by the theatre entrance. Traffic approached from all directions and began lining the streets a half hour or so before the theatre opened. Local police were assured plenty of overtime directing traffic during the drive-in season.

During my sixteenth summer, I worked as an usher at the H.O.T. Long before show time, we lined up early arrivals bumper-to-bumper and three abreast in the entrance driveway. When the "doors" opened, half the ushers formed a human barricade on the other side. Cars came through like horses out of a starting gate. They had to be funneled into a single file, then shagged in a sharp U-turn around the end of the inner fence.

The remaining ushers were stationed along the inner aisles and the entrances to the parking rows. Arms waving continuously, we shouted an endless litany to the drivers: "Straight ahead, sir. Take it all the way up, please." The object was to fill the parking slots in an orderly fashion, starting with the front rows and working back.

I never understood the logic of this. It meant that folks who arrived early and waited patiently to get a good spot were steered to a position directly beneath the screen. Their reward would be eye strain from trying to focus and sore necks from craning and twisting to take in the whole picture. Most customers turned down the aisle where we directed them – then continued on down the lane and out at the far end. Then, unimpeded by the annoying ushers, they went looking for a spot of their choice.

On weekends, the "house" would be better than half-filled by dusk. The cartoons flashed onto the screen. Vendors hurried on their rounds hawking refreshments. By the time the previews ended, the ushers were using flashlights to direct latecomers. It was dark enough then to begin the feature film, even if it was a black-and-white. Lovers started to snuggle. Those who were actually there to see the movie adjusted their speakers and settled back to enjoy the show.

Increasing operating costs and tough competition from other media took their toll on the nation's open air theatres. By the mid-1980s, only about 3,000 were still operating. Rising land values had

made it too tempting for many owners not to sell. Where once I directed motorized moviegoers there now stands another unromantic shopping center (with a 6-screen multiplex indoor theatre, by the way).

After a nervous period when many drive-ins switched to skin flicks, most of the survivors resumed offering family fare. Others, counting the teen audience as their best source of revenue, specialize in ax murder horror films and gross-out nerd comedies.

Attendance is respectable again. But revenues continue a slow decline, and the long-term future of drive-ins is uncertain. The more stable theatres attract new and residual patrons with second and third screens and innovations such as sound tracks transmitted via AM car radios.

One fellow at our dinner gathering related that he had proposed to his wife during an outdoor screening of the original "Ocean's Eleven," starring the Sinatra rat pack. They've returned to the drive-in on that same date every year since.

"It's kind of like having two anniversaries," he explained, with a conspiratorial wink to the other males. "Helps keep the romance alive, if ya know what I mean."

His better half agreed with the significance of the anniversary, but demurred on the romantic aspect. "Since he became a grandpa," she confided, "Mister Romance has all he can do to keep from nodding off halfway through the movie. If he comes snuggling over to my side, it's not my body he's after—it's my popcorn."

"Clang, Clang, Clang!" Went Those Trolleys

Remember the Toonerville Trolley?

Remember the streetcar named Desire?

Remember when Judy Garland went to spend a jolly hour on a trolley?

Viewers of late night TV or the old time movie cable channels no doubt are familiar with Judy Garland's famous "Trolley Song" scene in the film classic "Meet Me In St. Louis." But young readers may not actually remember streetcars, or perhaps only foggily recall them clanging and swaying through the streets of their home town.

In this area, the South Shore Line and the Skokie Swift probably are the closest surviving ground-level descendents still operating commercially. Both, however, have been modernized to more of a "rapid transit" status, even as routes and services have been curtailed over the years.

Chicago's famed elevated train system, though similarly metamorphosised, is still an integral part of the city's public transportation network. Raised about two stories above street level on iron-girder stilts, "the L" (as natives call it) fans out from Chicago's downtown Loop area to all parts of the city and O'Hare International Airport on its northwest suburban fringe.

The nation's first commercial electric line operated in Cleveland, Ohio, as early as 1884. It was followed three years later by the more widely heralded system in Richmond, Virginia, constructed by industrial tycoon Frank Sprague.

Professionals within the transportation industry referred to them as "street railway systems" or "electric street railways." The rest of us just called them streetcars or trolleys. They evolved naturally from their horse-drawn predecessors when the development of the dynamo-driven motor made it practical to electrify the cars.

Though clumsy in appearance, trolleys formed the nucleus of public transportation for much of the U.S. back when even a single automobile was a luxury for most families. The local lines provided quick, reliable service in most large cities for a surprisingly low fare. In the streetcar's prime, Chicago had over 1,100 miles of track criss-crossing through its main streets.

Contrary to its reputation as a progressive city, Chicago was a relative hold-out. At the turn of the century, smaller towns such as Elgin, Peoria and Rockford had already committed to the electrified cars. Although several entrepreneur firms had started up small lines within the city, horse-drawn trolleys and the newer cable cars still dominated in Chicago.

By 1906, the city's trolleys were all electric, but service was provided by a hodgepodge of independent companies. Schedules were not coordinated and switching lines often required an additional fare. Financial difficulties, buy-outs and mergers resulted in confusing changes for passengers and made regulation by the city difficult.

Crew members pose with their early (1915) Chicago streetcar. (photo courtesy Margaret Leengran)

In 1913, the city passed what was called the Unification Ordinance. It brought the four remaining trolley lines under the management and operation of what became the Chicago Surface Lines. When the unification became effective on February 1, 1914, Chicago had the largest street railway system in the world. Thanks to the liberal transfer policy of the CSL, Chicagoans could travel almost anywhere in the city, and sometimes into neighboring suburbs, for a single fare.

The trolleys' interurban counterparts linked nearby towns and the countryside in between. By the early 1920s, Chicago boasted interurban lines radiating out in many directions.

The Chicago, Lake Shore and South Bend Railway did a substantial business between South Bend, Indiana, and the Illinois Central Railroad's downtown station at Randolph Street. The Chicago, Aurora and Elgin line linked western suburbs to Chicago's Loop. And the Chicago North Shore and Milwaukee interurbans transported passengers between the Loop and Milwaukee on luxury limiteds that included parlor-observation cars and diners. Almost 300 trains daily made the trip, in as little as two hours and ten minutes. Vying for commuters from the steam trains' patrons, the CNS&M's billboards challenged: "Did you ever travel 80 miles an hour?"

Thanks to the interurban trolley systems, a shopping trip or a holiday in the city ceased to be a major undertaking for small town folk and farm families. Singly or in trains up to five or six cars, the interurban lines gave stiff competition to the dusty and less conveniently scheduled steam railroads. When high-speed cars came into fairly common use, a rail journal reported: "The deluxe (traction) trains overtake and pass steam trains...to the great amusement and gratification of the interurban passengers."

At the peak of their popularity, 80,000 trolley cars in the U.S. traveled on 45,000 miles of track, carrying 11 billion (yes, *billion*) passengers annually. Folk in St. Louis, Milwaukee or Chicago could travel all the way to New York City via electric railway – if they did not mind transferring a few times en route.

Yet the trolley knew its place and stayed there. Accidents were few. Because of their limited speed, the generally flat terrain and regular maintenance of rails, trolleys almost never jumped their tracks. No automobile was ever stuck by a trolley while its driver kept to his designated strip of the road. On the rare instances when a motorman misjudged his stopping distance, passengers waiting to board stood out of danger on platforms or raised concrete "safety isles."

Streetcars provided a unique blend of comfort, speed and dependability. Grown-ups often took them for granted. Kids made an adventure of each trip. In Chicago, where my boyhood pals and I gamboled away our youth, the old "Red Rocket" trolleys of the 1930s and 1940s represented transport to a ball game, a movie, Riverview Amusement Park and the Lake Michigan beach, among other destinations.

A Chicago Surface Lines streetcar lets passengers off in front of an Andes Candies store. At right, a lucky kid out shopping with his mother gets pulled in his Radio Flyer wagon. (photo by T. H. Desnoyers, Krambles-Peterson Archive)

Sometimes my friends and I spent our whole journey huddled on the rear platform, observing the conductor at his work. As passengers boarded, he accepted their transfers or fares, performed magic with the shiny coin changer clipped to his belt and rang up a passenger tally on the overhead counter. Sometimes he gave a hand to a lady boarding with an armload of shopping bags. Then he leaned out to make sure that no one was making a late dash for the streetcar before he pulled the cord that gave a little "ding, ding" signal to the motorman to proceed. When otherwise idle, he might punch up some transfers to be dispensed to the next few boarding passengers. If we were well behaved and asked politely, he usually would give us a handful of used transfers for our collections.

The most coveted spot on the streetcar, however, was the window corner on the motorman's left. Two average boys—or three very skinny ones—could squeeze in there and survey the trolley's progress. On a hot summer day, the little window would be raised, providing a refreshing breeze as the car rolled along. Mostly, though, we stood awed in the presence of the man who controlled that giant electric conveyance.

At the "Six Corners" intersection of Milwaukee, Irving Park and Cicero Avenues, two "Red Rocket" trolley cars pass each other on Milwaukee. On left is the Portage theatre, a frequent matinee choice of the author and his pals. The Sears, Roebuck store is on the Irving Park/Cicero corner, just out of the picture at right. (Chicago Surface Lines photo, Krambles-Peterson Archive)

Unlike the often garrulous conductor, the motorman spoke only to remind disembarking riders to watch their step, or to reassure an uncertain passenger that, "Yes, ma'am, this next stop coming up is Pulaski Avenue." Indeed, a sign overhead warned sternly: "Motorman may not converse with passengers while car is in motion."

The safety of his passengers, as well as careless pedestrians and motorists, demanded the motorman's full attention. Frequently, he stomped the pedal that sounded a loud warning clanger out front. But when the coast was clear for a couple of blocks, he would sometimes give the electric traction motors their head. With a whine of power, they would propel the streetcar at up to 30m.p.h. – a seemingly breakneck speed!

How easy it was to close your eyes and imagine yourself in the motorman's place, a street-bound Casey Jones, rocketing to some desperate rescue over rails heated red hot by the friction of those speeding wheels! On one rare trip when I was traveling alone, such fantasizing caused me to miss my stop and have to walk back, feeling like a dunce.

At the end of the line, you could watch the fascinating ritual of the change-over. The conductor walked through the car to the front (now the rear), flipping the reversible backs of each wicker seat so that passengers now would face the opposite direction. The motorman got out and pulled down the trolley's current pole in the rear (now the front), securing it to a hook atop the car. Then he loosed its mate at the other end of the car and, as its spring mechanism tugged it upward, he gently guided the current collector wheel to the overhead electric line by means of a control rope. A motorman with a steady hand could touch wheel to wire without a single spark flying upon contact. Kids, of course, would prefer to see that shower of sparks.

The front motor was now idle and the rear motor activated . The motorman and the conductor exchanged positions. Now the streetcar was completely reversed, a mirror image of its former self. With a simple switch-over to the parallel track, it would begin its next run in the direction whence it had come.

The ultimate end of the line for street railway systems in general came into view about 1950. Many lines, victims of excess competition, poor management or the Great Depression, folded during the 1930s. Most of the others actually got a lift from the gas rationing during World War II. But the proliferation of private automobiles after the war put a severe crimp in ridership. Most of the surviving lines began experiencing a serious profit squeeze.

Then the manufacturers of those new-fangled "motor coaches" (buses) began doing some high-powered lobbying among city officials and transportation authorities. Buses, they said, would operate more efficiently. They would eliminate the annoyance of tracks in the road and trolleys interfering with the growing auto traffic. They offered more versatility and mobility and required only one driver.

During the early 1950s, streetcar track was already being taken up or paved over in many cities. Some newer steamlined models, their cost not yet amortized, resisted the trend for awhile. The last of Chicago's "Green Hornet" model returned to the barn June 21, 1968. (Meanwhile, though, many were being converted to elevated/subway cars.)

In some instances, trolley buses initially took advantage of the existing overhead power supply. One problem with the "more versatile" buses quickly became apparent. Drivers often misjudged their distance when pulling to the curb for passengers, causing the collector wheel to part company with the overhead electric line.

By 1960, however, these and the remaining trolley cars had been phased out by propane-fueled buses in most municipalities. In cities throughout America, "Progress" gradually took its toll of the street railway systems.

At what price? Well, the "limitations" of the streetcar included its limited ability to disrupt traffic, since its path was unwavering. Its "more efficient" successor can efficiently block two lanes of auto traffic repeatedly while fighting its way into and out of boarding zones. Its fumes can efficiently nauseate both motorists and pedestrians who pass within half a block of its wake. It becomes stuck in snow drifts that never phased the electric cars, and it stalls in all kinds of weather.

In downtown Chicago, buses reportedly average about 4 to 5m.p.h. during peak periods. The typical pedestrian can walk at a speed of 3m.p.h.

In a society burdened with countless forms of air pollution, the streetcar creates virtually none. As for energy conservation, streetcars burn no fuel at all while they idle; and they can be lighted, air conditioned and heated with relatively little power.

Streetcars never were rendered obsolete technologically. (Many other countries, including our neighbors in Canada, still utilize them extensively.) They simply were put out to pasture as a result of our love affair with the automobile and the unwarranted conclusion that gas-powered buses were a superior mode of transportation. Today, bus passengers and motorists alike are caught up in gas-guzzling, time-consuming traffic jams twice every workday. Many older commuters must mourn the loss of the dependable traction cars that once whisked them to work in hassle-free comfort.

Trolley fans in some cities are more fortunate. Boston, Cleveland, Dallas, Newark, New Orleans, Philadelphia, Pittsburgh, San Diego, San Francisco, Seattle and Portland (Oregon) all have maintained at least part of their street railway services. In 1974, they carried 200 million passengers.

The following year, Boston and San Francisco expressed their satisfaction with their respective trolley lines by ordering 230 new cars from the Boeing-Vertol Company – the first cars to be built in the U.S. since 1952! Meanwhile, the U.S. Department of Transportation held a national conference to explore the potential of trolley lines as a partial solution to the nation's mass transit woes.

Purists among trolley buffs might not approve of the new "light rail transits" (or LRTs). Streamlined to look more like modern "rapid transit" cars, many will even receive their power from a third rail. Sacrilege! Even so, on local non-express routes, they should manage to evoke some of the romantic aura of our old Green Hornets. In any case, they will be quieter and quicker than buses.

Given the challenge of our modern mass transit problems, streetcars probably never will effect a complete role reversal with those noxious smelling buses; but they can assuredly provide a valuable auxiliary service. For the LRTs of today still offer the same basic advantages of the old fashioned trolley cars of yesteryear: dependable transportation for large numbers of people; non-polluting; more rapid and more economical then the gas-fueled buses.

Besides, streetcars are more fun. Did you ever hear of anyone who went to spend a jolly hour on a motor coach?

Afterthought: Those with fond memories of trolleys, and young folk who never had the pleasure, can see and ride vintage cars at many railway museums around the country. Easily reached from the Chicago area, both the Illinois Railway Museum in Union and the Fox River Trolley Museum in South Elgin have cars representing many long-gone lines. Lovingly restored by volunteer crews, the cars are open for inspection, and selected streetcars will take passengers on periodic runs.

Chicago old-timers and trolley enthusiasts of any era can enjoy a trolley trip back in time with "A Century of Chicago Streetcars," by James D. Johnson. Much of the historical background in the above piece came from this book, which also is lavishly illustrated with vintage photos.

And here's a late breaking news story. As we go to press, a U.S. Congressman, the son of a Chicago streetcar conductor, is proposing the return of streetcars to selected streets in Chicago, with some routes extending to western suburbs. Among the touted advantages: replacement of polluting buses; renewal of economically depressed areas; still useable rails buried just below some paved roads. Among the likely roadblocks: opposing vested interests; political haggling; funding.

Stay tuned...

A Six-Cornered Shopping Trip

Anticipation gripped me as soon as I awoke and remembered. Yesterday school had let out for the holidays. Today Mom and I would go on our big Christmas shopping trip.

I reviewed my finances as I dressed. The bottom line hadn't improved. After months of saving a portion of my allowance, I had ten dollars. Normally, I would count myself rich, but on this occasion, by my calculations, I was about a dollar short.

There were my two brothers to buy for, four aunts and uncles, three cousins, two grandparents and two best buddies. I was allocating fifty cents for each of them, and I planned to spend as much as a whole dollar on my folks. I figured I'd need a little extra for tax and any purchases that were a bit over my budgeted amount.

At breakfast, I broached the problem to my father. He came up with a business-like solution. He would advance me a dollar and deduct a dime from my allowance for ten weeks. That was relatively painless. I had braced myself for a proposal that would require me to perform some extra chores to earn the money.

My mother, meanwhile, extracted a more unwelcome concession: that I would wear my long johns on our excursion.

Mom got pushy about the long johns only on really cold days – like today was forecast to be. But no matter how bitter the weather, those scratchy woolen drawers were akin to wearing burlap leg warmers. When obliged to wear them, I often cut short my sledding or other outdoor winter sports rather than endure the discomfort.

Today I had no choice; and it would be a long day. So I came up with the clever ploy of wearing my cotton pajama bottoms under the long johns. Had we been in an accident that day, Mom no doubt would have been mortified when they undressed me at the hospital.

A four-block walk brought us to Irving Park Road. The wind was indeed icy cold as we stood at the unsheltered bus stop. Briefly, at least, I appreciated the warmth afforded by my long johns

Mercifully, a Chicago Surface Lines shuttle bus soon arrived and took us as far as Neenah Avenue. There we transferred to a waiting streetcar. A wisp of heat from beneath the reversible wicker seats melted a trace of snow from our shoes. Seated by the window, I watched familiar landmarks pass by: the Patio movie theatre, Andes

Candies, the now deserted Portage Park swimming pool and playground. More than half of our fellow passengers debarked with us at our destination – the intersection of Irving Park, Cicero and Milwaukee, known to most Northwest Siders as "Six Corners."

The Sears, Roebuck store, occupying about a square block, was and is the anchor of the busy "Six Corners" shopping area at Irving Park, Milwaukee and Cicero Avenues on Chicago's Northwest Side. (Lake County [IL] Discovery Museum, Curt Teich Postcard Archives)

A Sears, Roebuck & Company store dominated the bustling multi-cornered intersection. Several floors tall, it occupied a square block at the northeast corner. The next block east was a huge parking lot for Sears customers (but with no signs warning that others would be towed). Woolworth's, Walgreen's and dozens of smaller, less famous stores were within a block or two along the three main streets.

We began our quest at Sears, pausing outside to admire the gay holiday scenes in their display windows. A Salvation Army group sang carols at the entrance. Mom dropped a coin into their large copper kettle.

Inside, we helped ourselves to two of the free shopping bags offered by Hillman's Bakery. (Hillman's operated a store in the basement of Sears, a novelty that I never quite understood and never saw duplicated anywhere else.) Mom's shopping came first, and I tagged along patiently for awhile. When I began getting twitchy, she steered me to the toy department to wait for her.

Christmas is coming, and this 1940s store window display gives kids much to dream about and wish for. (Retrofile.com)

The toy section at Sears overflowed with so much good stuff that any girl or boy could fill a wish list four or five times over. For me, though, the main attraction at Christmas was the train display. During the holidays, Sears set up an impressive oversized electric train lay-out. A Lionel train and its economy-priced Marx counterpart ran on parallel tracks through an elaborate town and countryside. The tracks criss-crossed at two points, and I marveled at how the trains continued endlessly on their respective routes and never collided.

When Mom returned with one shopping bag filled, we headed for Woolworth's. My limited funds made the "five-and-dime" chainstore our logical choice. It was a relief to get outside and walk a block. The long johns were starting to itch right through my pajama bottoms.

Everything I needed to complete my list turned out to be available and affordable at Woolworth's. Brothers, cousins and buddies would receive such universally appreciated things as comic books, bags of marbles, paper doll cut-out books, Old Maid playing cards and Big Little Books. Aunts got nail polish, powder puffs, hankies, even knitting needles. Much of this was suggested by my mother, since I was basically clueless about buying for adult women. (Some things don't change as we get older. Am I right, guys?)

For my uncles, I selected such manly items as razor blades, smokes or shaving soap. I didn't really know their brand preferences, so I selected Burma Shave in appreciation of their roadside signs, Raleigh cigarettes because they sponsored one of my favorite radio comedians and Gillette Blue Blades because I liked their catchy singing commercial.

Mom helped me pick out two pairs of socks for Dad. While she was busy at another counter, I beckoned to a saleslady.

"That's my mother over there," I told her. "Can you help me pick out some stockings for her?"

She smiled knowingly and replied, "Sure, hon. Let's look over here and see if we have something in your price range." We were in the halcyon years after World War II, and my dollar was able to purchase a pair of real nylons in a shade that the helpful saleslady thought would suit my mother.

When I rejoined Mom, it was about lunch time. We ate at the Woolworth's lunch counter, sitting on the stools with those tapered chrome supports and the red padded swivel seats. My grilled cheese sandwich was complimented by their generous cup of hot chocolate, topped with whipped cream. Then we continued our shopping at several other stores until mom completed a few more purchases. Having seen much of what she purchased, I was sworn to secrecy.

I proudly took charge of the shopping bags for the trip home, lugging them a bit clumsily on and off of the streetcar and the bus.

When they started to bump on the ground, Mom relieved me of the heavier one for the last two blocks of our walk.

We arrived home in late afternoon. My first act was to dash to my room and shed the hated woolen underwear. I made sure the door was closed, lest my mother look in and spot my makeshift pajama liner. Then, as Mom started supper, I carefully hid away my purchases.

Wrapping and tagging would be done on Saturday morning as I listened to Smilin' Ed, Let's Pretend, The Adventures of Frank Merriwell and the rest of my radio favorites. On Christmas day, as my gifts were opened, I would be rewarded by both the surprised thankfulness of brothers and cousins too young to be giving presents and the over-acted but sincere joyfulness of adult relatives.

It would be reward enough to almost erase the unpleasant memory of those scratchy long johns.

Mellow Musical Memories

Husband: "As a boy, I wanted to play the piano terribly."
School Teacher Wife: "Your grammar needs work, but
you got your wish."
                          —-variation on a Joe Miller joke

Norman Rockwell often portrayed freckled face youth trapped in music lessons and yearning to join friends playing outside their window. That undoubtedly happened at times. But none of my peers in Rockwell's *Saturday Evening Post* days had their arm twisted to begin or continue lessons. The budding musicians I knew all did so by their own choice.

Bobby actually had to plead for trumpet lessons. His father initially said no. He worked a graveyard shift and needed a quiet house in order to sleep during the day. With gentle coaxing from Mom, however, Pop finally relented and even produced a borrowed horn from somewhere.

Bobby readily agreed to practice only in the evening. The lessons went well for about six months. One day during summer vacation, Bobby planned to see a White Sox night game with friends. That morning he began practicing around ten o'clock. Pop awoke, of course, and threatened to fix bobby's lip so that he could not even blow bubble gum.

After that, Bobby stuck to the agreement for another month or so. Then his enthusiasm got the better of him and he tried to cheat again, but this time playing softly, in the basement. His mother quickly shut him off, but his father could be heard grumbling in the bedroom.

That night, when Pop left for work, the trumpet evidently went with him. Presumably it was returned whence it came. Wise for his years, Bobby resisted the urge to inquire.

Jimmy may have been a prodigy who missed his calling. At a young age, he yearned to play the violin. Skeptical, his parents urged him to start by joining the school band.

Bands do not include violins, of course. Jimmy became a cornet player, which seemed to satisfy his musical bent for the next five or six years.

207

When he progressed to high school, he signed up for band and was tested on several brass instruments. The band director was delighted to find that he had a talent for the sousaphone. It became Jimmy's instrument throughout high school and a tour of duty with a U.S. Army marching band.

For Jimmy, the horn named in honor of John Philip Sousa was a source of both enjoyment and frustration. When he told people that he played the sousaphone, they invariably looked puzzled. Describing it proved to be a waste of time, so he took to carrying a picture of himself playing the instrument. But when he showed the photo to someone, the response always was, "Oh, it's a *tuba!*"

"No," Jimmy insisted indignantly, "it *ain't* a *tuba*. It's a *sousaphone!*"

Katie attended a parochial school. After classes, she and her brother Howard took piano lessons (separately) with one of the nuns. Classical only – none of that raucous "pop" music here.

Katie suffered near mortal embarrassment when Sister scheduled them for a recital and Howie refused to play a duet with her. She always suspected that Howie kept up his lessons only because Sister never applied a ruler to the knuckles of one of her future Paderewskis.

During lessons, if Katie hit a clinker, she became distressed and froze with her fingers poised over the ivories. She shook her head in exasperation, searched frantically for the right keys and muttered, "Wait! Wait! Wait!"

Sister sat patiently, her hands clasped in the folds of her habit. Straight-faced, she replied, "I'm *not* going anywhere, Katherine."

Katie had considered becoming a classical pianist. But in high school she discovered a new extra-curricular activity called dating. Alicia de Larrocha's path to the concert stage became just a tad more secure as Katie bowed out of the keyboard competition in favor of more…eh…romantic pursuits.

In the days of five-cent candy bars, boys seldom received singing lessons except as part of a choral group. Sam was an exception.

Sam's mother tutored in French. She had worked out a barter arrangement with a local spinster who gave voice lessons to young people. Since Sam had to accompany his mother to Miss Peterson's home, he ended up being trained in both subjects. He rather enjoyed the singing, but it was forty years before he took a trip to Europe and was able to put his French to practical use.

Miss Peterson required seemingly endless scales, sung in English and Italian, in half notes. She provided piano accompaniment. Gradually, Sam progressed from simple songs to such classics as "The Road to Mandalay."

Recitals by Miss Peterson's pupils were given in her parlor. During one of these sedate gatherings, some inattentive ladies were chatting softly and began to giggle as Sam performed. He was certain that they were laughing at him and had to choke back tears to finish his song.

Enduring and overcoming such adversity helps to build self-confidence. Sam eventually entered the ministry. He later observed that without Miss Peterson's recitals and her insistence on breathing and projection exercises, he probably would not have passed the public speaking classes in seminary.

Pete's choice of instrument was the accordion. "The old go-to-me, come-to-me," or "Polish piano," his Uncle Stosh called it. While still in short pants, Pete began learning on a 12-base model. As he grew, he moved up to the full size 120 base.

Many of Pete's relatives were musically inclined. At family gatherings, they entertained each other. Grandpa, another accordionist, once joined Pete in a medley of duet numbers at a birthday bash. After several tunes, Pete asked, "Gramps, how come you don't look at the music?"

Gramps shrugged. "These're all old standards," he replied. "I know 'em by heart."

Pete was awed. Playing from memory was a concept as yet unknown to him. His already great regard for his grandfather went up another few notches.

For one of his recitals, Pete and a female student performed a duet. Halfway through the ever-popular "Lady of Spain," Pete's middle "C" key fell off. The spirited tune afforded no pause to retrieve it. Pete gamely finished the piece without it. Thanks to his partner's lively playing, the audience seemed not to notice the occasionally missing note.

Such showmanship prompted Pete's mother to take him to the downtown Chicago studio where the Morris B. Sach's television amateur hour held try-outs. From stage left, the producer and a secretary conducted the low-budget auditions. Pete played up a storm and thought he'd done very well. But the producer just shook his head once and waved the next kid forward.

As Pete left the stage, the secretary scratched his name from the list on her clipboard and said kindly, "Sorry, hon."

Pete's mother shared his disappointment and asked, "What's wrong? Didn't he play beautifully?"

The producer nodded. "The kid's good," he agreed. "But he's too stone faced."

A few years earlier, when the amateur hour was broadcast only on radio, Pete might have been picked as a contestant and had hundreds of listeners calling in to vote for him. But this new visual medium demanded both talent *and* personality. Pete was too reserved to make it big on the small screen.

TV's rebuff didn't deter Pete from joining a small band in his teens. The group landed numerous jobs in the local area. Most "gigs" ended at midnight. One of the fathers dropped the boys off and picked them up in a station wagon.

Once the band was hired for a party at an affluent location near Chicago's lakeshore. It would last until *2a.m.* This was the big time!

As part of the deal, the band was promised transportation home, but something went wrong. When the party broke up, there was no ride.

At two o'clock in the morning, no one in the band wanted to call his parents for help. So they hauled all their equipment—including music stands and a full set of drums—across town on the Chicago Surface Line. Fortunately, they had one of the famed "Red Rocket" streetcars almost to themselves.

My own musical "career" didn't begin until I was almost 12. That's when my family acquired a used upright piano. With juvenile logic, I enrolled at a music studio where my pal Wayne was taking electric guitar lessons—never mind that they catered mostly to guitar and accordion pupils and it would require an hour-long trip from my home.

The school's token piano teacher was an elderly fellow who had played in the nickelodeon and burlesque theatres years ago. Mr. Golding could still play a mean honky-tonk piano.

Unfortunately, his teaching method involved the use of chords for the left hand. It was a short-cut to playing simple tunes. However, it meant not learning to sight read the bass notes. That becomes a handicap when you progress to more sophisticated sheet music on which chord names aren't printed above each measure.

The first year, Mr. Golding provided me with over 100 mimeographed sheets of pop standards. They were all "oldies," presumably in the public domain genre and subject to copying at will. If not, who was I to ask my grandfatherly teacher if "Daisy, Daisy" still carried a valid copyright?

Once I began buying printed sheet music from the school's large rack, the cost of lessons almost doubled. My taste ranged over such Hit Parade memorables as "Harbor Lights," "Gone Fishin'," "Halls of Ivy," "St. Louis Blues," "Foolish Heart," "Bewitched," "Orange Colored Sky," and "Too Fat Polka" (with a great cover photo of Arthur Godfrey playing his ukulele).

During my fourth year, I realized that my training had plateaued. Mr. Golding had honed my modest talent to its fullest. Now, he made only occasional suggestions for jazzing up the more lively tunes. Mostly, he sat back, puffed on his cigar and enjoyed listening.

Out of loyalty to my teacher, I stayed on until the next school recital. I practiced for weeks my own jazzed-up rendition of "Maple Leaf Rag."

On recital day, I was prepared but, as always, nervous. It did not help to find that, because I was Mr. Golding's oldest and favorite pupil, he'd arranged to schedule me last on the program. I paced backstage with sweaty palms for two hours.

Stage fright notwithstanding, I think Scott Joplin would have enjoyed my performance. The audience's applause echoed sweetly in my ears as I donned my coat backstage, my heartbeat slowly returning to normal.

Suddenly, Mr. Golding scurried backstage and glanced around the milling group of performers. Spying me, he grinned. "Wait, Danny," he ordered. "Take off your coat. The folks want an encore from you."

Encore, my clavicle! I'd rehearsed only *one piece*. I'd have run in panic, but my teacher already was pushing me back onto the stage.

What should I play? What *could* I play? My brain was doing its Mortimer Snerd imitation. Thank goodness my back was to the audience. They couldn't see my hands shaking. I closed my eyes and did an introductory chord run, stalling for time.

In that last instant, my subconscious latched onto "Body and Soul." I'd been practicing it lately, embellishing with fancy trills and crosshand rolls. Somehow I got through it with no flubs, although the tempo was a bit fast.

The audience rewarded me with warm applause. A deep bow, a hasty retreat; and my public performing ended on that high note.

Since my teen years, I play infrequently and usually in private. Being able to play for my own entertainment is ample reward for four years of lessons. An added bonus is that, when stresses build up, it's a wonderful way to relax and unwind.

Good reason for all of us who were "enriched" by music lessons in our youth to thank the folk who juggled budgets to pay the bill and endured those hours of dissonant practicing. Reason, too, to be open-minded when one of our offspring comes around as ask, "Mom and Dad, can I get a set of drums?"

They Don't Make 'Em Like They Used To

Ronald Colman suggested this column to me. Sort of.

Jack Benny's long-suffering neighbor was portraying George Apley on a Sunday TV matinee. In one scene he struggles to communicate via one of fellow actor Don Ameche's new inventions – the telephone.

It was an early vintage wall-mounted device. Its mouthpiece protruded only six inches from the wall, with no evident adjustment for height. The receiver, with its long handgrip, had a very short cord, presumably to keep the user positioned close to the mouthpiece. A crank on the side "rang up" the operator, who would then come on the line to inquire: "Number, please."

In my preschool years, telephones were considered a luxury rather than a necessity. My family and many others in our neighborhood got along quite well without them for many years.

The first telephone ever to intrude upon my boyish view of the big world was at my maternal grandparents' house. Proudly on display and prominently located in the dining room, it sat upon a table designed for the use, with a drawer to store the Chicago directory. (That volume was then less than an inch thick.)

Like Ford's early automobiles, its color was basic black. One of the tall goose-necked models, it had a lamp style base. The mouthpiece swiveled up and down atop its long neck. The earpiece hung just below in a cradle on the side of the neck.

Grandma and Grandpa Farr's telephone was one of the new improved models with a rotating dial. If your call was local and you knew the number, you no longer had to jiggle the cradle arm to signal the operator for assistance.

The evolution of telephones is grist for a column of its own. Do we really need such modern "conveniences" as call waiting, call forwarding, cordless phones, voicemail, etc.[1] ad infinitum? But George Apley's encounter set me pondering many other benchmarks of "Progress"— things that ain't what they used to be...and not necessarily for the better.

---

[1] And, since this piece originally appeared, the infamous cell phone?

213

As a boy, I brushed my teeth with Pepsident tooth powder. It came in a metal can shaped like today's hand lotion containers, minus the pump. Its shaker head was covered by a pop-off cap. To use the powder, you poured some into your palm, then sopped it up with the moistened bristles of your tooth brush.

The transition to tooth paste had its merits. Powder sometimes was spilled around the bathroom. But it's a challenge to measure out enough paste and not too much. (A cynic might suggest that the manufacturers had thought of that.) Like words spoken in anger, excess tooth paste can not be returned to its source.

At least the original tinny metal tubes could be folded over at the bottom and would stay folded. As you emptied the tube and continued folding upward, you eventually had the satisfaction of knowing that you had squeezed out the last useable smidgen.

Now we have plastic tubes possessed of an annoying elasticity. Roll them as tightly as you can. They will nonetheless unwind immediate upon their return to the medicine cabinet. Or try to get that last squeeze out of the neck. It's easier to drop the last ball into the clown's eye socket in one of those pocket-size skill toys.

Helping Mom open a new can of coffee used to be a treat. It required peeling off a metal band that sealed the lid to the can.

A "key" was lightly welded to the bottom of each can for this purpose. The key actually was a thin length of metal formed into an oval-shaped handle with an inch of shank extending at a 90 degree angle from one side. At its tip was a small slot. It accommodated a tapered end of the can's metal band to get the process started.

Excess air had been pumped out of the can in the packaging process. Your initial twist of the key broke the seal and there was a *whoosh* of air rushing in to fill the void. This was true of all brands, but one manufacturer capitalized on the fact by boasting that its coffee was "vacuum-packed for freshness."

One needed a steady hand to strip away the entire band in one unwrinkled coil. If done successfully, the result would look somewhat like the spring inside a wind-up toy. But if the band twisted sideways and tangled on itself, finishing the job was difficult. It also increased the chance of cutting a finger on the sharp metal edges.

When you proudly presented the opened can to Mom, you got to keep the key. Removing it carefully from the wound-up metal band, you added it to the collection of discarded and found keys that you kept on a long key chain.

Some kids saved can-opener keys on a separate chain. You never knew when Mom might lose or break one and you'd have to come to her rescue with a spare. The advent of electric can openers and plastic lids made key-opened cans all but extinct. Once they held such diverse products as sardines and Crisco shortening. During a recent undercover investigative foray to our local supermarket, I found only one item still packaged this way: canned hams.

Anacin and Bayer aspirin once were sold in handy pocket-size metal packets of 12 tablets. The "tin" had twin dimples at the rear of the box and the lid, which served as hinges. Small matching bulges in front provided a snug fit. Snap the lid down, it stayed securely shut. Press the rear edges between thumb and forefinger, it popped open.

Kids coveted the empty Bayer and Anacin tins. They were perfect for storing small quantities of change and other small flat treasures. (Also for hiding and passing secret messages to your fellow members of Captain Midnight's Secret Squadron or Nick Carter's "Inner Circle" for junior detectives.)

When I first began going to the movies *sans* parents, I was very nervous about losing my limited funds. I had to continually check to see if the loose coins in my watch pocket were all still there. Then I hit upon carrying them in a Bayer tin.

The makeshift coin container was a solid presence I could feel and know that it was still there. When I walked, it gave audible reassurance with a continuous metallic clicking sound.

Headache remedies are still available in 12-packs. But they are flimsy cardboard flip-top boxes, like sawed-off packs of Marlboros. You wouldn't risk carrying your week's allowance in them.

Some throat lozenges are still available in metal boxes with snap-tight lids. Likewise, Band-Aid bandages, although the last time I checked only a few selected sizes were in "tins," the majority coming now in paper boxes. But these are much larger containers and meant for different treasures. You can't conceal them in a watch pocket.

Back when my brothers and I were consuming literally hundreds of peanut-butter-and-jelly sandwiches annually, these deliciously

215

compatible foodstuffs were akin also in the way they were packaged. Both came in decorative "tumblers" that became drinking glasses when empty.

The jelly glasses were illustrated with nursery rhymes. Jack and Jill, for instance, would go hand-in-hand up the hill on the front of a glass, then tumble down the reverse side, spilling their pail of water.

Our favorite peanut butter, a brand that's still popular, depicted the story of Peter Pan's magical adventures. The manufacturer kept coming out with new ones, so a "full collection" probably was not possible. My best guess is that our family accumulated 30 or 40 over time, with some broken along the way. Mothers had to remember which ones they had in their kitchen cabinets so as to avoid selecting duplicates when they shopped. Otherwise, there would be distressed cries of, "Mom, we've already got that one!"

These tumbler style containers had metal lids that were crimped on. Because the lids had to be pried off, they never fit snuggly afterward. The Board of Health probably prefers today's screw-on lids. But both products were stored in the "fridge," and the contents were used up rapidly. I never knew anyone to get ptomaine poisoning from jelly or peanut butter.

At least half of Mom's "everyday" glasses had once contained peanut butter or jelly. In thousands of homes like ours, kids drank their milk a bit more willingly while twirling glasses that told the tales of Simple Simon, Little Bo Peep, Humpty Dumpty et al.

In my view, the change-over from tin to aluminum cans for beer and soda pop has proved too costly to be classified as progress. (I'll not dwell on the satisfaction of collecting discarded Coke bottles in the 1940s and turning them in for the two-cent deposit.)

"Tin cans" were, in fact, made of thin sheet steel plated with a coat of tin to prevent corrosion. Their capacity to preserve foodstuffs for an indefinite period was a tremendous boon to food processors, merchants and housewives. Not to mention millions of GIs, who otherwise might never have savored the opportunity to dine on those incomparable K-Ration meals.

Early tin beverage cans were opened by punching a hole in the top with the pointed end of a hand-held can opener. A second hole on the opposite edge permitted air to enter as you drank, thus allowing the liquid to flow more smoothly.

I received one of my earliest ecology lessons while fishing on Lake Springfield with my Uncle Mac and Uncle Leo. We had a cooler in the boat with beer and soft drinks in tin cans. When I drained a can of Coke, Uncle Leo had me use the church key to make a small scratch on its side before submerging it in the water.

Bottles thrown into the water sometimes broke. Shards often washed into shallow water, where swimmers could step on them. With our tin cans, Uncle Leo explained, the oxidation process began even as they sank to the bottom. Soon they would rust away to nothing, their elements returning to the earth whence they came.

Unfortunately, this doesn't work on aluminum cans. They can be recycled but are otherwise all but indestructible. Casually discarded empties blight streets, lawns, parks and country landscapes. Waste management experts worry over the dwindling number of sites for new landfills.

Aluminum cans are an extreme example, but a lot of life's simple pleasures have bit the dust in the name of Progress. Do you suppose you'd get any obscene phone calls if we all still placed our calls through a live operator? And wouldn't you like to pour your next Pepsi Cola from a 12-ounch returnable bottle into a Peter Pan tumbler?

Now that would really hit the spot!

Afterthought: For those too young to remember, Pepsi Cola came onto the market as an unknown. It made an incredible dent in the market share of reigning king Coca Cola by introducing a 12-ounce bottle for the same price that Coke charged for its familiar 6-ounce size of "the pause that refreshes." The young upstart's motto was "Pepsi Cola hits the spot!" Radio airwaves were flooded with a jingle that went:

> Pepsi Cola hits the spot.
> 12-ounce bottle, that's a lot.
> Just five cents for a bottle, too.
> Pepsi Cola is the drink for you!

Morning Comes Early
(At A Kid's First Church Camp)

In the summer of my tenth year, my parents decided that two weeks at a church camp would be a good experience for me. Although it was discussed over the supper table, I wasn't so much consulted as informed. I knew some kids who had been to camps and had a good time, so I was easily persuaded that it would be a lot of fun.

Just getting there was a bit of an adventure. On a Saturday afternoon, we rode a bus, then a streetcar, to the Northwest Side of Chicago and the Methodist church where my mother had once attended Sunday school. About three dozen boys and girls waited with their parents as the church's adult chaperons checked a list and signed them in. Like me, each carried one suitcase stuffed with clothing and personal items.

Soon we all kissed our parents goodbye and the leaders lined us up for one last roll call. Then they marched us several blocks to a Northwestern train station.

The train ride was short but fruitful. It enabled me to get slightly acquainted with several of my companions and observe that "city kids" were interested in a lot of the same things as us kids from the sticks.

We got off the train at the Des Plaines station. Still lugging our suitcases, we walked about a mile along a gravel road in a shady wooded area. When we passed two-by-two through the camp's front gates, I was awed by what I beheld.

The campground encompasses 30 acres and was like a small city. Streets named for famous Methodists were lined with whitewashed cottages where Methodist families lived from Spring through Fall. There were numerous other buildings for meetings, crafts, storage, etc. The focal point of it all was the immense Waldorf Tabernacle, where hand-clapping, foot-stomping camp meetings were held. The wood-planked, 16-sided worship hall was designed with no center pillars so that everyone has a clear view of the altar. Such notables as Dwight L. Moody and Billy Sunday had preached here, and years later, Mahalia Jackson sang to the glory of God.

Enclosed by a wire fence, the campground also was surrounded on three sides by forest preserve. The dense growth of bushes and trees kept it well hidden. A small section of its southern perimeter faced out on a two-lane highway, giving a view of the swimming pool and just a glimpse of what lay beyond in the wooded area.

At the main assembly area, we were greeted by full-time camp personnel. We parked our suitcases, merged with other church groups and received a tour of the grounds. In addition to a ball field and volleyball court, the recreational facilities included a swimming pool, with high and low diving boards. At the end of our tour, girls and boys were separated and dispersed with their assigned leaders to a row of two-story dorms.

The dorms were similar to army barracks, but less austere. Each double-decker bunk was flanked by a dresser with four drawers. Whoever slept on a top bunk took the top and the third drawers. Alternate drawers went to the bottom bunkee. With our junior-size suitcases of belongings, most of us could have done with just one drawer.

We had time to freshen up and get settled in before a clanging bell signaled the evening meal. A mob of kids swarmed out of each dorm, followed by adults calling after them: "Take it easy. Slow down."

We filed into the mess hall and were seated at tables of ten, with one place reserved for a counselor. As the last stragglers found seats, one of the counselors stood, called for quiet, and led us in a grace.

Camp dinners were served family style. Our chorus of "Amen!" was the signal for the cooks to burst forth from the kitchen. They carried trays and dishes of food that were quickly dispensed to every table while the food was still steaming.

I experienced a moment of panic. I was a finicky eater and this wasn't Mom's home cooking. What if we were served veggies that I normally would pass up at home and everyone was forced to eat them?

To my great relief, the leaders did not push us to take portions of anything we did not choose for ourselves. This first meal, at least, was the meat and potatoes variety that I thrived on. The corn on the cob was a bit chewy (what Grandpa Farr called "horse corn"), but tolerable.

Good manners were encouraged by a game in which kids watched for anyone at another table who had his or her elbows on the table. If an offender was spotted, everyone at your table would chant: "Joey, Joey, strong and able, get your elbows off the table!"

Then Joey would have to get up and march around his table while the whole room clapped and sang: "'Round the table you must go, you must go, you must go. 'Round the table you must go, with your greasy elbows!"

After supper, two youths from each table were singled out to be cooks' helpers. This meant clearing the tables, carrying everything to the kitchen and helping wash the dishes, glasses and silverware. Cooks did the pots, pans and cooking utensils.

The rest of us were marched down a path to an assembly hall. We settled into wooden folding chairs in a huge circle. Two college-aged counselors led us in singing some familiar rounds and folk songs. One tune was new to me, but as the week progressed I realized it was quite appropriate for camp. It was called "Morning Comes Early (and bright with dew)."

When the cooks' helpers rejoined us, an adult leader gave us an official welcome to the camp and outlined the activities that lay ahead of us. A few more fun songs and we were excused to our dorms or the main camp area until 8p.m.

At that time, we hiked a little way through the woods and reassembled in a large clearing for vespers. We formed a circle and squatted Indian fashion. A large woodpile was stacked in the center, ready to be ignited. We sang a couple of familiar hymns. Then the evening's leaders began to teach us some traditional campfire songs.

At dusk, the campfire was lit. The leaders dispensed marshmallows. Under close supervision, we were allowed to come forward and roast them on sticks. Our singing continued as darkness swallowed everything outside our circle. Within that circle, the blazing fire and the warmth of our fellowship shielded us from the evening chill.

To conclude vespers, we sang "God Be With You 'Til We Meet Again." We dispersed to our dorms in high spirits, still singing and laughing. But we were more tired than we knew. In our bunks, the excited chatter lasted only ten or fifteen minutes after "Lights out." Then our voices gave way to the crickets' chirping.

On Sunday, we rose at seven. We had an hour to make our bunks, line up at a row of sinks to brush our teeth and vie for space in the crowded shower room.

Breakfast was at eight. Different menu, same routine: grace, announcements, "volunteers" selected to help clean up. We had an hour of free time afterward and were "encouraged" to use it writing letters or postcards to our families.

At ten, we met in small Sunday school groups. At eleven, we convened in the chapel building, along with all the adults currently staying at the campground, for a full-blown hour-long church service. The resident pastor preached a sermon that drew "Amens" from adults, yet did not go entirely over the heads of the 8- to 12-year-olds in his congregation.

The afternoon was devoted mostly to recreation. There were volleyball and softball games, horseshoes, swimming, sit-down games. An hour before supper was again devoted to letter writing. Counselors collected letters each evening and dropped them at the Post Office. In a few days, we began receiving replies from home.

Before vespers, we met in an assembly hall for a movie. It was a forgettable Biblical drama, but for our endurance and good behavior we were treated to a couple of short subjects. (I suspect the college-aged counselors enjoyed them as much as we did.)

The weekday routine was rather structured. Our morning Bible study/discussion hour usually centered on one of the Old Testament heroes. (Heroines, as I recall, got short shrift.) Another hour was devoted to a wide array of craft projects. Afternoons afforded a couple of hours of recreation, some prescribed and organized by leaders, but mostly individual choice. Easy access to a swimming pool was a luxury for me, so I spent a lot of time there. Actually, my "swimming" consisted mostly of dog paddling and the dead man's float. But I befriended a couple of fellows whose aquatic skills were likewise limited. We had a good time hanging on the pool sides, dunking each other and jumping into the almost-deep water to see who could create the highest splash.

Two grandmotherly ladies opened a sort of camp store for a couple of hours each afternoon. It offered such sundries as soap, tooth powder, stamps, stationery, postcards and penny candies. The latter commodity was by far the most popular item among those of us blessed with any pocket change.

There were several hikes into the forest preserve area that bounded the camp. I was impressed with our counselors' ability to name plants and trees. It was a thrill to me to observe chipmunks, rabbits, squirrel, occasionally deer and all sorts of birds roaming their natural habitat. Our path often trailed alongside the Des Plaines River, where a few years later I would spend countless summer days with my pal Wayne, fishing for bullhead catfish.

The Methodist Camp Ground swimming pool is well maintained and not much changed since the author dog paddled there during summer camp in the 1940s.

Time can drag or it can fly by, as our perspective dictates. My two weeks at church camp was a mixed bag of emotions and experiences.

Other than visits with relatives, I'd never before been separated from my family overnight. In just a few days, I acquired a vivid understanding of a word I'd seldom heard before: *homesick.*

Although the food was mostly good, increasingly I hungered for Mom's home cooking. One day we had chocolate pudding, my most favorite dessert. I could accept the fact that the taste left something to be desired. (It probably was a generic mix prepared in a five-gallon vat.) But whereas Mom's pudding was smooth as silk, this had *lumps* in it!

Because I was a tag-along in this church group, it took much of the two weeks to overcome my outside status. But toward the end I was pleased to realize that I'd actually become pals with a number of boys my age.

Mike and Steve, two fellas who probably weren't at camp by their own choice, took a liking to me for some reason. Once I'd gained their confidence, they explained to me a trick call short-sheeting. During one of our free periods, we sneaked into the next dorm while everyone was out. We rearranged the sheets on five bunks and remade them before we heard someone coming and made a hasty retreat out the back door.

That night, five campers climbing into bed next door found that they could get only halfway into their bunks. We knew our joke had succeeded. In the otherwise quiet evening, we could hear the ruckus through the open dorm windows. We had to bury our faces in our pillows to stifle our laughter, lest we give ourselves away as the culprits. (I hope that dorm's counselor doesn't read this. He was heard to declare, "I'm going to find out who did this, and when I do they're going to be in *big* trouble.")

The "religious" activities at camp were mostly low key, but upon reflection I later realized that I had acquired some new knowledge of church history and beliefs. Our campfire vespers exhilarated me. Only when I was a bit older did I understand that the camaraderie was at least as responsible as the singing itself.

Had I been given a preview of those two weeks and a real choice in the matter, I probably would have shrugged and declined. The terrible homesickness alone would have elicited a "no" vote.

Yet, in my early teens I accepted an invitation to join some of my Presbyterian peers at another camp. It was the greatest week of the whole summer! We made friends with dozens of kids from other churches and strengthened our own bonds of friendship in the process. Many of us met again at camp in succeeding years. On Sunday morning, I prayed that the buses coming to take us home would all break down.

That week made a confirmed camper of me. But it was several weeks before an important revelation struck me: I hadn't been homesick once!

River Bank Gambollers

Non-participants tend to view fishermen as a bit tetched, and parents view their offsprings' teen years as a period subject to various forms of nuttiness. Perhaps that's why no one ever raised an eyebrow over all the summer days that Wayne and I spent fishing at the Des Plaines River.

Having checked the previous night's sky ("Red sky at night, sailors delight!"), we'd arise about 4a.m. Tip-toeing through the house so as not to wake my family, I ate breakfast standing up. Between bites, I dressed and filled a Thermos bottle with steaming coffee.

Wayne was always speedier than me and would be whistling at my back steps by 4:30. Fishing rods were already tied to our bikes. We stuffed sack lunches, coffee and a can of bait worms indiscriminately together into a flour sack, which I strapped into my bike basket so it would not bounce out. We'd be on our way before 5a.m. to take advantage of the good early morning fishing.

From my house, it was an easy 2-mile ride to the river. A forest preserve bridle path followed the river, atop a steep embankment of trees and bushes. Narrow footpaths provided access to an occasional level clearing along the bank. When we located one to our liking, we would skid down on our bikes.

It took just a few minutes to untie our gear and prepare our rod and reel outfits. A fairly heavy weight went on the end of the line. (Store-bought weights were pear-shaped and had swivels to tie onto, but in a pinch a large hex nut would do.) We tied the hook about a foot behind so it could rise a little off the river bottom. Once we had a nice juicy night crawler mounted on the hook, we cast out to the middle of the murky river.

We reeled in just enough to make the line taut, then rested the rod on a Y-shaped prop fashioned from one of the many fallen tree branches. Fishing "deadline" (without a bobber) allowed the line to settle in the deep water, where we hoped some "lunker" might pass by. A nibble would cause the end of the upright rod to jerk and bend dramatically, signaling us to take action.

For now, we could relax and enjoy our first cup of coffee. Always the best one, it scalded our tongues as the metal cups burned our lips.

We always bet a quarter on who would get the first bite. I declined to bet on who would land the first fish. Wayne was a better fisherman, and seldom failed to hook his fish once he got a solid bite.

If we'd picked the right spot, the action would begin shortly. The prospects were limited, because we were not far from the river's northern origin. There were some carp, occasionally fairly large. Some patient black fishermen caught them on doughballs and actually cooked them, although they looked like pale oversized goldfish, not particularly appetizing. There were a few turtles, experts at stealing your bait without getting hooked. Sometimes we'd drag them up almost onto the bank before they reluctantly spit out the worm and slid back into the water.

Mostly, though, what we caught were catfish. Not the relatively clean "channel cat" found in large rivers and lakes (and today raised commercially on large fish farms). What we got were the ugly, fat, yellow-bellied, scavenging, aptly named "bullhead" catfish.

Although it's definitely not a keeper, the author proudly displays his catch of a bullhead catfish fresh from the Des Plaines River.

Typically, the catfish Wayne and I caught were in the 6- to 8-inch range. Downstream, around Kankakee, the Des Plaines became a

226

formidable river, both wide and deep. A wider range of species populated those waters and grew much larger. Local fishermen were sometimes pictured in the papers with the big brothers of our catfish. Often five or six feet long and weighing 70 or 80 pounds, they had to be hauled into the boat with a gaff.

In our neck of the woods, where you could portage easily in the dry season, a bullhead 10 or 12 inches long was a real catch. But regardless of size, they were scrappers! An 8-inch bullhead was as exciting to pull in as a 2-pound bass. They also had a penchant for swallowing the hook. We had learned to carry a long-nosed pliers with which to remove the hooks. Even so, we often were obliged to cut the line and release one back into the water with the hook still in him. The hooks would dissolve rapidly in the bullhead's stomach acids.

When the fishing was slow, we could seek amusing diversions along the bridle path. One good spot was behind the fence (easily scaled) of a run-down cemetery. Some of its tombstones were very old and bore some intriguing inscriptions. A bit farther along, the path bordered a Boy Scout camp. Often we could spy a troop of future male leaders setting up pup tents, preparing meals over a fire or otherwise seeking to earn outdoor merit badges.

We might migrate to Dam No. 4, a mile or so north. Fishing usually was good just below the dam. If not, we could take off our shoes and socks and walk across the dam. The dam was a low one, almost level with the riverbank just before the drop-off. The water flowing over the top was only ankle deep, but the stone surface was smooth and slippery. A young boy once drowned doing this. So although we presented each other with an air of brave nonchalance, we walked very carefully.

Daredevil bike games were great fun, too. A favorite involved getting up speed on the bridle path, then plunging down one of the footpaths to the river's edge. The trick was to hit the brakes at the last second, cut the front wheel and skid to a halt on the clearing before you took a bath in the muddy water. Our balloon tire bikes took a lot of abuse that would destroy today's skinny tire lightweights.

Once I did go in up to my pant legs. I removed my shoes and socks and propped them on rocks near our campfire to dry. Then I got engrossed in our fishing again. When I remembered to check, the socks were burning and the shoes had smoldering holes in the soles. Fortunately, the shoes were my old knock-abouts. I disposed of the socks, fairly certain that Mom wasn't keeping count. But I wore the shoes with strips of cardboard stuffed inside for about six months lest my parents ask what became of them.

Our supplies on these excursions included plenty of snacks, and we munched freely. When the sun was about at its peak, we ate lunch, usually sandwiches with an apple or banana. Often we built a campfire (like the one that consumed my socks) and cooked wieners, or maybe roasted marshmallows or walnuts.

When we ran out of coffee, the many picnic areas in the forest preserve each had a pump that provided cool well water. Nature calls were no problem in the woods, of course. If we'd misjudged the weather and it rained, there was always a bridge or a picnic pavilion nearby for shelter.

Since we were required to be home for supper, we missed the good fishing at twilight. Even so, Wayne and I caught literally hundreds of the Des Plaines' uneatable bullheads.

These days, my fishing trips are farther from home and fewer, but usually a week long. With brothers Al and Rich, I fish several lakes in northern Wisconsin from the comfort of Rich's bass boat. When the fishing is slack, Rich's house boasts a patio that is perfect for playing cards and watching TV. Best of all, we catch countless bass, northern and walleye pike and sundry pan fish that are "keepers" – and fireman Rich is an excellent cook.

For us aging fishermen, who have trouble baiting a hook even in bright sunlight without our glasses on, it's the way to go. Still, it's no more exciting or enjoyable than the days I spent with Wayne on the banks of the Des Plaines River, chasing those spunky bullheads.

Let's Go To The Pay Show

Perhaps prompted by an article about once-great movie theatres that are no more, a *Nostalgia Digest* reader has written the editor to pass along word of a noteworthy exception. After a period of hard times, the Patio theatre has been completely refurbished and is making a comeback. For yours truly, this welcome news evoked a warm nostalgic glow.

For a period of about eight years in my carefree youth, I spent probably four out of five Saturday afternoons at the movies. Wayne, Chuck, Bobby and I were matinee addicts. Two or more of us made weekly pilgrimages to one of the dozen theatres scattered around Chicago's Northwest Side.

Unless some competing double bill was especially appealing, the Patio was our first choice. From our remote starting point in a semi-rural suburban neighborhood, it simply was the most accessible.

Folk who listen to his weekly radio rebroadcasts probably have heard Chuck Schaden mention that as youngsters we called the Patio "the Pay Show." This had nothing to do with the cost of admission, which was the same at all neighborhood theatres. It came about because none of the kids in our gang knew what a patio was. (They weren't a common feature of back yards in our neck of the woods.)

Our young minds, often inquisitive about things that were none of our business, found no reason to question the names of theatres. (Who knew what a "rialto" was?) But in making our weekly decision about which show to see, it was a problem not being able to pronounce one theatre's name.

Georgie, whose older sister was in high school, was picking up snippets of Spanish from her. Proudly drawing upon his second-hand foreign language education, he informed us that the word was pronounced "pay-show." That made as much sense to us as many of the other theatre names. And so it was that the Patio became the Pay Show.

Interestingly, none of our parents ever corrected us on this score. Those were the days when parents didn't worry about what film their kids were going to see. Mothers would ask which theatre we had selected so as to have some idea about when we should be due back home. They knew what we meant by "the Pay Show," but apparently

229

accepted it as a kids' code word or a nonsense nickname we'd assigned to the Patio.[1]

The standard matinee schedule at most neighborhood theatres was: "Doors open (meaning tickets go on sale) at 12:30. Show begins at 1p.m." It was about a 45-minute trip to the Patio. That meant eating an early lunch and leaving no later than noon. Our goal was to arrive after the ticket line had diminished, but in time to buy candy and select seats before the house lights went out.

First we walked four blocks to Irving Park Road, the closest main street. There we waited for a Chicago Surface Line shuttle bus, which arrived at about 12-minute intervals. This smaller model of the standard oblong-shaped big-city vehicle took us as far as Neenah Avenue, just a few blocks inside the Chicago city limits.

The bus unloaded its passengers directly in front of the entrance to the old Dunning State Home. The home was a repository for the mentally disturbed and old folks grown senile. A few of the unkempt older inmates would be at the iron fence, reaching out and shouting gibberish at passersby. Some of their younger cohorts would plead with wary kids coming off the bus: "Hey, son. Here, take this quarter to that tavern over there and bring me a pack of Camels. Would ya do that for me, please?"

Of course, we all had been warned by parents never to get close to those poor folk in Dunning, and none of us would have had the nerve to set foot inside the tavern anyway. Nor were they likely to sell us any cigarettes. So we averted our eyes and pretended we were deaf or in a hurry to catch the streetcar.

Neenah was the western end of the line for the Irving Park trolley cars. Here they switched to the parallel tracks and the motorman repositioned the current bar to the overhead power line while the conductor flipped the seat backs so that passengers would be facing forward. Then they traded places, and the streetcar was ready to begin its return trip into the city.

---

[1] Some of us were in high school before we bothered to look up the word *patio* and learn its definition and the correct pronunciation. On the eve of his wedding, knowing that Chuck loved to reminisce about "the good old days," I took him aside and set him straight, lest he embarrass himself in conversation with his new bride during their honeymoon.

We boarded the familiar "Red Rocket" car at the rear and presented our transfers to the conductor. In the solidly comfortable reversible wicker seats, we sat and watched various landmarks pass by as the streetcar rocked and clanged along on its tracks. Dunning Station Post Office. Merrimac Park. The shoe store with the big Buster Brown display in its window.

When we passed Saint Pascal Roman Catholic church and its parochial school, it was time to start moseying toward the front compartment. As the Austin Avenue traffic lights loomed ahead, we would instruct the motorman in our most grown-up voices: "Next stop, please."

The Patio theatre, where the author and his pals attended countless Saturday matinees, and some midweek shows during summer vacations. In its later years, the upright portion of the marquee had been removed after it became structurally unsafe. (Sulzer Regional Library, Chicago Public Library; donated by Bob Krueger, Ravenswood Historical Society)

The streetcar screeched to a halt, the motorman moved a lever that slid the front door open and we debarked to a safety island. From this vantage point we could view the panorama of shops and shoppers along both sides of Irving Park.

It was a scene typical of the era. A bakery, deli, cleaners, drug store, hobby shop, neighborhood pubs on either side of the street, a shop that sold and *repaired* radios, a storefront branch of the Chicago Public Library. Most of the buildings had upper stories which housed a second business, served as offices for the business below or provided apartment space for the store owner. Although the buildings all were flush against their neighbors, no two brickworks were the same color.

To our eyes, the focal point of the entire block was the blinking marquee of that second building from the northwest corner – the Pay Show.

When the traffic light turned green, we hurried across the street. Outside the theatre, we paused to examine the "stills," glossy photos of scenes from today's feature.

The glass front doors, usually propped open for the first rush of customers, were now closed to hold in the air conditioned coolness. Only a few kids were in line ahead of us as we stepped up and produced the price of admission for "children age 12 and under."

The ticket booth was centered in the outer lobby. Directly overhead, a huge chandelier hung on what seemed an inadequate chain from an ornately decorated ceiling. The Patio's interior was designed to have an open-air Moorish appearance. At the second floor level, the interior façade was a series of tall, round-domed "windows" such as might look out from a palace, each with an imitation balcony.

An usher tore our tickets in half and returned stubs to us as we passed into the main lobby. The walls here had tall glass enclosures that displayed posters ballyhooing future feature films. Two wide staircases at left and right were roped off as usual at matinees. Signs draped over the ropes proclaimed: "Balcony closed." At center stage, girls and boys crowded around the concession booth in ill-formed lines.

We waited our turn in line to make the difficult choice of what snacks to munch on for the next three or four hours. With a dime allotted for this, I usually spent five cents for a box of buttered pop corn. The remaining nickel went for lemon drops, licorice Nibs, Milk Duds, Dots or Raisinets – always something that could be eaten one or two at a time.

By the time we resolved the inevitable debate about how far down to sit, the house lights would dim. The matinee always began with a cartoon, and we added our voices to about 800 others in shouting our gleeful approval.

Tom and Jerry were favorites of my generation, along with Heckle and Jeckle, Little Lulu, most of the Disney characters and the Looney

Tunes bunch. Many of the same cartoons that had us howling at the Pay Show are entertaining kids today on TV and in home videos.

After the cartoon, came the weekly episode in the current serial. I was a sucker for these "cliff hangers" – even the one that featured Brenda Starr, whose comic strip adventures I skipped over when reading the Sunday funny papers. When my favorite comic heroes, Batman and Robin, showed up in a serial, I was in heaven. Once that one began, it did not matter what films were showing on the Patio's main bill. I had to be there every Saturday to see how my heroes would escape each week's close encounter with danger and death.

We would be on the edge of our seats as the narrator wrapped up the episode with his urgent reminder: "Don't miss Chapter 7, 'The Lightning Bolt Strikes'!" But we had a chance to regain our composure as a colorful panorama appeared on the screen with searchlights criss-crossing left and right. A fanfare blared in the background and the screen filled with the words "Previews of Coming Attractions."

This was the introduction to a series of typical Hollywood teaser scenes from both of the movies that would be appearing next Sunday through Wednesday. These were preceded by a brief banner declaring: "Sunday, Monday, Tuesday, Wednesday." Next, again with the banner, came a similar treatment of the double bill for Thursday, Friday and Saturday.[2] If a blockbuster film was scheduled for a few weeks hence, there might be a bonus Coming Attraction dubbed "Coming Soon."

After all this, the first feature film would begin with its introductory fanfare for the studio that produced it. Because the Saturday matinee usually was a packed house of junior film fans, the Thursday-through-Saturday bill had to be something that would appeal to juvenile tastes. Typically, we might see the latest Abbott and Costello laugh riot paired with "The Falcon in Mexico." Or a John Wayne war movie with "Thunderhead, Son of Flicka." The

---

[2] Perhaps because they were fearful of losing the slow-witted, the coming attractions banner never said "Sunday through Wednesday." It was invariably "Sunday, Monday, Tuesday, Wednesday." Likewise for the films later in the week: "Thursday, Friday, Saturday." Some theatres, presumably those suffering lower attendance, changed their feature three times weekly and had a Tuesday, Wednesday, Thursday offering. These were generally selected to appeal to adults. During the school year, at least, kids attended mostly on Saturday and Sunday.

233

management tried to include one film that could be enjoyed by both smallfry and adults, since they couldn't count on kids to fill the seats on weekdays and at three evening screenings.

As the feature's title flashed on the screen, our half-pint horde would give a cheer and settle back to munch on our cavity-makers. Most features were between 75 and 90 minutes long. With the short subjects, viewing time was likely to run about three and a half hours. Then, likely as not, we would sit through the cartoon and the serial again, and maybe the previews if they were really interesting.

Following a stop in the downstairs washroom, we would exit the Pay Show, checking the posters again and comparing the illustrations to what we had seen in the previews. Outside, we would catch a westbound streetcar and re-hash the best parts of the show en route home.

This westbound Irving Park streetcar might have been carrying the author and some of his pals homeward after a Saturday matinee at the Patio theatre, at far right. (Hammill Studios, Roger Hammill collection)

The Patio theatre opened on January 29, 1927. Its premiere screening was a forgettable film called "The Blonde Saint," but the theatre itself was impressive.

Chicago's local movie house business then was dominated by large chains such as Balaban & Katz and Essaness. The Patio's original owners went all out to build a theatre that could hold its own against these deep-pocket competitors. Ornate cornices were adorned with Grecian urns, and the Moorish décor gave an overall sense of elegance. The Barton pipe organ was the largest of any local theatre at the time.[3] The Patio also boasted an orchestra pit and its own small house orchestra to support the vaudeville acts that augmented its film attractions.

In the 1940s, when I was attending countless matinees, vaudeville was dead (although some of its performers made short-lived comebacks in the early days of television). The Patio, like most other local movie houses, had taken to showing two feature films "and selected shorts." Its elegant décor was lost on me, although the inner theatre's blue ceiling with its hundreds of small lights made a lasting impression. A device of some kind projected a soft white light moving over the ceiling. It gave the effect of clouds drifting across a star-filled sky.

But my pals and I were little concerned with ambiance. We came to the Pay Show to be entertained; and we were. By literally hundreds of Hollywood's A, B and C offerings, along with cartoons, serials and, occasionally, even by a newsreel. None of them would have been any more enjoyable had we seen them at one of the opulent movie palaces in Chicago's downtown Loop theatre area.

In recent years, a decline in movie attendance and other factors have killed off many of the local movie houses in Chicago, as well as the once regal Loop theatres. Most of those remaining have been sliced up to create multi-theatres – essentially long, thin rooms with gray walls, cramped seating and doors at each end. Lacking atmosphere or personality, they have a claustrophobic effect on many patrons.

For a time, it seemed that the Patio would be obliged to follow suit or close altogether. Now it has been blessed with new owners who have restored it from a run-down state to its former elegance.

---

[3] While the theatre itself was being refurbished, a small group of volunteers, led by a Hammond Organ Company engineer, lent their know-how, parts and labor to rebuilding the dilapidated organ. Occasional concerts have been performed by such talented soloists as Pearl White, Dennis Scott and Hal Pearl. In addition to popular and classical selections, the concerts usually include a demonstration of the background music once provided for silent films. All the performers agree that the Barton has been restored even beyond its original visual and acoustical grandeur. Thanks to a generous group of organ donors.

The Patio was built in a period when movies were this nation's predominant source of entertainment. This splendid example of neighborhood theatres from that by-gone era is worth preserving. Loyal patronage by its neighbors can make that possible.

It's a longer ride for me now, but I plan to check out the revitalized Pay Show soon. Who says you can't go back?

Afterthought: Later feedback indicated that the Patio had managed to survive into the new millennium. Showing second-run films at an admission rate of two dollars, it struggles to attract enough hungry patrons to the concession booth, which represents the make-or-break profit for most theatres. Occasional "blockbuster" films draw larger crowds that help make the difference in paying the bills.

A recent report on the Chicago theatre scene stated that there are but three single-screen movie houses still operating on a regular basis in Chicago: the Broadway (owned by the giant Cineplex Odeon chain), the Adelphi (which now shows only Indian films, in Hindi)—and the Patio.

Matinee Madness

For my eleventh Christmas, Aunt Evie gave me a booklet of admission coupons good for all the Balaban & Katz movie theatres in and around Chicago. Although I received some other neat stuff that year, that gift excited me most.

The Balaban & Katz chain dominated Chicago's thriving movie theatre business from the 1930s well into the 1950s. B&K operated such elegant downtown movie palaces as the State-Lake and Chicago theatres. At the Chicago, first-run films often shared the bill with live stage performances by such stars as Danny Kaye, Betty Hutton, Frankie Laine, Les Paul and Mary Ford.

Balaban & Katz also ran a chain of up-scale movie houses scattered throughout Chicago and the surrounding suburbs. The little "Happiness Books" they offered sold for $1.00, $2.50 and $5.00. The mid-priced book I received from my aunt would get me into ten local theatres, or I could combine tickets for the higher priced downtown shows.

During a period that spanned most of my grade school years, I shared with my pal Chuck a mutual addiction to Saturday matinees. Barring any preemptive family events, we early on ceased even asking, "Ya wanna go to the show?" The question became, simply, "What show you wanna go to?"

In pre-television days, a volcanic eruption of "B" pictures flowed endlessly from a raft of Hollywood studios. A lesser flood of quality films featured real plots and top rated stars. Even with double features and midweek showbill changes, no one theatre could present the entire array.

Chuck and I established a Friday evening routine. We'd huddle over the *Chicago Sun* or *Daily News* movie section, evaluate the listings and narrow the choices. When we agreed on one, we'd decide what time we needed to leave so as to reach the particular theatre shortly before show time.

Scattered around the Northwest Side of Chicago, two dozen or more movie theatres were reasonably accessible from our semi-rural suburb. All required a shuttle bus ride on Irving Park Boulevard to Neenah Avenue. There, across from the entrance to the sprawling grounds of the awesome Illinois State Hospital, we boarded an eastbound Irving Park streetcar.

Several theatres were located at intervals on Irving Park. Others that we frequented required another transfer to a northbound or southbound trolley.

Part of the ritual of attending Saturday matinees was to get there early enough to be fairly near the front of the line that would form outside the ticket booth. When tickets went on sale, you bought yours and rushed inside to elbow your way to the pop corn and candy counter and buy your snacks. Then you hurried inside to lay claim to a seat in your favorite section.

Kids line up for a Saturday movie matinee. They came by bus, by streetcar, on foot and riding bikes. None of the bikes parked at the curb were locked, but four hours later they all would still be there waiting for their respective owners. (Library of Congress photo)

Most ticket booths opened at 12:30. Chuck and I needed almost an hour to reach even the closest theatre; up to an hour and a half or more for the most distant ones that we frequented. This meant that we often gulped down a quick lunch as early as eleven o'clock. Our mothers would shake their heads with uncomprehending displeasure. Yet they insisted that we eat before leaving, lest we stuff ourselves with "junk" at the movies and come home with stomach aches.

In another column, I eulogized the Patio theatre, which has made a welcome revival after some lean times. Us kids called it "the Pay Show," because we didn't know how to pronounce it. (Shucks, we didn't even know what a patio was.)

Least distant from our homes, the Patio enjoyed a major portion of our youthful patronage. If no other listing really thrilled us, we'd end up by saying, "Aw, what the heck. Let's just go to the Pay Show." (Those of us who grew up before television often boast of how kids had to use their imagination to entertain themselves. Strange, then, that Chuck and I did not seek some other creative outlet for spending a free afternoon. Yet the lure of the movies was such that the thought of *not* going was seldom considered.)

To me, one major attraction of the Patio was an Andes Candies store on the nearby corner at Austin Avenue. The Andes confectionary chain once blanketed Chicago and suburbs. It went out of business in the 1960s. Today's closest equivalent is the Fannie May chain. But it lacks a special feature that distinguished Andes.

Tucked into a rear corner of most Andes stores was a small soda fountain. They mixed some of the thickest, richest malts and shakes in the city. Time and finances permitting, I always would suggest a visit to Andes after a matinee at the Patio. Chuck's sweet tooth was akin to mine. He seldom declined. Sometimes, if my funds were limited, I endured a double feature without pop corn or other goodies so as to savor that Andes chocolate malt later.

A bit farther down the Irving Park line, one encountered the renowned "six corners" intersection of Milwaukee and Cicero Avenues. Here the busy Sears, Roebuck store dominated a square block on the northeast. In both directions, each of the three main arteries was crowded for two or more blocks with business establishments of varying kinds and sizes. Facing Sears across Irving Park was the staid Northwest National Bank building. An old fashioned cigar store occupied the triangular corner formed by Cicero and Milwaukee on the north side of Irving Park.

During most daylight hours, a uniformed policeman helped to keep the congested traffic moving with authoritative hand and whistle directions. Debarking via the rear platform of the streetcar, we crossed to Milwaukee on the traffic cop's signal. Walking a block north, we reached the Portage theatre, named for the city's Portage Park district.

Given the nature of motion pictures, entering any theatre is like stepping into a world of make-believe. This was particularly so at the Portage because of the usual hubbub outside. At holiday time, especially, sidewalks would be so jammed with shoppers that one often had to step into the street to keep moving.

If we left the Portage with time to spare, we could do some wishful window shopping or roam through the toy section at Sears or Woolworth's. A mom and pop record store across from the theatre was a favorite stop.

The store had several soundproof booths where you could listen to records before making a selection. (This was before the age of headphones, tapes, CDs, etc.) The owners never objected to letting a couple of kids audition eight or ten of the latest pop singles, even though we seldom had the wherewithal to make a purchase.

By transferring to a Milwaukee trolley car, we could ride about a mile north and take our pick of three–count 'em–three theatres within blocks of each other. Away from Chicago's downtown Loop area, it was a rare feat for three movie houses to survive in such proximity.

The Gateway was a block east of Milwaukee on Lawrence Avenue. A Balaban & Katz theatre, it had an edge on its neighbors, showing first-run films in a well-maintained, clean atmosphere, just a tad more ornate than most independents. We visited the Gateway infrequently, though, since their features usually played at more accessible places, albeit perhaps a few weeks later.

Back on Milwaukee, just a block north of Lawrence was the Times, and a block south the Jeff. Along with Chuck and several other buddies, I spent countless hours in these two obviously older facilities.

Mere survival may have been a 4-star achievement for both, even in those days of high movie attendance. While not exactly dingy, neither of them sparkled. Wads of hardened chewing gum adorned the undersides of many seats, while still sticky gobs on the floor lay in ambush for unwary shoes. Seats with broken springs, ruptured upholstery or a sideways tilt were common.

Both theatres stayed alive, I believe, primarily by attracting kids— lots of kids—to Saturday and Sunday matinees. Kids consume large quantities of sweets, and concession sales make or break most theatres.

The Times theatre's gimmick was a weekly offering of triple features, usually older films, and almost always with a common theme:

> Abbott and Costello in "Buck Privates"
> Laurel and Hardy in "Chumps at Oxford"
> Olson and Johnson in "Hellzapoppin'"

There might be three action films, three cowboy films (Gene Autry, Hopalong Cassidy, Roy Rogers), three detective films, etc. For kids who (like me) enjoyed having the pants scared off them, the triple horror show was irresistible:

> "Curse of Dracula"
> "The Wolfman Returns"

"Frankenstein Meets the Mummy"

Occasionally, they varied the format and presented just two features – preceded by *15 color cartoons*. The Saturday morning TV line-up can't compare to that Times theatre potpourri of your favorite cartoon characters. Non-stop animated slapstick. Big screen. Contagious laughter from hundreds of hyped-up kids. And no commercials.

Down the street, the Jeff theatre showed only two features, usually of related genre. Two war dramas. Two mysteries. Back-to-back westerns. Depending on the features' length, the Jeff generally offered two to five cartoons.

What helped the Jeff attract a nearly full house almost every Saturday was a weekly door prize of a shiny new balloon-tire bicycle. Ticket stubs went into a huge fishbowl. At an intermission between features, the manager got someone from the audience to come up on stage and draw a winner. Each week some lucky girl or boy got the thrill of her or his young life.

My pal Bobby claimed these drawings were rigged. He said winners always were relatives or friends of the management, and the same bikes were "won" week after week. When I questioned the logistics of such a scam, Bobby insisted that he knew "someone who knows it for a fact." It's tough to argue with such insider information, but I still felt those weekly winners had to be terrific actors if they weren't legit.

If my buddies and I stayed on the Irving Park trolley past the "six corners" area, we soon reached the Irving theatre. I never quite figured out if it was so named because the owners thought it clever to name it for the street it was on, or just because all the other good names had been taken. It was next to a street that also puzzled me because it couldn't seem to make up its mind what its name was. Here at Irving Park, it was Pulaski; a couple of miles south, without warning, it suddenly changed to Crawford. Didn't that cause people to get lost?

The Irving was about four blocks from my maternal grandparents' home. As the house lights dimmed, I sometimes was awed by the thought that my mother and her brothers and sisters had walked to this theatre when they were young. On weekends when I had stayed over with my grandparents, Aunt Florence had taken me to the Irving and treated me to such films as "Lassie Come Home" and the early "Jungle Book," starring Sabu. (Yes, even in those days long before Cher and Madonna, we had stars with only one name.)

An added attraction of the Irving was its location across from the Buffalo Ice Cream Parlor. For years, the Buffalo ranked as one of the city's best ice cream shops, certainly the Northwest Side's top contender. During my high school years, I had the good fortune to obtain a part-time job working behind the counter. The pay was modest, but the fringe benefits were delicious.

Still farther along on the Irving Park line was the Commodore theatre. Another relatively old structure, it seemed misplaced amidst a mostly residential block. It never seemed to draw a capacity crowd. In later years, it became a foreign language house and eventually was closed. Because of the long ride, we usually went to the Commodore only to catch movies we'd missed closer to home.

When the Patio began a serialized Batman and Robin adventure, it was a "must-see" for a devoted Batman fan like me. Yet, halfway through, I was sick one week and missed a chapter. The Commodore saved me from a bat mania attack by running the serial a week behind the Patio schedule.

I could not have identified its famous namesake when we attended the Will Rogers theatre. It required two transfers and a southbound streetcar ride on Central Avenue. The theatre was on Belmont Avenue, a block west of a busy shopping area at the Belmont/Central intersection.

The Will Rogers is most memorable for its floor plan. Unlike most theatres, it was situated on a corner. The ticket booth faced out on a diagonal. The entry area and outer half of the lobby formed a triangle. This resulted in a departure from the normal layout for concession booth, washrooms and doors into the theatre proper.

Other theatre names come to mind. The Luna was noted for its almost exclusive showing of old horror and western films. The Pickwick was in the neighboring suburb of Park Ridge. We could walk to it if we started early, but getting there via public transportation was not possible. The Logan was named for its Logan Square locale. The Mont Clare, in nearby suburban Elmwood Park, was accessible but not exactly convenient. A Milwaukee Road railroad track ran directly behind the theatre. When a train rumbled past, the screen shook. The rippling effect often gave an amusing perspective to whatever action was taking place on screen.

Lewis Wilson and Douglas Croft portrayed Batman and Robin in this 1943 serial produced by Columbia Pictures. The film's low budget was evident in the Dynamic Duo's costumes. But for an avid fan like the author, that was no deterrent to catching every episode at least twice. (Photofest/ICON)

All of these were back-up choices. They were more difficult to reach than our five nearest mainstays. The Harlem Avenue bus route ended about five blocks from the Mont Clare; an easy hike in good weather, but rough if you came out and found it raining or snowing. For the Pickwick, we usually begged some adult to drive us – not an easy chore in times when cars were a luxury and parents not accustomed to being their kids' chauffeurs.

If you grew up in Chicago or any other big city in the first half of the Twentieth Century, you probably have similar memories of a dozen movie theatres where you spent Saturday afternoon with friends. (I haven't touched on our trips downtown to those elegant Loop theatres with their exciting film and live stage show offerings.)

Readers from small towns and rural communities no doubt had a different experience. As an avid movie buff, I can't imagine living in a town like Texasville with only one picture show. I'm told that such theatres often changed their films three (sometimes four) times a week. Even so, the limited choices would cause you to miss a lot of good films – until decades later when they came on late night TV.

In many small towns, the population could support only one movie theatre. If the management wanted to be open daily, the bill of fare had to change every couple of days. (Library of Congress photo)

A glance through today's newspaper reveals that the Portage, Pickwick and Patio are still operating. (Maybe theatre names starting with "P" are blessed with some sort of lucky charm?) Most of the others have been boarded up or razed as neighborhoods underwent various changes.

Meanwhile, the once unincorporated village in which I grew up has grown and prospered. It now boasts a split-screen Loews theatre that offers six films simultaneously. Thank goodness it wasn't there in my youth. The weekly allowance I received on Friday would not have lasted through the weekend.

My Quintessential Grandma

"Paul?"

No answer

"Yoo, Paul!"

Still no answer

"That boy!" Grandma muttered.

Her slippers swished softly along the bare floor as she returned to her kitchen. Tantalizing breakfast aromas drifting up the stairway had already wakened me. The others in our bedroom had not yet stirred.

Mom and Dad were in the iron frame double bed. My brothers, Alan and Dickie, shared a twin-size. My slim cot formed an "L" with their bed at the corner of the room.

"That boy" was my Uncle Paul, who now began making wakeful sounds in his room across the hall. On this summer morning, he was about 17.

From the foot of the stairs that divided our rooms, Grandma tried again. "Paul? You're going to be late for work, son."

"Okay, Ma," Uncle Paul answered at last. "I'm up." His voice had a still-half-asleep tone, but creaking bed springs and feet thumping on the floor supported his claim.

After allowing Uncle Paul time to dress and use the house's lone washroom, I quickly dressed and followed him downstairs. My brothers and our parents straggled down one by one and found places set around the kitchen table.

At home, we boys usually opted for cold cereal, toast and hot cocoa. Having reared ten children, Grandma McGuire was used to serving a boardinghouse menu. Our choices were hot cereal, pancakes or waffles, eggs, bacon and sausage.

Grandma's cold cereals tended to be wholesome brands such as Grape Nuts and Raisin Bran – not big favorites with kids. As a result, we ate more cooked items when visiting her. I learned to actually like fried eggs – as long as they were served over easy so I could sop up the yolk with my toast. In lieu of cocoa, Grandma served chilled orange juice, freshly hand-squeezed.

Uncle Paul had eaten quickly and was gulping down a cup of coffee as we got seated. A moment later, he gave Grandma a hasty kiss and left for his summer job as a Springfield Gas Company meter reader. He wore a military looking jacket with epaulets and a nametag on the breast pocket, and he carried a long, five-battery flashlight. I was impressed. I could hardly wait to see our meter reader at home.

"You know what?" I'd tell him. "My uncle's a gas man, too!"

I was even more awestruck when I saw Uncle Paul's Cushman motor scooter. The classic sun yellow model, with its squarish body and small wide wheels, was a national favorite. Unlike sporty models that became popular a half century later, the Cushman was designed to be practical, economical and safe. I vowed that I would own one by my senior year in high school, but by then the company had ceased production.

One day Grandma sent Uncle Paul on an errand uptown. Knowing I was fascinated with the scooter, he said, "Wanna ride along, Danny?"

Mom probably would have nixed the idea, but she was out back with my brothers. I looked to my father for approval. He nodded and said, "Sure, go ahead. But sit straight and hold on tight."

I straddled the black leather passenger saddle behind my uncle and, with my arms wrapped around his middle, got a firm grip on his belt. As we putt-putted down the street, I closed my eyes and imagined that I was already driving my own Cushman.

Coming home, we stopped for gas at a Marathon service station. Uncle Leo was a regional sales manager for Marathon Oil, so all the family patronized its stations whenever possible.

Uncle Paul knew the station manager and introduced me. The manager gave me a grown-up hand shake and said, "Glad to meetcha. Say 'Hi!' to your Uncle Leo for me." I was impressed with the McGuire clan's status hereabouts, and the more so when Uncle Paul filled the Cushman's tank himself. He paid with a half dollar – and got change back!

Uncle Paul did not keep late hours, but he evidently slept soundly. Grandma's efforts to wake him proved to be a regular weekday ritual during our visit.

She, however, was up at about 5:15 every Monday through Saturday. After a light breakfast, she walked about seven blocks to attend the six o'clock mass at Saint Peter and Paul's Catholic Church. This schedule enabled her to be home in time to feed her youngest son

247

and see him off to work. On Sundays, she indulged herself by sleeping until 6:30 or so and being picked up by other family members to attend a later mass.

My grandparents (both devout Roman Catholics in an era when church doctrine was never questioned) were blessed with ten children over a 20-year period. My father, Raymond, was the eldest. Then came Leo, Ursula, Cecilia, Maurice, Francis, Vincent, Kathleen, Mildred and Paul.

Grandma McGuire and her family gather for a photo record on daughter Mildred's wedding day. From left: Grandma, Cecilia, Leo, Grandpa, Raymond (author's father), Maurice, Paul (holding photo of Francis), Ursula, Kathleen, Mildred, Vincent. April 4, 1944.

Uncle Paul was just six years older than me. I found it difficult to remember that he was my uncle, not an older cousin.

I once wondered aloud how that modest home had accommodated such a large family. Aunt Kathleen allowed that, yes, it was crowded at times. Boys slept in one of the upstairs rooms, girls in the other. At times, a little "parlor" on the first floor could do double duty as a bunk area for two. But all ten children were never there at once. When Paul was born, at the height of the Depression, Leo and Ray had left for Chicago in search of jobs.

Grandma's house on south Pasfield Street was the sixth and last that my father's parents shared in their 46 years together. It was a white frame, tall and square, probably build circa 1900. Three concrete steps led up to a porch half the width of the house and only a few feet deep. That porch was one of my favorite spots when we visited in Springfield.

A very young Uncle Paul stands guard over the front porch swing.

It had a wooden railing just the right size for a kid to lean against, sit on or straddle. A bench swing was suspended on chains from the overhanging roof. In that confined space, adults would just rock gently without lifting their feet from the floor. Kids could kick against the railing and swing about a foot in each direction. More than that and the swing banged against the wall behind you.

It was impossible for exuberant boys not to get carried away and crash against the wall occasionally when they swung unattended. Yet, for all the times I was guilty of this offense, Grandma never chastised.

Immediately on the right, as you entered through the front door, was a room that had been the master bedroom, albeit a small one. In that uninsulated house, it was chilly in winter and caught summer sun from windows on two sides. It had evolved into a modest living room, usually referred to in those days as a parlor.

On the left, a large open area had been the original parlor. Grandma's bed, dresser, nightstand and accessories now were in the less drafty rear half of this room. An arrangement of draw curtains gave her a degree of privacy.

Furniture that did not fit in the pseudo-parlor—chairs, end tables, a magazine rack—filled the front half of the room. Much of it was decorated with handmade doilies. Near a side window were a chair and a table that held a black cradle style telephone and the Springfield directory. Here Grandma made daily contact with two or three of her children or their spouses. Until Uncle Maurice moved his family to California years later, all my father's siblings remained in the Springfield area. Thus Grandma could keep abreast of all the doings of her family at large for the price of a local phone call.

At the far end of this area, past the upstairs stairway, an open doorway on the right gave entry to the kitchen. Probably because the house had no dining room, the kitchen was half again the size of the fairly large one in our house.

On your right was a closet area and Grandma's sideboard (which we then called a buffet chest). At the corner on this side was the washroom entry door. Situated under the upstairs stairwell, the washroom had a sloped ceiling over the toilet that could be hazardous to anyone over six feet tall. The limited space left over for the sink and medicine cabinet also made bending over the sink a challenge. There was no tub or shower. Bathing took place in the basement, where a tub sat near the drain. No plumbing was attached. Hot water from the laundry tub was transported and poured in from pails.

I thought this arrangement was rustic until my father explained that the tub actually was a relatively new luxury. As children, he and his siblings took turns bathing in a round metal wash tub in the kitchen.

The house originally had no basement. With a little help from his eldest son, Grandpa McGuire had cleared out and leveled the area under the house. He brought cement mix home a wheelbarrow load at a time. Over several months, he methodically laid small sections of concrete until a floor was completed.

From the entrance hall at the back door, he constructed stairs to the basement. Before his health failed, he had installed a laundry tub and plumbing for his wife.

The two outside kitchen walls, apart from a window in each, were taken up almost entirely with sink, stove, counters and the once popular porcelain-finish metal cabinets. On the basement hallway door hung a fly swatter and one of Grandma's ever-present religious calendars. In that corner space near the door stood a shining white GE refrigerator, a group gift from her children and one of her newest and most prized possessions.

In the basement hallway, not to be wasteful, she still maintained her old icebox. It held items not used regularly that would not result in frequent openings. Sometimes she would assign me to prop a square sign in the front window to let the ice man know that she required another 25 or 50 pounds of ice.

Since the kitchen was also Grandma's dining room, its center piece was her large dining table. With its leaves in place, she could serve a dozen people. With only Uncle Paul still living at home, she took pleasure in our visits and invited at least one other family from the clan to join us each evening.

A specialty of the house was Grandma's "Mulligan stew." I was never able to ascertain who Mulligan was, but it obviously originated as a meal to feed many mouths on a small income. The main ingredient was ground beef. It was heavy on kidney beans and contained more vegetables than I could name – including some that I probably would have rejected if served separately. Everything was cooked in a huge pot with a thick brown gravy. It was nourishing, filling and, by golly, just plain delicious!

A simpler treat, but much appreciated by my brothers and me, was the bottle of water that Grandma kept in her "fridge." A brick-shaped half-gallon bottle, with a screw-on cap, it had begun its life cycle as a juice container. Now Grandma kept it filled with water, and anyone who emptied it halfway was expected to refill it. The cold water tap could run for five minutes and still not satisfy a kid-sized thirst. On sweltering summer days, a slug of the "ice water" really hit the spot.

Even though Springfield is our state capitol, my grandmother's house and neighborhood seemed more small-townish to me than the semi-rural Chicago suburb where my family lived. Around the corner, for instance, there was a mom and pop grocery store. It sat smack between two homes, rather than off on a main thoroughfare along side other stores. The butcher kept live poultry out back. Its wooden floors were always covered with reddish sawdust.

A lady across the street had two sons who owned a farm. She sold eggs, butter and other dairy products to her neighbors. Grandma bought eggs from her because, she said, "They're fresher than at Piggly-Wiggly and cheaper than around the corner."

Grandma McGuire chats with a neighbor as Uncle Leo heads for the back yard, probably carrying a can of fishing worms. Note the wartime "V for Victory" banner in window.

Grandma's upstairs bedroom windows were similar to those I later observed in Abe Lincoln's Springfield home. Only a couple of feet off the floor, they extended almost to the ceiling. With both sashes open halfway, you enjoyed the maximum benefit from any breeze that stirred on a steamy summer night.

About six blocks away, a railroad track ran parallel to Grandma's street. It apparently was used only by freight traffic. I never saw a passenger train in all the times we crossed it. Sometimes I woke in the wee hours to the rumble of a passing train. In the otherwise still night, it would sound as though the train was clattering right through Grandma's alley.

During our stays with Grandma, there were many side trips to visit with aunts, uncles and cousins scattered around Springfield. Grandma often tagged along, especially on Friday or Saturday nights, when several McGuire families were likely to gather for a card game.

Grandma was an ardent card player. She loved Pinochle and a game called Michigan Rummy. (I remember it as similar to a game we played years later that was known as Rummy Royale.) She also was a savvy Poker player. In the family's penny ante games, she played conservatively, usually left the raising to others and "folded" early as often as not. But if she held a good hand, there was no bluffing or scaring her out. When she actually raised the bet, Uncle Vinnie would raise his eyebrows and caution everyone, "Uh oh, folks. Look out. Ma's got a powerhouse." Most nights she went home fifty cents to a dollar richer than she had arrived.

Our visits with Grandma were infrequent in my preteen years, when we did not own a car and had to travel by train. In between, I wrote to her and reported on school, kid stuff and family activities. She responded with long, newsy letters about McGuire family goings-on.

I long harbored the secret notion that I was her favorite grandchild. I was the first, and hogged the spotlight unopposed for three years until Uncle Leo and Aunt Thelma's Joanlee arrived. For years, Grandma saved and mailed to us Uncle Paul's useable outgrown clothes. They'd be too big at first. Mom stored them in her cedar chest until I could "grow into them." I kept hoping that someday I'd inherit Uncle Paul's meterman jacket. (It didn't happen, but eventually Uncle Sam gave me my very own Eisenhower jacket.)

Our trips to Springfield became more frequent after the war and into the 1950s. My love and admiration for Grandma McGuire increased as I matured. I came to view her as the quintessential grandmother.

From my earliest recollection, her hair was gray. In the style of her youth, it grew to her waist. During the day it was pinned neatly around the sides and back of her head. No fuss, no bother. At night, she brushed it out with at least 100 measured strokes.

Soft spoken and small of frame, she appeared frail but possessed an endless energy in caring for home and family. She was a good neighbor, a patriotic American, a faithful church-goer whose Bible did not gather dust on the shelf. She was not shy about speaking her mind or correcting a wayward child. Yet I can not recall her ever saying an unkind word to or about anyone.

Grandma died in 1960. Uncle Paul had recently married. The house finally became too much for her and she moved in with Aunt Ursula and Uncle Carl, who had no children at the time.

She may have simply decided that she had done her duty by all her children and it now was time to join her departed husband in Heaven. I'm certain that her arrival there must have been the occasion of many a joyful embrace from relatives, friends and the angelic welcoming committee.

Riverview: Let's Ride Again!

The streetcar stopped in the middle of the 3300 block. Almost everyone but the motorman and conductor filed out and across Western Avenue. Bobby, Chuck, Wayne and I formed part of a mass exodus that streamed under the red, white and blue entrance arches and through the turnstyles of the "World's Largest Amusement Park." It was 2-Cent Day at Riverview!

Ahead of us lay two and a half miles of midway filled with thrill rides, games, fun houses, food and refreshment stands. Most rides normally cost 35 cents or less. On 2-Cent Days (Monday, Wednesday and Friday), when admission for all ages was reduced to two cents, the prices of all rides were greatly discounted. Some of the less exciting ones cost only two cents. The same was true of 5-Cent Nights (Tuesday and Thursday).

Whatever the price, my pals and I were ready for action. We'd all been saving up for this outing and were well-heeled for a day of adventure.

Just inside the main gate, we veered right around the beautiful landscaped flower garden with its tall flag pole. You could head left or right as you entered. We never made a conscious decision, but in all the times I was there, regardless of who my companions were, we always took the counter-clockwise route.

Perhaps it was the appeal of the twin roller coasters that you immediately encountered. Both had covered cars that kept passengers safely enclosed. The Blue Streak was the milder ride, its main thrill being a section of track with a surprise double dip. The Silver Flash climbed higher, had a steeper first hill and thus ran faster. Usually, we elected to ride the Blue Streak first and build up to the more exciting Silver Flash.

At a 5-Cent Night outing with our folks, Wayne and I once coaxed both our fathers into riding the Silver Flash with us. Wayne's Dad was a transplanted country boy who had never before ridden a roller coaster. As he came down the exit ramp on shaky legs, he observed to my father, "By golly, a feller could do a good business if he was to set up a booth right here and sell fresh underwear."

255

Passersby on the Riverview midway watch as the Blue Streak begins its first dip. (Lake County [IL] Discovery Museum, Curt Teich Postcard Archives)

With our legs still unsteady from the two coaster rides, we stopped to recover in the Penny Arcade. A raft of skill games were playable for a penny or a nickel. The Steam Shovel had a sand pit inside a glass case. Apparently valuable prizes, such as a watch or diamond (?) ring, lay in the sand along with many worthless trinkets. The object was to pick up something with an overhead claw and drop it down a chute before time ran out and the mechanism shut off. Most players got a marble, a whistle or a clawful of air.

Chuck and I were hooked on the machine that dispensed post cards with movie star pictures. We bought them not to mail, but to collect and trade. (At one time, I had eleven different pictures of Margaret O'Brien. She was my first Hollywood heartthrob in those years when we both were still kids.) Evidently, Chuck and I weren't alone. The Arcade sold 1,750,000 cards per year.

After donating about 25 or 30 cents apiece, we left the "penny" arcade. Across the street, we decided to ride the Tilt-A-Whirl. Even though it was a ride found at many carnivals, it was always a thrill to get bounced and spun around, feeling as though our necks would snap. We skipped most other carnival style rides, like the Ferris

Wheel and Carousel. Although prepared to spend every cent in our pockets, we were selective about where.

The Red Devil locomotive wasn't unique either, but we elected to invest in a ride. It traveled around the entire park. En route, we observed the various attractions and discussed which ones were "for sures" and which were "maybes."

(When we returned as teenagers, the park train had succumbed to Progress. The old steam engine had been replaced by a diesel, and the "streamliner" was renamed the Riverview Chief.)

We paused to gawk with the crowd in front of the Palace of Wonders sideshow. A strongman dressed in a leopard skin was driving a nail into a 2 x 4 board with his bare hand. The wonders inside (tattooed lady, rubber-skinned man, snake charmer, etc.) sounded enticing as touted by the barker, but we couldn't spare the time.

The Dodgem was on our "must" list. Its oval-shaped 3-wheeled cars were protected by thick rubber bumpers all around. (The ride's name later was changed to Bump'Em.) They were electrically powered by a wire screen overhead. Tall poles extended from the back of each car to make contact. When all the cars were occupied, the operator threw a control switch. Sparks zipped around the ceiling as drivers stepped on the "gas" pedal to draw current.

The operator repeatedly instructed us over a speaker: "Move in a clockwise direction." This was to avoid jam-ups. But the real fun was in trying to sideswipe your pals and knock them off course. If you veered too much out of the traffic pattern and had a head-on collision, you were out of action until an attendant came and pushed the cars apart. They had no reverse gear.

Mill of the Floss (better known as the Tunnel of Love) was a slow boat trip channeled through landscaped lagoons and some dark tunnels. It was popular with married couples, ladies in groups and, of course, young romantic couples. Usually, we weren't interested. Today we decided to try it, just to spy on any couples necking in the tunnels. Only one sailor tried to kiss his date, and she was too shy to permit it. Phooee! Chuck and I got a laugh from our buddies, though, when we mimed a couple who couldn't coordinate their embrace to complete a kiss.

257

Shoot the Chutes was a water ride more to our liking. The "boats" were shaped like miniature Navy landing craft, with high sides and a raised shield in front. A canal and another tunnel took us to an elevator that slowly raised us to a high tower. A recorded message on a P.A. system repeated warnings posted on intermittent signs: "Keep hands and arms inside the boat. Remove eyeglasses while riding this device. Remain seated. Do not rock the boat."

When we reached the tower platform, we had about six or seven seconds for a great panoramic view of the park from our high perch. Then the rear of our boat tilted and we began a swift descent on the 45-degree waterway. Our boat hit the small pond with an impact that gave everyone a brief shower. Then the driver (who somehow stood up in the rear throughout the ride) steered us toward the edge. A helper docked us with the aid of a long hooked pole.

Riders of Shoot the Chutes could count on a cooling "shower" when their boat hit the water at a 45-degree angle. (Sharpshooters Productions, Inc.)

Continuing along the midway, we passed Kiddyland, with its miniature rides, just right for the smallfry. Riverview also boasted a roller skating rink, miniature golf course, go karts, a paddle wheel showboat and sky cable cars. All this was years before the advent of theme parks.

Nearby was the Whip. We gave it a whirl, literally. It looked relatively tame, but its wicked 90-degree curves gave us the feeling that our heads were being snapped off.

Next came the Comet, a somewhat rougher roller coaster than the Blue Streak or Silver Flash. Then the Strat-O-Stat. These bullet-shaped planes, strung by suspension wires from a revolving tower, soared over the crowds at a 45-degree angle. And finally we arrived at one of my personal all-time favorites, the Flying Turns.

Even if the line was a bit long here, I felt it was worth the wait. The Flying Turns had been acquired from the 1930s era World's Fair. Riders scrunched down on the floor of squat open-topped cars, and were not strapped in. The train was cabled up the usual starter hill. Then we shot downward into a barrel-shaped tunnel.

At breakneck speed, we zoomed through a series of treacherous twists and turns. The car rode up the sides of the tunnel until we were traveling almost upside down. Centrifugal force was all that prevented the cars from crashing or the riders from flying out.

On most of the thrill rides at Riverview, there were signs posted that invited you to "Ride again. Ten cents!" As the ride came to a halt, operators repeated the invitation over the speaker: "Enjoy another thrilling ride on the Flying Turns, folks. Ride again for ten cents." Attendants passed by and collected dimes from those who took up the offer. Keeping a third of the riders on board enabled the ride to restart quicker and probably increased the day's overall take.

If my pals were willing, I'd stay on the Flying Turns for two or three rides. It probably was the shortest ride in the park (about 40 seconds once you started downhill), but for my money the thrill was worth every cent.

Somewhere in this area was one of Riverview's many fun houses, Hades. As we approached, there always was some weak attempt at risqué humor. "Hey, there's where my ma says all you guys are heading." Or: "Who the devil wants to go to Hades?"

Inside Hades' dark corridors, colored lights flashed, spooky figures leaped out at us, there were weird noises and fiendish laughter. At the back end was a fire exit. (Appropriate, right?) Naturally, we peeked out. Not ten feet away was the edge of the Chicago River, which formed the park's west boundary and from which its name derived.

After you've been through Hades, you should be ready for anything, right? Not Necessarily. Next stop was the test of young manhood – the Bobs!

In its day, the Bobs was the most intimidating roller coaster ride in the park – maybe any park. It was an open top ride that started off with a steep drop from 85 feet up. It was fast and it was a non-stop series of wicked curves and dips. Riders did very little waving to friends below. They were too busy screaming and maintaining white knuckle grips on the lap safety bars.

Usually, there were two trains running. On busy days, there were three. The controller had to time departures 30 seconds apart. Sometimes, if customers were slow boarding, a train had to be dispatched with some empty seats.

The Bobs, in its day, was the fastest—and the scariest—roller coaster ride anywhere. (Sharpshooters Productions, Inc.)

This day the line was long but moving well. My pals and I paused to discuss the pros and cons.

"Aw, it ain't so great as to wait in *that* line."

"Maybe we can double back later."

After five minutes, we convinced ourselves to move on with no one having to admit that he was scared to ride the Bobs.

Some version of this scene was repeated on all my outings to Riverview until I attended with a group of my Giles School classmates to celebrate our graduation. On that day, pride finally won out over timidity. After the thrill of my first ride, I rode again four times to make up for some of the fun that I'd missed in my chicken younger days.

Some tamer rides followed. The Flying Scooter was similar to Strat-O-Stat but had smaller, individually controlled planes. A large rudder up front enabled you to fly high or low.

Next, the Greyhound, a roller coaster with a mild ride but an extra long one.

Moon Rocket's cars formed a circle and raced around clockwise while a blue sky centerpiece turned counter-clockwise. As the ride gained speed, the whole contraption tilted on a 45-degree angle. The effect occasionally was too much for some rider who had consumed large quantities of assorted refreshments. Operators had a hose nearby for washing down the cars and platform.

The Boomerang's tub-shaped cars were hooked onto a spinning turntable. As it gathered speed, cars spun off one by one into a circular tunnel. Again our heads felt as though they were about to leave our necks.

Water Bug was an aquatic version of Dodgem. One or two people were seated in an enclosure atop a giant motorized inner tube. The steering device was difficult to master, but the fun really was in bumping other boats and being splashed.

Along about here our group entered another fun house, Ghost Train. It was a typical spook house, but here we rode through in cars on a track.

The Octopus, with its pairs of seats on long extended arms, was featured at lots of carnivals. But it was a dizzyingly fun ride, so we gave it a go. Likewise, the Roll-O-Plane, which rotated us straight up and down while simultaneously our "cockpit" did a tailspin. Midway through the ride, the up and down rotations would cease – and then resume, *going backwards*! This was another ride that could induce queasy stomachs.

Next we entered the huge barrel called the Rotor. We were instructed to stand with our backs to the wall. The barrel began revolving, and when it reached Mach I, *the floor dropped away*!

Once again, centrifugal force came into play. We were pinned to the wall. No one fell, but the screams heard outside undoubtedly caused some customers waiting in line to have second thoughts.

Near the end of our walk, we came to the one Riverview ride that I never patronized. The Pair-O-Chutes.

Looking like a giant Erector Set construction, the great steel structure stood 212 feet tall. The first free-fall parachute ride ever built, it originally was an observation tower called the Eye-Full Tower. It was converted to a parachute ride because the city inspectors declared its elevator unsafe for carrying large groups of people to the top.

On several occasions, I wrestled with myself about giving it a try. But just the thought gave me vertigo. The seat and back support were webbed canvas. Even the lap strap was canvas, rather than a bar. The most solid part of the seat was a set of rubber side bars. Most riders ended up clinging to these for dear life.

Brave patrons ascend and descend on the Pair-O-Chutes ride. In background, at left, is Aladdin's Castle, the granddaddy of fun houses. (Sharpshooters Productions, Inc.)

A long discussion ensued among our foursome. Chuck and I reluctantly admitted that we weren't quite ready for the parachutes yet. Wayne and Bob had already bragged that they were going to go (first time for both). Up close now, they weren't so certain. They still half wanted to but, like Cowardly Lion in "The Wizard of Oz," they half hoped that we'd talk them out of it. No such luck.

"You can only ride two to a chair, anyway," I pointed out with feigned unconcern. "You guys go. Chuck and me'll stay here and pray for yuz."

"Yeah," Chuck agreed. "That way if anything happens, we can notify your next of kin."

Finally, still uncertain, Wayne and Bob bought their tickets. After a short wait, they made it to the front of the line, got seated, and the operator gave them the usual instructions as he checked the safety strap. When they started up, affecting brave grins, Chuck got close to the operator and whispered, "Hey, how about giving those two guys a thrill?"

The operator knew what he meant, as they often had a little fun at the expense of couples riding up together. He grinned and nodded. When our pals' chair was about two thirds of the way up, he cut the power and the chair stopped. Wayne and Bobby leaned forward as much as they dared, looking down nervously.

The operator made signs as though he was having trouble with the motor. Chuck and I waved our arms at our buddies and acted frantic. Chuck leaned toward me and snickered, "I hope they don't wet their pants."

After a minute—which probably seemed like an hour to our buddies—the operator signaled that he'd got the "problem" fixed. The chair continued to the top and then began its slow, graceful descent, the white cloth chute billowing above. At the bottom, it took a high bounce as the unit's coil spring cushioned the touchdown.

Wayne and Bob ran off looking shaken but triumphant. Chuck and I draped our arms over their shoulders and congratulated them on their bravery, especially when the machinery "broke down." I had to avoid eye contact with Chuck lest I burst out laughing and give away our prank. It could have messed up a beautiful 4-way friendship.

Last stop on our tour was Aladdin's Castle, one of the best fun houses ever. In its day, the castle was the Big Daddy of them all. The fun began even before you got inside, thanks to a series of air jets hidden in the walkway from the ticket booth to the entrance. Long before Marilyn Monroe stood over the draft from that sidewalk grate, a blast from one of the air jets would "give a lift" to the dress or skirt of many an unsuspecting lady. Their embarrassment would be increased by the laughter of passersby on the midway who caught a glimpse of legs or undies. Some fellow got paid to handle the tough job of sitting in a control booth all day watching for likely victims.

Aladdin's castle began with a maze of screen doors that took forever to get through. Then there was a hall of mirrors, followed by a room with sections of the floor slanted in all directions. The latter didn't look difficult to navigate, but we never quite made it through here without grabbing one of the hand rails to steady ourselves.

There was a maze of dark hallways. A floor of round discs that twisted underfoot. A giant rotating barrel you had to walk through. Near the end was the "magic carpet," a long, wide, floor level conveyor belt. We sat down on a low bench. The operator pulled a lever and the bench collapsed from under us. Then we rode the carpet downhill as it moved over a series of bumpy rollers.

When we exited the Castle, we were again close to the main gate. We had timed our day's adventure well. We arrived when the gates opened at 11:30a.m. Now it was almost 8p.m. Our folks wanted us home by dark. We would just about make it.

The old Red Rocket trolleys, usually sort of fun in themselves, would be anticlimactic after the many exciting rides we'd enjoyed. As we handed the conductor our fares, Bobby waved a coin at us and echoed the chant we'd heard so frequently all day: "Ride again. Ten cents!"

Afterthought: Those of us who obeyed the billboard, print and radio invitations to "Laugh your troubles away at Riverview" never dreamed that such a popular amusement park would one day close. But close it did, after the 1967 season. No public explanation was ever made. Most folks presumed that increasing land values had led to an offer the owners could not refuse. Today, the sale price of 6.5 million dollars could not even reproduce the Bobs.

Chuck Wlodarczyk's book "Riverview, Gone But Not Forgotten" will evoke many thrilling memories for anyone who ever spent a day at that great amusement park. Even those who never had the pleasure will feel as though they are making a return visit. A beautiful photo history, the book includes background information on practically every attraction in the park.

Another nostalgic walk along the Riverview midway can be found in "World's Largest Amusement Park," co-authored by Ralph Lopez (a former Riverview employee) and Derek Gee. This reminiscence is less lavishly filled with photos, but it affords a detailed history of Riverview, from its beginning as a family picnic grove to an informed account of the most likely explanation for its demise. Lopez and Gee also offer pictures, history and other folks' memories of the park on their website: **riverviewparkchicago.com.**

If August Comes, Can School Be Far Behind?

Between the ages of 6 and 14, my schoolmates and I viewed August as a sort of eleventh-hour month. When we dashed home with our final report cards in May, summer's possibilities seemed unlimited. But the first week of August signaled a countdown period of our precious remaining vacation days.

School resumed on the Tuesday after Labor Day. It varied with the calendar. Yet, inevitably, the arrival of August brought a day when one unwelcome fact was unavoidable. One month from today we'd be back at our desks in James Giles Elementary School.

To paraphrase one of my first children's books: *A* was for *August, anticipation* and *anxiety. A* was for our *ambivalent approach* to and *adversarial attitude about August.*

All during June and July, my pals and I strove diligently to enjoy the seemingly endless days of freedom at our disposal. Spontaneity was our watchword. A rubber ball, the steps of a front porch and two players were enough for a makeshift ball game.

If two or three more players arrived, we could move into the street, switch to a bat and softball and play peggie-move-up. A few more players would prompt a jog to the schoolyard diamond. Twelve kids was enough to pick teams and play pitcher's hands and right field out.

Three players could while away hours at Old Maid, Sorry, Chinese Checkers, Parcheesi or a dozen other board or card games. For larger groups, there were more active games: Hide and Seek (in half a dozen variations); Statue Maker; Red Light/Green Light; Mother, May I?

We ran the gamut from two kids playing War with a double deck of cards to mini-battalions waging fierce battles between the American and the Germans. (After the war, this reverted to cops and robbers or cowboys and Indians.)

In between activities, we might spend an hour on someone's back steps, discussing the crucial question: "Well, what'll we do now?"

"I dunno, Wayne. Whadda you wanna do, Chuck?"

"I dunno, Danny. You guys wanna play radio station?"

"Nah. You always get to be the M.C. What *is* an M.C., anyway?"

266

"It stands for 'Mister Charles.' 'N' I'm the only one whose name is Charles. So I *have* to be the M.C."

Often, if nothing special presented itself, we just roamed the neighborhood looking for inspiration. We walked. We rode scooters. We pushed each other in wagons. In later years, we rode bikes. And we donned roller skates.

Not shoe skates with laces and wooden wheels. These were clunky, expandable metal skates that fit onto the bottom of your street shoes. With straps that went around your insteps. Metal wheels that would hold up on the streets and sidewalks. Clamps that you screwed tight over the tops of your shoes.

Comedian Shelley Berman observed years later that certain words and phrases can enoke waves of acute nostalgia. Phrases such as: *skate key*.

Thus did most of our waking moments in June and July involve: a) enjoying ourselves in one activity or another; b) plotting what fun stuff to do next; and c) staying on the move to avoid being recruited for work details. (Parents seemed to share a universal notion that idle children were bound to get into mischief. Or, at the very least, that it was in their best interest to find some task to end their idleness.)

Suddenly, the sultry "dog days" of August were upon us. After two months of working feverishly at having fun, it was tempting to spend some time just lazing in the shade. But now our days of carefree sport were numbered. We must respond to the challenge.

Everything we'd neglected to do, or wanted to do once more, took on a new urgency. As Chicago's weather grew more humid, a day of swimming rated a high priority.

In our younger years, this meant a trip to Portage Park, the closest Chicago park that boasted a pool. Our swimming abilities varied, but we all knew how to dog paddle and leap into the pool so as to direct a tidal wave into our pals' faces.

Before and after swimming, we worked out on the park's tall swings. At the corner where we caught our streetcar to go home, there was a large bowl-shaped water fountain with six continuously flowing drinking spouts. A favorite prank was to cover several of the spouts while one of your buddies was taking a drink. With increased water pressure diverted to his spout, it would suddenly erupt with a heavy stream straight into his face.

267

When we were older, our parents permitted us to journey to Chicago's Montrose Avenue beach. It involved transferring three times and about two hours in transit. Mothers packed lunches and we bought soda from beachfront vendors. Of course, we had strict instructions not to go into the water for an hour after eating.

For the author and his buddies, a day at Chicago's beaches required about two hours en route via bus, streetcar and Ankle Express. But on hot, steamy, summer days, the cool water of Lake Michigan attracted kids like a magnet. (Library of Congress photo)

Chicago's beaches were less crowded in those days. We played catch with a rubber ball in and out of the water. Non-swimmers had plenty of fun jumping over or diving into the waves. Even at its warmest, Lake Michigan is still cool. It felt great on our sweaty young bodies.

We saved the cost of changing in a beach house by wearing our suits under our clothes. They'd be a little crusty on the trip home, but the cool dampness felt good and reminded us what a swell day we'd had.

Wayne and Bobby were Cub fans. They made it to Wrigley Field about eight or ten times each season. I enjoyed listening to Bert Wilson's radio play-by-play, but I got enthused about actually attending a game only when time was running out. Then I made sure to tag along with my buddies, regardless of who the Cubs were playing or what their chances were of winning.

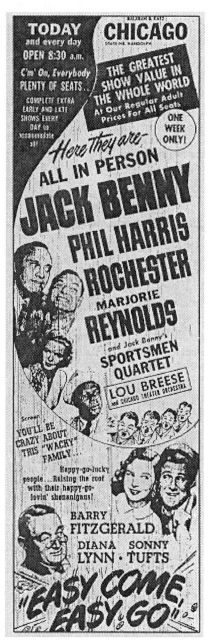

I recognized only a few of the best known players. I often needed Bob or Wayne to explain a ruling on an unusual play. While most kids prayed for a foul ball to come their way, I dreaded the possibility, knowing that I'd most likely embarrass myself by dropping it – or, worse yet, letting it go through my hands and bean me.

Even so, as I munched on my hot dog and sipped my ice cold Coca Cola, no one got more into the spirit of the game than I did. The one drawback was a nagging suspicion that I might be a jinx to our home team. Never once did the Cubs win a game when I was in the stands.

Chuck was a frequent patron of the Chicago Theatre, where live acts shared the bill with first-run movies. He especially liked to wait in the alley between shows to collect autographs of his favorite stars when they stepped out for a breath of fresh air or to have a smoke.

I sometimes joined Chuck, even though my enthusiasm for stage shows didn't equal his. Because this was something we could do on weekends all year long (or any time during summer vacation), I often took a pass. But come August it was on my "must do" list as one more semi-special event.

In retrospect, I must credit the Chicago Theatre (and the Oriental, which also featured live stage acts) with introducing us to many future headliners who had not yet achieved star billing.

Wayne and I were avid fishermen. As often as possible, we coaxed our fathers into taking us to the Fox River, Chain O'Lakes or any other fishing spot within easy driving distance. When we acquired bicycles, we spent many days pulling bullhead catfish and occasional carp or turtles out of the Des Plaines River.

August demanded a special excursion, though. One year we rode on Illinois Route 42A out to where farms prevailed. Then we headed east until we reached Skokie Lagoon. We'd been told that it was stocked regularly with large crappie and bass. Maybe so, but we caught only bluegill. It was a long grueling ride to catch a few pan fish.

Another August, with sack lunches and fishing poles tied to our bikes, we pedaled up Illinois Route 12 all the way to Lake Zurich. (Probably about 30 miles of riding on the highway, but back then auto traffic was slower and much less plentiful; and if we annoyed any motorists, road rage in those days took a much milder form.) Once there, we found that the lake was surrounded by private properties. The only public access was a commercial park geared to picnickers and swimmers.

Undaunted, we rode back to the Des Plaines River. En route, we stopped at the roadside stand of an orchard that advertised itself with a gigantic red apple balanced on a tall pole atop the building. For ten cents, we each had a glassful of homemade (non-alcoholic) apple cider. Delicious! And the day's muddled outing was perfect for including in our "What I Did This Summer" essays.

For most of my gang, one more day at Riverview was a must. We'd raid our treasure chests, beg some extra change from the folks, and go on a Monday, Wednesday or Friday – "2-Cent Days." Admission to the "World's Largest Amusement Park" would be two cents and most rides would be at greatly reduced prices.

The imminent resumption of school made it mandatory: one more trip to Riverview for a day of fun at "the world's largest amusement park." (Lake County [IL] Discovery Museum, Curt Teich Postcard Archives)

Knowing it was our last visit of the year, we rode almost every attraction, even those we normally deemed "baby stuff." There were restaurants that served sandwiches and other real food, but as a point of honor we survived the day on hot dogs, candy, frozen treats and soda pop.

Departing Riverview was perhaps symbolic of our impending return to the school routine. After Labor Day, the park would close for the season. There would be no more loud speaker invitations of "Ride again, ten cents" until next summer.

Eventually, Labor Day arrived. For most folks, it meant family gatherings, usually with a back yard picnic. During the afternoon, my pals and I visited each other's groups and mooched various ethnic snacks between meals.

A couple of years my family turned it into a 3-day holiday. Braving the traffic horde on Route 66 (remember Route 66?), we drove 200 miles to Springfield and spent the weekend with Dad's relatives. Either way, it was a fitting finale to a kid's vanishing vacation.

271

Returning to school wasn't as bad as anticipated. On the weekend after Labor Day, we breathed a sigh of relief for making it through the first week of the new school year. After racing to do a little of everything during that last month, it was sort of nice to have your schedule laid out for you.

We all understood that getting educated was an important occupation. Still, we never lost sight of that other goal which held a high priority for all kids: having fun. Very soon, we began planning how to more judiciously allocate our vacation time next year.

Stripped For Action

Chester Gould surely started something. Cartoonist Gould, who died May 11, 1985, is widely credited with beginning the trend of "serious" comic strips with a continuing story line.

According to a Smithsonian Institute anthology, comic strips – sequenced drawings that tell a story, with dialogue enclosed overhead in "balloons" —were already popular in Europe and emigrated to American newspapers about 1890. Early on, some cartoonists presented stories that extended over many days. If any were of the dramatic variety, however, they apparently were short-lived.

Mr. Gould, a native of Pawnee, Oklahoma, moved to Chicago in 1921 and spent ten years in various art department jobs with five of the city's newspapers. In 1931, he succeeded in selling a strip called "Plainclothes Tracy" to the Chicago Tribune-New York Daily News syndicate. Daily News publisher Joseph Patterson gave Tracy the first name Dick, because it was a common slang term for a detective.

Neither Gould nor Patterson could have foreseen Tracy's impact on comic strip history. In that Depression era of bootlegging, gangland killings and crooks scoffing at the law, Dick Tracy's blood-and-guts battle against master criminals was a nationwide hit. Publishers picked up on the readers' response and began adding all sorts of adventure strips to what we nevertheless continued to refer to as "the funny papers."

During the 1940s, when I was learning to sound out words of more than one syllable, my family subscribed to home delivery of the Chicago Sun. (The Sun, a morning paper, later merged with the afternoon Times. Renamed the Sun-Times, it survives today as the only competitor to the dominant Chicago Tribune.) I soon became addicted to the action-packed tales of several comic strip heroes.

Superman was high on the list. The "Man of Steel" was created in 1932 by school chums Jerry Siegel, who wrote the story lines, and Joe Shuster, who did the illustrations. Surprisingly, in view of its subsequent success, the strip was rejected by newspaper syndicates for six years. It finally saw print in 1938 in the first issue of Action Comics (now a valuable collector's edition).

Faster than a speeding bullet, Superman pushed Action Comics sales close to a million copies a month. More powerful than a locomotive, a spin-off bi-monthly Superman comic book soon exceeded the million copies mark. As easily as leaping over tall buildings in a single bound, Superman branched out into radio (and, later, television), the movies and—of course—newspapers. By 1941, the Superman comic strip ran in 230 papers nationwide.[1]

As Dick Tracy had inspired a trend to action comic strips in general, Superman became the prototype for a host of costumed super-heroes. For my money, he always was the greatest. Certainly, no one ever surpassed his super-human powers.

Superman had only two weaknesses. His X-ray vision could be stopped by lead shields. More important, he had to avoid Kryptonite like the plague. Kryptonite was a meteorite substance from the planet Krypton, the Man of Steel's original home. (His father, Jor-El, sent his infant son to Earth in a tiny rocket ship shortly before the dying planet exploded.) Proximity to the smallest chunk of Kryptonite caused Superman to lose his powers and become weaker than Earthmen.

During World War II, Superman alternately came to the rescue of the Allied Forces and kept the streets free from crime here on the homefront. I wished he could end the war by capturing Hitler, Mussolini and Hirohito; but it was rumored that the Axis leaders never went anywhere without a chunk of Kryptonite secreted in their hip pockets.

Batman made his solo debut about a year after Superman. He very quickly became the second most popular comics hero. Created by Bob Kane, The Bat-Man (as the strip initially was titled) was really Bruce Wayne, a millionaire dedicated to fighting crime because his parents had been killed in a hold-up. Already armed with wealth and high intelligence, Wayne became a self-trained strongman and

---

[1] Sadly, Shuster and Siegel did not reap the riches generated by their creation. As employees of DC Comics, they sold the rights to the strip for a reported $130. When they later requested, and then sued for, a larger sum, they were fired. After repeated losses in court, they took their case to the general public in 1975. Warner Communications, which by then owned the rights, bowed to the higher court of public opinion. Both men were granted lifetime pensions of $20,000 (later increased to $30,000), and none too soon. Siegel was then working as a clerk typist. Shuster, legally blind, was being supported by a brother. Copies of that first Action Comics have sold for $4,000.

acrobat. For his vigilante role, he donned a bat-like caped costume designed to prey upon the fears and superstitions of criminal minds.

The newspapers referred to them as the Comic Section. Kids called them "the funny papers," or just "the funnies." (Retrofile.com)

When I met him in the Chicago Sun, he already had adopted Dick Grayson, an orphaned circus acrobat. Dick became Robin, the Boy Wonder, and the pair soon acquired the nicknames of "the Dynamic Duo" and "the Caped Crusaders." With their gymnastic skills, an array of clever devices (which they somehow always managed to have packed in their black utility belts at the right time) and the incredibly equipped, rocket-powered Batmobile, they were a match for the most fiendish bad guys. (Some of their outlandish adversaries became as well known as the heroes themselves: The Joker, The Penguin, Catwoman, The Riddler.)

If pressed to name my favorite action comic strip, I would have to choose Batman. For all the gimmickry they utilized, the Dynamic Duo were mortals who could (heaven forbid!) be killed. Yet they fearlessly did battle with a host of public enemies, besting them with their fantastic athletic abilities, their keen intellects and their bare – well, actually, gloved– hands. Moreover, since kids identified with their comic heroes, I had two for the price of one. I could imagine myself as the young Robin, or as Batman, whose role I would assume when he grew old and I was in my prime.

Even so, Tarzan was a close second. From my first exposure to a Tarzan movie starring Johnny Wiessmuller, I was a devoted fan. (A dozen or more of Hollywood's muscular male types have portrayed the ape man on screen, some rather well, but for me Wiessmuller always stood out as the real Tarzan.)

Nevertheless, after struggling through a couple of Edgar Rice Burroughs' books, I realized that the comic strip character was much closer to the author's original hero. "The Lord of the Jungle" was born to titled English parents. As an infant, he survived a plane crash in Africa in which his parents perished. Raised by apes, he later returned to England and completed his education. Afterward, he forsook an easy, sumptuous life as Lord Greystoke to return to the jungle.

This was no "Me Tarzan, you Jane" ape man. Though he conversed with animals and many native tribes in their language, he reasoned in English, and very intelligently. In movies, he was armed only with a knife. In the comics (and Burroughs' novels), he usually carried a bow and arrows—much more effective for hunting dinner. He slept in trees (for safety) because he usually was on the move. There was no permanent-residence treehouse, and no sign of a Jane or Boy to slow him down.

However, like Wiessmuller's movie Tarzan, he could run, swim, climb trees and swing on vines with great skill. And, yes, he did beat his chest and give the victory cry of the bull ape after a kill. To a city-bound boy in short pants, his adventures among humans and animals alike were a source of great admiration.

These three, Tarzan, Batman and Superman, topped my list of favorite comic strips in the action category. No doubt I was influenced by their presence in the newspaper that we received daily.

Readers whose papers carried other strips may have become avid followers of Terry and the Pirates, The Lone Ranger, Mandrake the Magician, The Phantom, Brenda Starr (a rare strip featuring a heroine rather than a hero) or a host of others. (I'd be pleased to hear which was your favorite and why.) A few years down the road we were introduced to more sophisticated series such as Mark Trail and Steve Canyon.

Occasionally, my folks bought a Sunday Tribune. When they did, I took the opportunity to check on Dick Tracy's adventures, but I never became a real fan, perhaps owing to the lack of continuity. That did not prevent me from getting hooked when Tracy appeared in a 13-week movie serial.

Fan or not, I acknowledge a debt to Chester Gould, whose square-jawed, straight-shooting, tough-guy hero was syndicated in over 500 papers worldwide. Without the success of the Dick Tracy strip, my favorites—and dozens of others—might never have been published.

Mr. Gould retired to Woodstock, Illinois, in 1977, but he arranged for his history-making comic strip to continue, written and drawn by others. On behalf of all us action comic strip readers, young and old, hats off to you, Chester Gould. And long live "Plainclothes Tracy"!

When We Left Our Hero Yesterday...

During the years when James Giles Elementary School waged an uphill battle to educate my playmates and me, radio was a key ingredient of our after-school activities.

Coming out of the Great Depression, radio's basically cost-free nature led it to reign as our nation's primary entertainment medium. For kids, especially during the school year, it greatly influenced our weekday routines.

Most days, we came straight home and gratefully accepted an after-school snack from Mom. Then, unless the gang was doing something really exciting outside, we dutifully started in on our homework.

The goal was to finish by 4:30. Because from 4:30 until 6p.m., Chicago's major radio stations vied for the youthful audience with a continuous line-up of 15-minute serialized adventure programs. For radio-active kids like us, there were some painful choices as to where to set that "little green eye" (the glowing indicator on the dial that adjusted tuning).

Some choices were easier than others. I never was a fan of Little Orphan Annie or Dick Tracy in the comics. So I did not get hooked as a regular listener to their radio shows. The round-eyed Annie was a girl, after all. As for Tracy, I was skeptical of a hero whose pointed chin looked as though it could punch neat holes in a Pet Evaporated Milk can. Not to mention the cast of outrageously conceived villains with whom he did battle.

"Terry and the Pirates" fascinated me with its sing-song Oriental introduction. Storywise, though, I kept losing the drift. The plots weren't all that complex, but I listened sporadically. (Terry was an alternative choice when one of my regular shows dragged a little.) Also, I would get confused as to who were the good guys and bad guys among the many weird characters who populated the script.

It bothered me some that I wasn't more loyal, because Terry, Flip, Pat, Stoop, Dragon Lady and the rest of "the Burma bunch" were sponsored by Quaker Puffed Wheat and Puffed Rice. ("It's shot from guns!") The former was a regular on my breakfast menu. Some of my favorite shows, meanwhile, had sponsors whose products I seldom patronized.

Captain Midnight, for instance. To be the first kid on my block who received a mail order Secret Squadron decoder, I persuaded my mother to buy a jar of Ovaltine. Then I was obliged to force feed myself countless glassfuls of a drink that was nothing like the chocolate treat I had anticipated. Mom eventually dumped half the jar, for which wastefulness I received a parental lecture about the starving children in Europe.

Yet I was unshakably loyal to the mysterious midnight flyer. The program's intro made me fairly quiver. The deep tolling of a tower clock. (You *knew* it was 12 midnight on a cloudy, moonless night.) The drone of a propeller airplane coming from far off, then roaring overhead. Announcer Pierre Andre's inimitable voice, mimicking the plane's approach: "Caaap...Tiiiin...**Miiiiid**...nite!"

Another program that snared me with its dramatic opening had several voices shouting in turn, each one closer and louder: "Jack Armstrong. *Jack Armstrong.* Jack **Armstong**!" Then announcer Franklin MacCormack's erudite voice elaborated: "Jack Armstrong— the aaaallll American boy!" As if that wasn't enough, there followed that rousing theme song. "Have you *tried* Wheaties? The *best* breaskfast food in the *land*!"

Under the protective tutelage of their Uncle Jim, Jack, Billy and Betty traveled to exotic places around the world and continually became involved in bizarre adventures. Jack sounded as though he might be college age, but more likely senior high. Betty and Billy obviously weren't much older than me – junior high schoolers, at most. I never figured out how they could be gallivanting all over the world instead of being stuck in school like us ordinary kids.

Perhaps because I'm a lifelong sucker for horse operas, Tom Mix was on my "must listen" list. I also was vaguely aware that Tom was not a made-up character. He had been killed in a car accident in 1940, but before that had been a soldier/horse wrangler in the Boer War, a sometime cow puncher and rodeo star. He became famous as a movie cowboy, first in silent pictures and then in "talkies."

In later years, he chose to devote his energies to his Tom Mix Circus. When the radio series began in 1933, he agreed to have his part played by a radio actor. The closing credits would mention that "Tom Mix was impersonated," but most kids were flipping the dial by then. If we'd been paying attention, we wouldn't have known what "impersonate" meant, anyway.

Several actors filled the lead role, but it wasn't until after Tom died that the announcements were modified to include their names. The closing that sticks with me is: "Tom Mix was played by Curly Bradley." Bradley portrayed Tom during most of the years that I was a faithful listener. He was a veteran radio actor who had played other roles on the show.   He also was a talented Western singer. Scriptwriters often found ways to work in a song for Tom, and at Christmas he would host a party at the ranch and lead the cast in singing many holiday tunes.

While there was plenty of action in the stories, Tom Mix was not essentially a fist-fighting, shoot-out type cowboy. Rather, he was a sort of Western detective. In between resolving problems at the TM-Bar Ranch and among his rancher neighbors, he assisted Sheriff Mike Shaw ("Sassafras 'n' sourdough, Taum!") in unraveling mysteries that involved everything from disappearing cattle, to amnesia victims, to murder. Shaw, by the way, was played for awhile by Harold Perry, who later became radio's Great Gildersleeve.

Tom's sponsor was Shredded Ralston ("bite size and ready to eat"), a product I consumed regularly. Right off, of course, I was able to join Tom's Ralston Straight Shooters. Better yet, I was able to send in box tops and dimes for dozens of Tom Mix radio premiums. In today's collector market, their combined value would have thrilled the folk on PBS's "Antiques Road Show." But, silly me, I just played with them until they were broken or lost.

A short-lived series that I became attached to was "The Adventures of Tennessee Jed." I remember being upset when it faded from the airwaves. Yet I can't recall much about the details of the show except that Jed was a sort of easy-going, backwoods version of Tom Mix. His claim to fame was his deadeyed accuracy with a long range deer rifle.

VOICE: (Excited) There he goes, Tennessee. Git 'im.

SOUND EFFECT: Crack of rifle.

VOICE: (Jubilant) Got 'im, Tennessee. Daid center!

During World War II, I was a devoted fan of "Hop Harrigan, Ace of the Airways." With his mechanic sidekick, Tank Tinker, Hop Harrigan flew many a patriotic mission. The show dripped with propaganda. Once Hop and Tank bravely headed into a potentially deadly situation with two captive German pilots aboard. Says one German to the other: "Da more I see of zese Americaners, da more I realize vot fools ve are to be fighting dem."

If I got an early start on my dial twisting, sometimes I'd tune in "Just Plain Bill." Though actually a late afternoon soap opera for the ladies, it occasionally featured a robbery, or even a murder, in the normally laid back town of Sommerville, where Bill ran his little barber shop. (Maybe the writers hoped to hook a few husbands who arrived home early.)

With his gifts of gentle wisdom and observation, aided by his customers' penchant for gossip, Bill helped solve these and many of the town folk's other problems. Usually right there in his shop. While weighing the facts of a particularly muddled situation, Bill once spent 17 days (not counting weekends) shaving the same customer.

Oh, and talk about exciting openings. Whether you were a kid or a parent, if there was a radio in your home you can't help but remember the most dramatic opening of all.

ANNOUNCER: Faster than a speeding bullet!
SOUND EFFECT: Reverberating gunshot.
ANNOUNCER: More powerful than a locomotive!
SOUND EFFECT: Train charging down track. Whistle blows.
ANNOUNCER: Able to leap tall buildings in a single bound!
SOUND EFFECT: Rush of great wind overhead.
FIRST VOICE: Look! Up in the sky. It's a bird!
SECOND VOICE: It's a plane!
THIRD VOICE: It's Superman!

Of all the 15-minute after-school serials, I ranked Superman as Number One. Tom Mix was a close second. But I was a long-time fan of Superman from both his comic books and daily newspaper comic strips. Not to mention his appearances on the silver screen and in Big Little Books.

Regular readers may recall that Batman was my all-time favorite comic hero. Unfortunately, he had no radio series. In one Superman adventure, the Man of Steel was immobilized by a villain who had acquired a chunk of Kryptonite. What a thrill it was for me when he was rescued by the Dynamic Duo – Batman and Robin! If the matter had ever been in doubt, that episode would have sewn up my subsequent loyalty to Kellogg's Pep's flying hero.

My pal, Chuck, shared my high regard for Superman, but our tastes differed on other programs. If he called me out to play while Tom Mix was on, I risked alienating my best buddy by saying I'd be out later. The shoe was on the other foot, though, if I called him during Dick Tracy's air time.

With so many gripping adventures pinning us down in front of the radio's little green eye, it's a wonder that we ever got out to join the other kids on the block in the after-school fun and games. Of course, we could skip even our most favorite shows for one day and usually not miss much.

On Fridays, homework could be put off until the weekend. Other days we could play for an hour after school and defer homework until after supper. That might mean missing some prime time radio favorites, though.

We could try doing our homework while we listened. (Another of the advantages of radio: you "saw" what was happening without having your eyes glued to a little screen.) But don't let the folks catch your grades slipping because your mind was on Straight Arrow's latest dilemma instead of the assignment.

Talking about making tough decisions! Who says kids didn't have to deal with stress in "the good old days"?

Batman, You're Still The Greatest

In that long ago era when only kids read comic books, radio was still our primary medium of entertainment. The "theatre of the imagination" was an ideal stage for action-packed adventure programs.

Every weekday afternoon, versatile actors and actresses (aided by skilled sound effects men) brought to life such comic strip favorites as Dick Tracy, the Lone Ranger, Little Orphan Annie, Terry and the Pirates, Red Ryder, Superman and others. Archie Andrews and his pal, Jughead Jones, joined the Saturday morning line-up. Drawing on the popularity of Penny Singleton/Arthur Lake movies, Blondie and Dagwood earned a half hour in a family oriented evening time slot.

Youthful fans were loyal listeners, and many of these shows enjoyed long runs on radio. When television took over, the picture changed.

Most comic book series did not adapt well to TV. The characters and scenes so clearly envisioned by our mind's eye were difficult to recreate on the small screen. Superman episodes (although now treasured as cult classics of the era) were low budget efforts and could not begin to duplicate the Man of Steel's incredible radio feats. The show survived largely on the strength of its hero's wide-spread popularity.

The Lone Ranger was a notable exception. Its Old West setting already existed on Hollywood's back lots. It meshed well with TV's myriad other Western series and old cowboy movies. The Masked Man's long ride across the TV plains made Jay Silverheels perhaps the most steadily employed Native American (in those days we still called him an Indian) actor, and created a lifelong career for Clayton Moore.

Hollywood has cashed in on the popularity of many comic characters. In 1940s cliffhanger series, Dick Tracy, Superman, Brenda Starr, Batman, Red Ryder and Captain Midnight all survived a multitude of ingenious traps and assaults by the bad guys.

Tarzan had been a perennial favorite since Elmo Lincoln portrayed him on the silent screen. We've seen such diverse folk as Li'l Abner, Orphan Annie and Popeye given feature film treatment. With modern special effects making his exploits believable,

283

Superman easily flew to new box office record heights. A feature film starring Warren Beatty as Dick Tracy is reportedly "in the can" as we go to press and Hollywood soon will be ballyhooing its imminent release.

Meanwhile, this summer we've been bombarded with Hollywood hype for the action packed Batman flick starring Michael Keaton and Jack Nicholson. I couldn't be more pleased. Since the days when ten cents would buy me the latest edition, Batman has been my all-time unzappable favorite.

Tarzan was a close runner-up. I'd have loved to have the Ape Man's physique, be friends with the wild beasts and perform his feats of strength and courage. Yet I couldn't quite daydream myself into forsaking all of civilization's amenities.

Batman, however, did battle in an urban setting not unlike nearby Chicago. He was mysteriously awesome in his dark cowled garb. Out of costume, his life as millionaire Bruce Wayne was one I could readily adapt to.

Tarzan and Batman were both grown-ups, educated and experienced. Thus, my fantasizing required a giant leap of imagination. But Batman was aided by a young co-crimefighter named Robin.

Robin, "the Bob Wonder" (in reality Wayne's ward, Dick Grayson), was not much older than me. Like me, he had to attend school and adhere to various juvenile restrictions. These actually prevented him from accompanying his mentor on some adventures. But here's the good part. Sometimes, while out crusading alone, Batman would be captured by Penguin, Catwoman or Joker. After school was out, *Robin would come to his rescue.*

Batman usually was cool and calculating in the face of

dangerous situations. Robin's bravery was commendable, but often triggered impetuous actions that invited danger.

The Dynamic Duo was a perfect pair of heroes for me. I could identify with the Boy Wonder and dream of growing up to take over Batman's role.

Comic book heroes came in a wide range of sizes and styles. Most of my contemporaries had their own favorites. This sparked some spirited debates.

My steadfast defense of Batman and Robin was that they (like Tarzan) were mortal humans. However outrageous their derring-do might become, they had no special powers to prevent them from being killed by the villains.

I shared my buddies' enthusiasm for Superman. He ranked high on my list, too. Yet, there was no escaping the fact that he was…well…Superman.

He could fly, see through walls, catch bullets in his hand. Kryptonite (meteoric chunks from his home planet, Krypton) made him weak, but bullet nor knife still could not pierce his skin. The Man of Steel was most vulnerable to the penchant of his friends Lois Lane and Jimmie Olson for being captured by the bad guys and held hostage or in danger of being dispatched.

One of my best friends (whom I'll not embarrass by naming) thought that Captain Marvel was the last word in heroes. To me, he was a comic hero with the emphasis on the word *comic*.

The Captain originally was conceived as a satire on Superman. To the great surprise and good fortune of Marvel Comics, readers took him seriously. He soon rivaled Superman in popularity and circulation numbers.

Dashingly handsome in his sparkling red and gold costume, Captain Marvel was brimming with valor and patriotism. Compared to Superman, though, he came up short on cleverness and boldness of action. Perhaps his criminal opponents demanded too little of him. Apart from his arch enemy, a mad scientist named Ninevah, none was as ominously ornery as those Superman encountered.

Captain Marvel did have his vulnerable side. He was really Billy Batson, a young radio reporter. When his work led him to uncover crooked activities, he shouted "Shazam!" A bolt of lightning changed him from scrawny kid to muscle-bound hero.

The nonsense word *Shazam* was created from the initials of six mythical characters. In his costumed persona, Billy acquired their

great attributes. Had the bad guys ever wised up, they could have ended the series early on. They were forever sapping or gagging Billy when he'd only started to call for the transforming lightning bolt.

"Shaz—" *Bop!* "Oooooh."

Oh, and don't get me started on Mary Marvel and Captain Marvel Junior. These spin-offs of the Cappy character were really Mary Batson and Freddie Freeman, a girl reporter and a crippled news vendor.

Like Billy, Mary shouted "Shazam!" to be transformed into a super female. Admittedly, she looked good in her form-fitting costume with colors to match the Captain's. Because of her youth, she probably was a favorite of many female comics readers.

For whatever reason (perhaps to avoid confusing slow-witted readers), Captain Marvel Junior's costume was blue. Worse though, with no explanation that I'm aware of, was that Freddie had to shout "Captain Marvel!" to be transformed. It was twice the syllables, which didn't seem fair. Bad guys were always clubbing Freddie with his own crutch before he could get the words out of his mouth.

A big favorite with girls was Wonder Woman. As I approached puberty, I gave her high marks, too. Her outfit—red, white and blue, with stars—was essentially a tight bathing suit with hightop boots. On her, it did not defame the flag. Wonder Woman was definitely an all-American gal, but she carried a *magic lasso* and wore bracelets that deflected bullets. Come on.

Plasticman was kind of fun, but can you buy a hero with an elastic body that he can wrap around corners like a rubber band? He was kind of a one-trick hero, and it stretched thin after awhile.

The Shadow and Mandrake the Magician were interesting characters, essentially mortal. Yet they, too, had little tricks that shielded them from the bad guys' bullets.

Others come to mind. The Flash. Captain America. Submarineman. (This guy was so deep he was unfathomable.) Some were nominally human and/or mortal. But even Green Lantern couldn't hold a candle to Batman.

Batman and Robin captivated a large television audience of all ages in the 1960s. The Caped Crusaders' most colorful adversaries

were well represented. (I'd have liked to see the fellow called Ali Blabber. In the comic series, author Bob Kane went to extreme lengths to come up with stories that would enable him to use titles such as "Ali Blabber and the Four Tea Leaves.")

The 3-year TV series, and the movie it inspired, were heavy on melodrama and choreographed with visual *Biffs*, *Pows* and *Zowies*. The campy style was typified by outbursts from Robin such as "Holy cat litter, Batman! That felonious feline is playing cat and mouse with us!" Having

287

outgrown the comics themselves, I enjoyed seeing my favorite crimefighters still doing their hero stuff, but sort of tongue in cheek.

The new Batman movie is something else. Every bit as well done as the Superman flicks, it is crammed with the fast-paced high-powered action I remember from the D.C. Comics of the 1940s.

Michael Keaton gives a credible performance in both halves of his dual personality. In spite of body armor under his costume (a 1980s innovation), Batman still takes a few lumps. Jack Nicholson, as the Joker, is the real star. The screen has not presented such a delightfully demented villain since Richard Widmark pushed an old lady down a flight of stairs in her wheelchair.

Police Commissioner Gordon and the faithful butler, Alfred, are on hand, fairly true to character. But the scriptwriters omitted Robin in order to let the film concentrate on the brooding psychological side of Batman, the dark knight, and the romantic efforts of his alter ego, Bruce Wayne.

That works for me. I'm too old to identify with the Boy Wonder any more.

From Highway Boredom They Did Save
Many A Driver: Burma Shave

When gas rationing ended after V-J Day, the Chicago McGuires began visiting the McGuire clan in Springfield several times a year. In that era before divided four-lane super highways, it was a six-hour journey that included a lunch stop en route.

One thing that helped pass the time was watching for the series of small red signs, spaced short distances apart, that occasionally appeared beside the road. In a short, loosely rhymed cadence, they presented passing motorists with such thought-provoking messages as:

THE BEARDED DEVIL
IS FORCED TO DWELL
IN THE ONLY PLACE
WHERE THEY DON'T SELL
BURMA SHAVE

The first time I observed a set of these lyrical advertisements, I repeated it to myself as I absorbed the humor. Then I grinned and recited it aloud for my parents. "Did you see those signs?" I asked, thinking I'd made a great discovery.

Mom and Dad shared a chuckle over that. The Burma Shave signs had been gracing U.S. roads since before either of them began driving.

Although it was the comic verses we all came to love, early Burma Shave signs were strictly commercial messages. In 1925, Clinton Odell, founder of the Burma-Vita Company, was seeking ways to promote a brushless shaving cream. His son, Allan, suggested posting sequential signs along roads leading to towns where druggists were stocking the new product.

Clinton wasn't keen on the idea, but agreed to give it a try. The first signs were constructed from secondhand boards full of nail holes. Allan and his brother, Leonard, cut them into 36-inch lengths and used stencils to paint the slogans.

The boys contracted with farmers for the right to post signs at selected spots. They did all the digging and mounting themselves. A typical first-year set of signs read:

SHAVE THE MODERN WAY
FINE FOR THE SKIN
DRUGGISTS HAVE IT
BURMA SHAVE

To the surprise of the older Odell—and the delight of all—repeat orders began coming in from druggists in towns near where the signs were located. The trio immediately set out to utilize the new sales technique on a broader scale. In 1926, signs sprouted throughout Michigan, Wisconsin and Iowa. In 1927, they dotted highways in most of the Midwest. By 1930, they were amusing travelers from New England to the Deep South and from Atlantic to Pacific coasts.

The humorous content that caught my attention in Illinois crept in gradually as sales and the Odells' spirits continued to rise. One of the first comic verses, still fondly remembered by some senior motorists, appeared in 1929:

EVERY SHAVER
NOW CAN SNORE
SIX MORE MINUTES
THAN BEFORE
BY USING
BURMA SHAVE

Initially, Allan and his father composed all "copy." The catchiness of rhymed lines was evident early on. After a few tentative efforts, the basic format was established. In 1930, most of the straight commercial signs had been supplanted by the sing-songy sales pitches.

By the late 1940s, my brothers and I had become (for those times) frequent travelers. Besides family visits to Springfield, there were weekend fishing trips with Dad and a week in Wisconsin. Watching for Burma Shave signs became a ritual that added to the adventure.

Sometimes whoever spotted the lead sign would alert the others. Then we might all crowd the windows and read the verse in unison:

I USE IT TOO
THE BALD MAN SAID
IT KEEPS MY FACE
JUST LIKE
MY HEAD
BURMA SHAVE

Or we might take turns reading successive signs.

Alan:	WHEN THE STORK
Danny:	DELIVERS A BOY
Dickie:	OUR WHOLE
Alan:	DARN FACTORY
Danny:	JUMPS FOR JOY
Dickie:	BURMA SHAVE

Whoever got stuck reading the "commercial" invariably would demand, "I get to go first next time!"

Often we brought along books, cards or other diversions for the trip. Then we took turns being "Burma Shave lookout" and reading the signs aloud to each other. This necessitated periodic seat swapping, which had the indirect beneficial effect of minimizing arguments about who would sit where.

For a change of pace, one of us sometimes would look out the back window as we passed a series of signs on the other side of the road – and read them to us in reverse:

BURMA SHAVE
UNTIL YOU'VE TRIED
DON'T BE CONTENT
JOKES ASIDE
ALL LITTLE RHYMING

The other passengers would repeat each of the lines and mentally flip them around until someone came up with the correct front-to-back rendition.

The snappy verses by this time had several distinct categories. One was a pitch to smoother boy/girl relationships to be achieved via smoother shaves:

HE HAD THE RING
HE HAD THE FLAT
BUT SHE FELT HIS CHIN
AND THAT
WAS THAT
BURMA SHAVE

Some were more subtle, but just as pointed:

A BEARD
THAT'S ROUGH
AND OVERGROWN
IS BETTER THAN
A CHAPERONE
BURMA SHAVE

Many verses qualified as public service messages. Not surprisingly, given their placement, the majority dealt with safe and sober driving.

SLOW DOWN, PA
SAKES ALIVE
MA MISSED SIGNS
FOUR AND FIVE
BURMA SHAVE

Even such serious subject matter didn't prevent some outrageous puns from creeping in:

HER CHARIOT
RACED AT 80 PER
THEY HAULED AWAY
WHAT HAD
BEN HUR

BURMA SHAVE

Along our routes, any trains we encountered usually were running parallel to the road. Still, one cautionary poem so amused and impressed me that I remember it yet today:

HE SAW
THE TRAIN COMING
AND TRIED TO DUCK IT
FIRST HE KICKED THE GAS
THEN HE KICKED THE BUCKET
BURMA SHAVE

Even signs that simply plugged the product bore the light-hearted imprint of a company with the confidence to poke fun at itself:

ALTHO
WE'VE SOLD
SIX MILLION OTHERS
WE STILL CAN'T SELL
THOSE COUGHDROP BROTHERS
BURMA SHAVE

Burma Shave signs occasionally could even be educational. "What's 'the pentagon'?" I asked my father after reading:

IN SEVENTY YEARS
OF BRUSHIN' SOAP ON
GRAMPS COULDA PAINTED
THE PENTAGON
USING BRUSHLESS
BURMA SHAVE

Thus, I learned not only what and where the famous military building is, but why it's called The Pentagon.

The popularity and success of their roadside signs caught the Odells somewhat unprepared. By 1930, their creative juices were running dry as they strained to produce new copy.

They solved that problem with an annual contest that paid $100 to any entrant whose verse was accepted. Would-be versifiers came forward by the thousands. Many became repeat contributors. The Odells were obliged to hire a team of copywriters to help screen and select entries.

Installing the signs took on an almost military strategy. An advance man would tour an area seeking likely sites. After striking an agreement with the land owner, he notified the office. Soon a truckload of husky youths arrived and started digging post holes at premarked intervals along the roadside.

Signs were mounted at a precise height, a precise distance from the road's center and a precise distance apart. Early signs were spaced twenty yards apart. As cars became faster and roads wider, that gradually lengthened to about fifty yards.

The signs became a uniform size. A silkscreen process eliminated bleeding and running. Pressure-treated wooden posts proved more durable than rust-prone steel posts.

At first, signs were changed as annual contracts were renewed. Later, the routine became: inspect this year; replace next year.

For over two decades, the formula worked as smoothly as the brushless cream it promoted. But even as the motoring audience grew, Burma Shave was discovering potholes in its road to success.

By 1955, sales had plateaued. The addition of other products helped little. Likewise experiments with other media. Competitive shaving products were proliferating, and the signs were less eye-catching to folk traveling at higher speeds along wider divided four-lane freeways.

In 1963, the Burma-Vita Company was sold and became a division of American Razor. Clinton Odell had died in 1958. Allan and Leonard stayed on as consultant and president respectively.

Concurring with a corporate decision to adopt other advertising techniques, the Odells set in motion a plan to dismantle all signs. In the process, they reaped one last burst of media mileage.

As the signs disappeared, the *Saturday Evening Post, Reader's Digest* and newspapers everywhere featured nostalgic "end-of-the-road" articles about the company and its unique claim to advertising fame. By special request, Leonard presented a representative set of signs to the Smithsonian Institute.   He chose one that had been a favorite of all the Odells:

WITHIN THIS VALE
OF TOIL
AND SIN
YOUR HEAD GROWS BALD
BUT NOT YOUR CHIN
BURMA SHAVE

Many factors contributed to the demise of the little red signs and their clever verses. The impact of competitors' advertising on radio— and that new medium, television—took its toll. Faster cars and the rapid growth of super highways surely played a part. And, as Allan Odell simply but philosophically observed, "Times change."

True; and a world burdened with more serious problems has little time to mourn the passing of those quaint signs. But those of us who fondly recall them may sometimes imagine one more verse appearing along the roadside:

DRIVING'S
MUCH LESS
FUN WE THINK
SINCE THESE SIGNS
BECAME EXTINCT
BURMA SHAVE

Afterthought: For a fact-filled, entertaining and more complete history of the Burma Shave signs, read *The Verse By The Side Of The Road*, by Frank Rowsome, Jr., published by Stephen Greene Press.

Dan McGuire

Christmas Eve At Grandma's House

December 24, 1947. It is 4:30p.m. on Christmas Eve. My brothers and I have been dressed in our Sunday best for almost an hour. We must sit quietly and read so as to not get our clothes mussed.

In the street out front, our Uncle Harold's car appears. He is a supervisor at the Lakeview Post Office, and because of the Christmas mail volume, he has worked until 2p.m. He then hurried home for his family and delivered them to Grandma Farr's house. Now he will drive us so that we don't have to carry all our presents on the streetcar.

The Studebaker is long and roomy. It still has the aroma of newness. En route, Uncle Harold demonstrates its push-button radio and we are treated to continuous Christmas music selections.

Our long ride along Irving Park Road takes us past the block-long Sears, Roebuck store at the intersection of Irving, Cicero and Milwaukee (known to Northwest Side residents as "six corners"). Sears' many window displays include animated Christmas scenes involving Santa and his elves. A Salvation Army worker packs up his kettle as the Sears door is closed and locked behind some departing last-minute shoppers.

When we pass the YMCA, I know that we are almost there. Uncle Harold turns right at Tripp Avenue, and three blocks later we park behind Grandpa Farr's black Ford sedan. My mother's childhood home has a porch with steep steps and a bay window off to the left. A huge Christmas tree, overloaded with colored lights and decorations, fills the window.

Aunt Evie, who is unmarried and lives with my grandparents, opens the door before we ring. We shed our coats and galoshes in the hallway. Relatives who have already arrived mill around in the living room, waiting to greet us. All the parents marvel at how much their nieces and nephews have grown since last seen.

Grandpa picks up my brothers, Alan and Dickie, and they kiss him on his shiny pate. I'm the oldest and a little too heavy. He bends to give me a hug and tilts his head for a kiss.

Maude and Wilfred Farr pose in front of the family home. Grandpa Farr, an office manager in downtown Chicago, was seldom without his suit and tie. At informal family gatherings, on hot days, he sometimes could be persuaded to remove the coat and loosen his tie.

We go back to the kitchen to greet Grandma, who is busy preparing her usual elaborate Christmas dinner. Her graying black

297

hair is done up in a bun. She looks too small and fragile to have raised six children. But her eyes sparkle when she spies her grandchildren. We each get a warm hug, but only after she has carefully wiped her hands on her handmade apron.

Aunt Florence is helping Grandma. Our mother instinctively grabs an apron and pitches in. We boys are "under foot" now, so we are scooted out of the kitchen.

On one side of the crowded living room, we mingle with our cousins: Tim, Susie and Joan (Aunt Louise and Uncle Walt's children); Elaine and Alice (Aunt Florence and Uncle Harold's); Freddie, Faith and Frankie (Aunt Edie and Uncle Sven's). We exchange stories about our youthful adventures and what we hope to get for Christmas. Soon we divide into two groups and start up games of Old Maid and Uncle Wiggly.

Aunt Evie passes around a dish of candies. I score some points by declining. "Good boy. You don't want to spoil your appetite," she concludes. Actually, they are hard candies with soft, gooey centers, and I have never cared much for them.

Uncle Will arrives. He is single and still living with my grandparents. I was disappointed not to see him when we arrived. He has been a favorite with me ever since he took me for a ride in the bumpy rumble seat of his Ford coupe.

I wait for everyone else to greet him first, then step up to shake his hand in a grown-up manner. He shakes, solemnly, but then laughs and picks me up under the armpits, hoisting me up until my head touches the ceiling.

When he sets me down, he ruffles my hair and tells me what a big lug I'm getting to be. We go to admire the tree ornaments that have decorated Grandma's tree for as long as I can remember. Then we are at the bay window watching people walk or drive by. Uncle Will makes up fanciful stories about happy Christmas gatherings to which they are heading. As he talks, his face close to mine, I notice a strong, musty smell on his breath.

Aunt Evie and Grandma appear behind us. Grandma says something gently remonstrating. Only then do I identify my uncle's smell and realize that something is amiss. I come to his defense with the innocence of youth: "It's all right, Grandma. He's just a little drunk is all."

Uncle Will's shoulders begin to shake and he bursts into tears. Grandma and Aunt Evie hustle him away to the kitchen. Puzzled by the effect of my candor, I follow at a distance. As Uncle Will's mother and three sisters comfort him and urge black coffee upon him, I listen at the kitchen door. Slowly I comprehend. Uncle Will has been remembering some of his Army buddies who did not make it home to enjoy this Christmas with their families.

Chagrined, I tip-toe back to the living room. The men folk talk with enthusiasm of politics, sports, the Marshall Plan, inflation, last week's snow storm.

Aunt Evie, a school teacher, gathers the older kids around the new radio/phonograph console. She has a five-record 78-rpm album of music from The Nutcracker Suite and hopes to enrich us with some culture. She summarizes the story for us. Then we must close our eyes and try to visualize the dances described by the musical segments. After three or four pieces, our interest wanes. She observes our fidgeting and permits us to escape.

Aunt Louise summons Aunt Evie to help her set the table. Mom and Aunt Florence steer us kids to the two bathrooms to wash our hands. Mine are perfectly clean, but I know better than to say so. As we straggle back, Grandma calls from the kitchen: "Okay, everybody, sit. Pa, is your knife sharpened?"

The adults gather at the dining room table. A card table had been drawn up next to the kitchen table, and the kids will eat there. It is overcrowded, though, so for the first time, I am invited to sit with the grown-ups.

The women help Grandma distribute platters and bowls of food to both tables. Last of all, she personally delivers the huge roast turkey. ("As big as Tiny Tim," I think.) Its aroma is so mouth-wateringly delicious that I can taste it already.

As Grandma seats herself, she says, "You can say grace now, Pa." Grandpa, who is not a regular church-goer, gives a short but acceptable blessing.

He then whets the blade of his carving knife on a sharpening steel. His strokes are swift and smooth. He touches the blade to the tip of his thumb to test its sharpness. Then he calls for requests, first from the grandchildren, and deftly serves up large or small slices of white or dark meat to order.

Grandma is up and down throughout the meal, taking food to the children, refilling bowls, fetching an extra salt shaker. Her daughters take turns trying to outrun her and saying, "Sit down, Ma. I'll get it."

The honor of sitting with the adults is a mixed blessing. A picky eater, I hear several declarations of disbelief that I do not eat cranberries or rice pudding. Also, I miss getting to feed scraps to Brownie, the big cuddly Irish setter, who must stay in the kitchen. The younger kids toss tiny chunks of meat to her from their table. If the morsels come at all close, Brownie unerringly snaps them up in midair, never moving from her spot.

During dinner, Uncle Will seems to have regained his composure and is becoming his jovial self again. Once he makes a joking remark and winks at me.

The meal ends with ice cream and three kinds of pie, including Grandpa's favorite, mince. Everyone compliments and thanks Grandma for the delicious spread.

Now comes the most trying part of the evening. The ladies clear the tables while the men and kids adjourn to the living room. We must sit politely until all the dishes are washed. Grandpa makes it easier by playing some Christmas tunes for us on his ocarina. I do not understand why he calls it a "sweet potato." It does not look like any sweet potato that I ever saw.

At last, we are all assembled. Several of my cousins who are old enough to read are elected "elves." They get to pass out the multitude of presents arrayed around the tree.

Amid the excitement, I'm wishing that I could tell Uncle Will that I'm sorry I made him cry. But I don't know how. When he opens his present from me (a package of Gillette blades and some shaving soap), it's obvious that he likes it best of all. He calls me over to sit on his lap, and I know that everything is okay between us.

Finally, the last gift is opened and displayed to all. There is the usual aftermath of cleaning up wrapping paper. There are more thank-you's all around. Kids try to stifle yawns. ("I'm not tired, Mom, really.") They're reminded that they must be home in bed before Santa Claus can come.

Gifts are accumulated in shopping bags. People mill around and side-step each other getting their coats and boots on. We all exchange best wishes for Christmas and New Years. One last hug and kiss for

Grandma and Grandpa, then we step out into the crisp December night and another fresh inch of snow.

We load our new possessions into the Studebaker's trunk. One bag has to come up front. A few bulky toys are left in Grandma's care to be picked up another time.

To avoid crowding up front, Elaine sits in the back on my lap. I would be embarrassed if she were a female schoolmate, but because she is my cousin it's okay. When her hair brushes my face, it has a fresh, sweet smell like some sort of blossom. I wonder if all girls smell so nice or just my cousin.

We pass Sears, Roebuck again. The street is empty now, but the window displays continue their semi-lifelike pantomimes.

A trolley car passes with just three passengers aboard. Each sits staring out a window, looking lonely. I feel sorry for them, but then imagine them back with their families for The Big Day tomorrow.

In front of our house, we unload our bags, thank Uncle Harold for the ride and wish our relatives happy holidays once more. Cousin Alice doesn't hear because she has gone to sleep on her mother's lap.

Our street has no streetlamps, but the moon reflects brightly off the snow. My father has no trouble finding the keyhole and letting us in. Inside, our darkened tree looks forlorn compared to Grandma's.

My brothers and I are quickly urged into our pajamas. "Santa could be here any minute," my father warns, "and you guys had best be in bed, or he may pass up our house." As we snuggle down under our blankets, our parents move quietly through the house, only a couple of lights lit. Dad goes down to stoke up the coal furnace in our cellar. Mom says, "My goodness, it's eleven o'clock already."

Alan whispers across the bedroom, "Dickie, let's stay awake and watch for Santa." He gets no reply. Dickie, the youngest, already is breathing heavily.

Alan redirects his suggestion to me. But this year I learned something that is still a secret to my brothers. I lie very still and do not answer. When Alan repeats his whispered idea, I imitate Dickie's breathing. Soon Alan becomes quiet, too. I smile to myself, but my own eyes are growing heavy.

I feel myself drifting away to a larger, more lavish house than ours, a palace almost. Glancing at a mirror, I discover that I am a nutcracker dressed as a soldier. I am standing in an imperial ballroom, surrounded by sugar plum fairies with transparent wings and hair that smells of blossoms. I pick up an ocarina and begin to play a lively tune. Together, we all dance about gaily as the lights dim and the ballroom slowly fades into darkness.

With his cousin, Elaine, the author stands on the porch of their grandparents' home shortly before it was sold. After the grandparents died, their unmarried Aunt Evelyn lived there until her health necessitated moving to a nursing home. The house was occupied by Farrs for just shy of 100 years.

ACKNOWLEDGEMENTS

Since this is almost certainly the only book I will ever publish, I want very much to do the job right in acknowledging all those who played a part in causing the book to be written. But to do so would require listing people who comprise what Hollywood delights in referring to as "a cast of thousands." Many of them, in fact, I do not know by name, so I will fudge a little.

The list begins, of course, with my parents, my brothers and our extended family. Then there are my childhood playmates, their families and all the folk that we thought of as neighbors, even if we knew them only to say "Hello" in passing. There were our principal and teachers at school, P.T.A. ladies (and some men), scout leaders, Sunday school teachers and other church friends.

Policemen and firemen kept us safe. Bus and streetcar drivers got us to exciting destinations in the Big City. Theatre owners there welcomed us. Lifeguards protected us at beaches and park pools. Shop owners treated us like real customers, and some gave us jobs when we were older.

All these folks, and countless others, helped make life pretty good for kids of my era. Without them, I would not have these fond recollections to share with you.

In the present tense, there are three ladies to whom I owe much in bringing the book to fruition. My loving and incredibly patient wife, Joy, has endured countless hours of my clicking away at the computer keyboard, with only an occasional reminder about things that needed doing around our house. Daughter Laurie has lent her professional editorial expertise and advice. Without her sister, Jennifer, my jumbled collection of manuscripts never would have been successfully formatted and compiled into a document stored on disc and suitable for submission to the publisher.

When the initial draft of the book was done, I began Stage 2. This involved attempting to verify or correct various details, and the more challenging effort to locate illustrative photographs. In the 1940s, cameras were a luxury for working class folk. Those who had one tended to use it mostly for snapshots of family gatherings and vacations.

Early on I realized that specific photos of places and events in "the old neighborhood" would be scarce. Generic photos of the era are available from many commercial sources, but not at what a self-publishing author would refer to as "popular prices."

Our own Bensenville Library got me started on the right track. Kelly Watson and Jennie Cisna were helpful with both research information and some photo ideas. Lois Phelan and Tony White offered patient assistance to a novice web surfer after Bill Erves gave me my first solid lead: a website for the Library of Congress Prints and Photographs Division.

Part of the LOC collection consists of over 112,000 images dating from the Great Depression through World War II. I spoke to five different people at LOC during the weeks that I scanned these files and selected photos. I regret that Kenneth Johnson is the only one whose name I wrote down, but they all were uniformly knowledgeable, efficient and helpful. In addition to handling my photo requests, they provided me valuable information on copyrights and how to obtain a Library of Congress catalog number.

With the help of Glen Humphrey and Gloria Price at Chicago's Conrad Sulzer Regional Library, I viewed a number of vintage Northwest Side photos and came away with one of the Patio Theatre.

Back in the old neighborhood, at Harwood Heights' Eisenhower Library, there was nothing of what I hoped to find in their photo archives. But David Zigler knew half a dozen folk to contact who had been in the village since "the old days."

Anne Lunde, editor at the Norridge-Harwood Heights News, was not able to offer any photos because of the turmoil caused by a recent merger and relocation. But Ann knows a *lot* of people. My conversation with her resulted in the names and phone numbers of about two dozen people with Norridge roots or connections.

Whether we hit pay dirt or not, people at local historical groups all shared a common trait of being enthusiastic and accommodating. At the Theatre Historical Society, Manager Richard Skelnar and volunteers Bill Benedict and Bill Ikert could tell you almost anything you wanted to know about any movie theatre that ever operated in Chicago—*and* they have photos of practically all of them.

I looked through stacks of vintage photos with the aid of Janis Arquette of the Bensenville Historical Society, Sheri Caine at the Des

Plaines Historical Museum, Carolyn Jensen and Richard Lang of the Irving Park Historical Society, Anne Morong of the Wood Dale Historical Museum and Nancy Wilson at the Elmhurst Historical Museum. (Photos of the milkman who came in a horse-drawn wagon are fairly common, but Nancy turned up the only photo of a fellow with a 1940s truck.)

Debra Gust, at the Lake County Museum in Wauconda, Illinois, introduced me to the Curt Teich post card collection (the largest post card collection in the world). In addition to other "finds," this yielded some great photos of Chicago's legendary Riverview Amusement Park.

Derek Gee, co-author of "World's Greatest Amusement Park," provided additional photos from Riverview's glory days.

At the Norridge Community Center, village historian Myron Petrakis had reams of newspaper clippings and historical information about my old home town. Unfortunately, not many photos from the 1940s. However, he gave me another great lead, namely, Roger Hammill in nearby Franklin Park.

With his lovely wife Dorothy (not *the* Dorothy Hammill, she is quick to tell you), Roger operated the Hammill (photography) Studios and did freelance work for local newspapers for many years. He also proved to be a streetcar enthusiast, and turned up one of my favorite photos in this book. Moreover, he introduced me to a magazine called *First and Fastest* and put me in touch with Art Peterson, the president of Shore Line Interurban Historical Society, which publishes the magazine. From Art, I obtained a couple more great trolley photos.

Peter Mitchell, whose family once operated the Patio, had no photos but knew much about the theatre's early history. Among several neat photos submitted by Mary Fran Purse was one real prize winner: the only photo that anyone found of a scissors grinder. Margaret Leengran sent a picture of her father posing next to the Chicago streetcar on which he was a conductor. It dated from well before my time frame, but the picture was too neat not to use.

Dick Huske, Fred Lehman, Jack Leengran, Wayne Leengran, Gloria Royal and Judy Thomas all took up the search, but came up empty. Still, they each had ideas of places to try or people to contact. Mike Grogan, editor/publisher of *Heros from Hackland* magazine, offered several suggestions for possible sources that would not stretch a thin budget.

In the search for "old neighborhood" photos and information, Kathy Gaseor at the the village hall devoted a page of the village newsletter to my quest. Louise Hartwig's folks ran a mom and pop store in the area, and she located some good pictures. Eleanor Balco referred me to her friend Chief Dennis Stefanowicz at the Norwood Park Fire Department. The chief sat me down at a conference table with a box stuffed full of department photos, mostly loose and unsorted, dating back to the Year 1. I spent three engrossing hours looking through the stacks and came away with several treasures.

When I narrowed my search to James Giles Elementary School, things got even tougher. Kerry Leiby, the current principal, was most gracious in searching through dusty files in the basement, but could find only a few photos from "the old days." Virginia Snadden, a former teacher at the school, was able to provide newspaper stories from when John V. Leigh retired and when he died. She also was able to steer me to others who had taught or been involved at the school. June Orten, niece of Mrs. Leigh (who taught at the school while Mr. Leigh was principal), sent a treasure trove of clippings, memorabilia and photos, including my favorite of all the John V. Leigh photos. In addition to photos, Izetta Castiglia provided some fascinating background on James Giles, both the school and the man for whom it was named. Vera Fulhorst, whose mother was president of the P.T.A when we were kids, located the aerial photo of our Field Day exercises. And my former classmate, Nancy Gisselbrecht, dug up photos from both our grade school and high school years.

At the high school level, Mary Ellen Carlson, membership chairperson of the Steinmetz Alumni Association, provided several good leads. Alice Beyer, who tries to keep track of our graduating class, helped me track down several classmates. Charles Roehl saved me from embarrassing myself by pointing out that odd number classrooms were in the north hall and evens in the south hall, not vice versa as I originally stated. Sheldon Kruger, a long-time teacher at Steinmetz and unofficial historian of the school, located a partial image of the giant mural that once decorated the stage firewall in our school auditorium.

Several businesses responded generously to my quest. At Brach Confection, John Lux put aside competitive interests and directed me to Tom Burke at the Wisconsin headquarters of Andes Candies. With his Chicago roots, Tom was enthusiastic about my project and offered numerous suggestions. He connected me with Kathy Maass, who searched through the company scrapbook and sent me an assortment of 1940s store photos. George Kanelos, brother of the founder, was a storehouse of historical information. (The first few stores, named after his brother, were called Andy's Candies. As the business expanded, a supplier suggested it needed a punchier name. So it was changed to Andes, a mountain logo was adopted and the slogan became "the peak of perfection.")

Sarah Blake at Breyers Ice Cream (now the parent of Good Humor), searched in vain for a picture of the 3-wheeled cycle with a Good Humor Man aboard. But the photo she provided of an unmanned bicycle is a beaut! (That sentence has great pun potential, and I think I deserve credit for resisting.)

At Gem Comics in Elmhurst, Gloria Berman did not carry the vintage comics I was looking for, but she steered me to Comic Kingdom in Chicago. There, owner Joe Sarno proudly produced dozens of early editions from his huge collection.

Cara Lynn Orchard, at Lionel L.L.C., made me feel as if it was I doing her a favor. She sent me a disc from which I could take my choice of 1940s Lionel catalog covers.

My inquiries to commercial photo sources all proved discouraging until I connected with Roberta Groves at Retrofile and Howard Mandelbaum at Photofest. Not only were their prices within my limited budget, but they were determined to find for me what I was seeking. Their patience and cooperation with a first-time author was never diminished by the up-front knowledge that I was unlikely to be a repeat customer.

I am indebted to brothers Andrew and Paul Madsen, who referred me to 1stBooks Library. Justin Axelroth, at 1stBooks, patiently answered a stream of questions I posed before submitting my book. Once it was in production, Michelle Hubbard held my hand through the agonies that are a writer's version of childbirth.

Have I missed anyone? I hope not, but if so, let me know and perhaps we can correct the oversight in our second printing (after Oprah's endorsement).

Finally, I would extend a special thanks to my lifelong pal, Chuck Schaden. I've noted elsewhere that it was Chuck who prompted me to write these pieces; but he also was a major player in the good times that gave me something to write about. Without him, it would not have been as much fun.

ABOUT THE AUTHOR

Dan McGuire traces his interest in writing back to the compositions he turned in for extra credit at James Giles Elementary School. The die was cast when a story that he wrote in high school was published in *Boys' Life* magazine. That first flash of success was seldom equaled thereafter, but it confirmed him as a lifelong freelance writer.

His efforts have appeared in a diverse assortment of periodicals, including numerous big city and small town newspapers. Recognizing early that he was not destined to become the next Hemingway, he prudently pursued a day job in the customer service field.

In 1976, he began contributing occasional articles to *Nostalgia Digest* magazine. The favorable response, coupled with Mr. McGuire's penchant for reminiscing, eventually led to a regular column, which ran for eleven years. All of the pieces collected in this book appeared originally in *Nostalgia Digest*.